SHED SUPERSTITION

OUTMANEUVERING FATE

Also by Armando Benitez:
Fate, Coincidence, and the Outcome of Horse Races

SHEER
SUPERSTITION

OUTMANEUVERING
FATE

ARMANDO BENITEZ

HAMPTON ROADS
PUBLISHING COMPANY, INC.

for the evolving human spirit

Cover design by Brickergraphics
Cover Art by PhotoDisc

For information write:

Hampton Roads Publishing Company, Inc.
1125 Stoney Ridge Road
Charlottesville, VA 22902

Or call: 804-296-2772
FAX: 804-296-5096
e-mail: hrpc@hrpub.com
Web site: www.hrpub.com

If you are unable to order this book from your local
bookseller, you may order directly from the publisher.
Quantity discounts for organizations are available.
Call 1-800-766-8009, toll-free.

Library of Congress Catalog Card Number: 99-068068
ISBN 1-57174-180-1
10 9 8 7 6 5 4 3 2 1
Printed on acid-free paper in the Canada

dedicated to my daughters
Miriam & Patricia

Table of Contents

Chapter 1: Casting the Cards for the Pie Woman 1

Chapter 2: The Golden Touch 11

Chapter 3: Acquiring Wisdom by Improving Our Luck 21

Chapter 4: Coincidence and the Outcome of Horse Races 33

Chapter 5: *Lapsus Linguae* and Coincidence .45

Chapter 6: Walking up the Stairs Can Change Your Luck 55

Chapter 7: Getting Your Fair Share of Good Fortune 71

Chapter 8: Some Divining Methods to Spy on the Fates 83

Chapter 9: Time, The Fates, and Your Grandmother 95

Chapter 10: How Arcane Knowledge Leaks Into Our Life 109

Chapter 11: Lightning Bolts and Winning the Lottery 119

Chapter 12: Is Daydreaming a Dangerous Enterprise? 131

Chapter 13: Why You Should Avoid Peacocks 141

Chapter 14: Not All Rabbits' Feet Are Lucky 153

Chapter 15: Duplicated Horses and Identical Twins 169

Chapter 16: Evasive Maneuvers in a Foreign Language 177

Chapter 17: The Luck of the Baloney 185

Chapter 18: Foods That Make Us Wiser 197

Chapter 19: Almost All Heads Are Unlucky Foods 209

Chapter 20: Wise Decisions by the Flip of a Coin 227

Chapter 21: The Honeycomb of Alternate Realities 239

Chapter 22: Spinning the Thirty-Million-Dollar Dream 255

Chapter 23: "Of Divination, What Good Has Ever Come to Men?" 269

Chapter 24: Incursions Into the Future to Beat the Lottery 279

Chapter 25: The Last One to Remain Clinging to the Wall 289

Chapter 26: Struggling Against Ourselves for Our Future 297

Chapter 27: Storming the Mysteries Sideways 309

Chapter 1

Casting the Cards for the Pie Woman

Four or five years ago, after I thought I had finished this book, and was assiduously looking for a publisher but receiving one brusque and impolite rejection after another, I finally received a favorable reply from a small press. They thought my book was wonderful. They couldn't offer an advance that was worth mentioning, they said, but they did want to publish it. They included their phone number so I could call back at my convenience to discuss the matter.

In the midst of my exhilaration at the prospect of having finally found a publisher, I took note of a small but disturbing detail: the said phone number had a certain unlucky double digit in it, repeated twice. Then I noticed that the press had a new address, which also included that same number. And to top all this off, I had received their reply on a very inauspicious date. After a week or so of deliberation, I decided that with so many ominous portents lurking in the offing, nothing good could come of the matter. I would continue my search for a publisher.

Yet, in the back of my mind was the nagging doubt: Could this perhaps be carrying a belief and a conviction to extremes? To pass by the chance I had been seeking for over a year! All because of an unlucky number. Maybe this was a prime example of the "monumental folly," the "disastrous fallacy" of superstition that Sir James George Frazer spoke of in *The Golden Bough*.

Are we, the superstitious, really complete fools? Could it be that our beliefs are utterly devoid of logic and reason? The superstitious person, much as he may force his reason to consider this possibility, will nevertheless still be reluctant to relinquish his superstitions. While non-superstitious people unconcernedly flout the most commonly known taboos with no evident ill effects, we, the superstitious, cower and shudder at every such intromission of these things in our lives.

We refuse to relinquish our superstitions because deep within recondite layers of our consciousness we feel that there is a rational and logical reason for them. We are no more capable of giving up these beliefs than are religious persons capable of renouncing their belief in God. Moreover, we continually undergo experiences that reinforce our superstitious convictions. Take the matter of that small press, for example. Over the months following my decision not to pursue the matter of publication by—let us call them Black Cow Press—I came to realize that my book was riddled with defects. It contained unresolved contradictions; it was poorly constructed; it was repetitious; it was badly written in many parts (maybe it is still all of these things). I have since read a book or two put out by Black Cow Press and have noticed that they apparently publish them without editing of any kind. If they had published my book, it would have become little more than a source of embarrassment for me. So I was right to heed my superstition.

There have been many other instances in my life when I would have done well to act in the same manner. Yes, superstition can be carried to excess, just as religion can be carried to excess. But the superstitious person should never try to eradicate it from his soul. It serves a useful purpose, and, as suggested above, it has a logical, rational, and legitimate basis and origin, which I will try to delineate in these pages.

I inherited my own superstitious nature from my mother. The earliest memories from my childhood are of my mother worriedly tossing spilled salt over her left shoulder, or commenting, in a grave and concerned voice, upon a dream of ill omen she had experienced the previous night.

My father, on the other hand, believed in nothing, continually railing against the folly of organized religion and the stupidity of superstition. He came to an untimely end, incidentally; the victim of an accident with a tractor. He had not listened to my mother, when she warned him about many ill omens she had received concerning a new job he was taking with the Works Projects Administration, urging him to look for something else, although this was during the years of the Great Depression in the San Joaquin Valley of California, and jobs were extremely scarce and hard to come by.

There is another memory from my childhood I would like to share with the reader. In the otherwise flat and dispirited landscape of the San Joaquin Valley, a bright and salient feature was our nearest neighbor, Mrs. Duncan, an elderly widow known to us as the Pie Woman. She lived not far from us on the outskirts of the little town of Firebaugh and she supported herself and her grandchildren, two little boys nearly my age, from the proceeds of her home-made pie business. Her daughter, the boys' mother, was in Tehachapi prison for women, and the father had gone West, so to speak. She made delicious pies—apple, lemon-meringue, mincemeat, and in fall, pumpkin—which she sold, if I recall correctly, for twenty-five cents each. She was my mother's friend. The best possible kind of friend my mother could have, I thought, because sometimes, when she and her grandchildren were glutted on unsalable left-over pies, she would pass one or two of them on to us.

Mingled with the thought of those delicious pies is the memory of the predicament Mrs. Duncan finally got herself into, from an ill-controlled inclination towards self-indulgence. She mortgaged her house—it was a large shack, actually—to buy a car, trading in her 1930 Chevrolet for a brand-new 1936 model.

Mrs. Duncan had had a choice. She could have waited another year to trade in her old car and then gotten the new one without having to resort to a bank loan. But if she did this, her old car would drop considerably in trade-in value. She chose the option of the bank loan, thereby gaining, she thought, more than one advantage: getting a better price for her old car, and taking possession of the new one quicker.

She had not plunged into the deal too blindly. She had first taken the precaution of consulting my mother, who had the hobby of fortune-telling with Spanish playing cards, to see if everything would turn out all right for her. After casting the cards my mother told her, no, the time was not right. There were too many *bastos* in her future, she told her, and the *sota de copas* had come up head down, which, according to the way my mother predicted the future, was very bad. *Bastos* are the clubs in the Spanish deck, and the *sota de copas* is the Jack of Hearts. But Mrs. Duncan had apparently resorted to my mother's prescient abilities only as a polite and condescending gesture. She went ahead and bought the new car anyway.

The new car had something called knee-action I recall (though my memory could be somewhat faulty on this point) and a radio, which I think were things new in automobiles. The day after Mrs. Duncan got it, the children invited me to ride with them as their grandmother delivered her pies. We sat in the back seat as she sped down the road away from town at the unheard-of velocity of sixty miles per hour, her pies stuffed in the trunk, and some of them beside her on the front seat, the radio blaring a new song called "Red-headed Mama."

But perhaps Mrs. Duncan had not grasped the subtle differences between the old cars and the new models. Maybe it was that "knee-action" thing. At any rate, while she was simultaneously negotiating a turn and singing along with the radio, precisely at that point in the song that said, ". . . can't make a fool out of me-ee," she lost control, and sent her new car flipping and rolling off the road. Miraculously, no one was hurt, but the consequences were devastating for Mrs. Duncan, nevertheless.

I was very little, and the memory I retain has no doubt been edited and selected in its details as most memories are. I have a recollection of waiting with my mother for Mrs. Duncan, as a loan officer expressed his regrets to Mrs. Duncan for the action that he saw himself forced to take, and Mrs. Duncan tearfully pleading with him, begging him not to take away the roof over her head, not to leave her grandchildren homeless, because their mother was at present in no situation to take them in. She couldn't take them in because she was in prison, of course, but Mrs. Duncan didn't mention this.

I recall, over the subsequent days, my mother sorrowfully commenting on her friend's situation, frequently referring to her as "poor Mrs. Duncan," a term which puzzled me. If anyone should be called "poor," I thought, it was us, and not rich Mrs. Duncan and her grandchildren, who even in the midst of her tribulations were still supping and dining, as I knew from personal observation, on such exotic foods as chicken, and beef, and pork, to say nothing of the leftover pies they had every day. We, on the other hand, knew no meat other than an occasional jackrabbit, or fish caught in the irrigation canals of the valley. My mother explained that she meant "poor" in another way. And she added that Mrs. Duncan deserved to be called poor in yet another, pejorative sense because she had been poor in judgment when she got herself into such a fix. She had had a perfectly good car; she should never have hocked the roof over her head just for the pleasure of driving a new car.

This was a long time ago and, as I have said, my recollection of the events is hazy. But I can say with certainty that the sad predicament had a happy ending. Mrs. Duncan somehow or other found the money she needed, paid off the bank loan, and continued to struggle with her pie business.

The drama of Mrs. Duncan's situation impressed me greatly at the time, and its elements have remained with me ever since. At the time all this happened, I did not entirely share my mother's opinion that Mrs. Duncan had been foolish to so brashly go against what the cards had told her. Being very little, perhaps my superstition, though firmly ingrained in my genes, was overridden by hearing my father scoff heatedly at these beliefs and state emphatically that Mrs. Duncan had gotten herself into her fix because she had recklessly hocked the roof over her head. A prudent person will not do such a thing, cards or no cards, my father constantly repeated. A prudent person knows that when we place our home and the future well-being of our family on the block, we had better make sure that the outcome of the operation is entirely beyond the vagaries of chance and luck.

With the passing of the years, however, my genes asserted themselves, and I now accept the fact that my mother was just as right as my father. Maybe more so. I now believe that, although prudence is very important for a happy life, we cannot be prudent if we do not have the good fortune to have been born that way in the first place. Prudence cannot be learned. (It can, however, be *acquired*, and I will go into that subject presently.) If we were born without prudence we are like that Max Shulman character who prided himself on his wisdom. He was once kicked in the head while crawling under a horse. He was subsequently kicked in the head again, but not while crawling under a horse. He would never commit the same error twice, he boasted.

The above example is not as extreme as it may appear. This is the way many of us who were born unwise and unfortunate are. We can only learn to act wisely and prudently in selective instances, where experience has already taught us. We never truly become wise and prudent, although if we live long enough and experience enough hard knocks we do attain a passable semblance of wisdom and prudence.

But there is another, much better, way to attain this state, and thereby bypass a good many of those hard knocks—that can even have fatal consequences. This is where superstition comes in. For those of us who were under the table when prudence, forethought, and cautious wisdom were passed out, the observance of superstitious caution can serve in its stead very nicely. I might not mention superstition very frequently, but its essence will be there in every idea I propound in this book. All my ideas are sheer superstition, I admit.

In these pages I hope to show that we the superstitious are not necessarily fools. Superstition has been present in the human soul from the first stirrings of the human intellect. Rather than trying to shake it off, let us first try looking deeply into the reasons for this, to see if we can find the hidden logical basis for its existence.

People who are entirely free of superstition do not need it. They are fortunate people, blessed from birth with the sort of life that has never awakened in them the awareness of the hidden strings and signal flags that are attached to all actions and processes on Earth and in life. Everything these people do, rather than bringing them bad luck, only brings them more good fortune. The superstitious, on the other hand, are people who have been taught by many hard knocks and the vicissitudes of misfortune that theirs is a state which can be vastly improved through certain precautionary practices. It should not surprise us greatly if it is some day proved that many superstitious beliefs and practices have evolved as stratagems for the survival of the human species. Superstition can come in many guises. Many animals have behavioral habits that, since they are dumb unreasoning creatures, must surely be what in a human being would be superstitious behavior. That is to say, some behavior in animals, birds, insects, fish, and so forth, which contributes to their continued survival, is not the product of a calculated logic and reason, and therefore can only be classified as a sort of superstitious behavior.

There is a species of caterpillar, for instance, that has the habit, when feeding on the leaves of certain toxic plants, of first chewing through the vein that carries the toxic substance to the edible part of the leaf. This shuts off the pathway of the toxin from the stem to the leaf, and the caterpillar can then feed upon it without being poisoned. Now, of course, the caterpillar has never thought its actions through, to explain to itself why it first chews through the inedible vein. Where would the brainless little creature store such complex knowledge in a logical sequence? Its actions are surely only the product of a superstitious behavior, inherited in its genes. In ages past, this behavioral trait assured the continued survival of its species, and this caterpillar now unquestioningly follows its ancient tradition.

Superstitious behavior of this sort is also seen in higher life forms. When the polar bear crouches in the snow and ice for hours, waiting for an unwary seal to flap close enough to pounce on it, it covers its nose with its paws. It is not consciously thinking that it needs to cover its black nose, glaringly visible in the whiteness of the snows, so the seal won't notice it. It is merely observing, the same as the caterpillar, the equivalent of superstitious behavior. If the caterpillar and the polar bear were capable of thought, they would feel very uneasy about flouting their superstition, even if they had no idea about the practical reason behind it. In human beings, superstitious behavior is sometimes of equally obscure practicality. Our reason has already identified the areas in which any given behavior will expose us to the danger of being poisoned, being eaten by a wild beast, bitten by a poisonous snake, drowned in a turbulent river, or, more likely in this modern world, being crushed by a car. But other dangers remain: the hidden, invisible dangers from malevolent fate and destiny, from which no amount of reason and logic can shield us. Here, only the judicious observance of superstitious practices can keep us safe.

Chapter 2

The Golden Touch

The basic premise of all superstitions is that we have direct control over our destiny, that we can change our destiny, because we are free to choose the path we wish to traverse. If we walk under a ladder, our steps lead us to misfortune. But if we walk around the ladder we are taking a path that leads to other, more benign, results in our near future. We are, in effect, changing our destiny.

If a relatively young man habitually sweeps the dust off his feet with a broom, he is ensuring that he will marry an old woman. But, having been informed of the relationship between that event and his action, and having accepted its truth, he will, of course, stop doing that. Gradually, with time, the ill effects of sweeping his feet off with a broom may wear off and he will have a better chance of marrying a more appropriately aged female. He has caused a change in the destiny that was in store for him. Superstitious practices, therefore, are a tool with which we can change the future.

If we can change the future, then it should also be possible to change the past. In fact, to change the future to any appreciable degree we must first change the past. All our superstitions should, therefore, be observed with this view in mind. We want to change the past so that the present in which we find ourselves becomes a present with a subtle difference.

For the moment, let us proceed to another question: If we blunder into unhappy situations, is it our fault? The person blessed from birth with good judgment and sensible caution will of course say, "Yes, whose fault can it be but that of the person who commits these errors?" The person who habitually blunders, if he is also inclined toward a reflective turn of mind, might say, however, "It isn't my fault. I'm naturally unfortunate. My parents were dumb; *their* parents were dumb; so of course I too was cursed with the misfortune of being born dumb, and you are wrong to scold me for it, because this will not change the way I am."

The first person may be right, in a certain sense, but from this point on I will speak mainly from the viewpoint of the second, developing and stating his arguments for him. If we were born dumb—say we have been cursed with a lack of foresight and prudence from birth—then all the lectures and lessons in the world will not change this fact. That is, unless these are oriented, not towards teaching us to be smarter, but towards improving our luck in such a manner that we will naturally acquire that prudence, forethought, and wisdom that we were born without.

Just as there are different kinds of good and bad luck, so are there different kinds of wisdom. There is conventional wisdom, which is the intellectual capacity for analyzing and dissecting ideas and situations, accompanied by the propensity to select the proper course of action. And there is that wisdom which is usually considered as nothing more than dumb luck, that mysterious ability to unconsciously choose the correct option from among a varied choice, apparently unaccompanied by any special intellectual capacity. This ability manifests itself in a subtle way, so that the advantage of the correct choice is almost invisible, even to the wise person who chooses it. There is also that wisdom I have spoken of, that is acquired by hard knocks, and that manifests itself in specifically familiar situations.

There is one thing, however, that all kinds of luck and wisdom have in common. They all originate in a time and place over which we have no control at the time in which these things are apportioned. The very fact of being wise is, of course, the greatest of fortunes. The person who leads a fortunate life because he is honest, persevering, constant in his purposes, dedicated to the work ethic, and endowed with abundant common sense, is very fortunate; i.e., lucky, to have been born with these virtues in the first place.

At the same time, it can usually be seen that the misfortunes which befall many people can be attributed to their shortcomings of character—that if only those people would stop doing dumb things their luck would be different. Pursuing this thought one step further, it is evident that if we can change our luck by changing our character, then it should also be possible to change our character by first changing our luck.

This becomes, then, our primary goal. We want to change our luck. If this seems to be too shallow and grasping for the reader, let it be considered that it is not necessarily an objective in itself, but only a way to the more altruistic goal of correcting our defects of character for the ultimate good of all humanity.

Psychologists and other busybodies continually tell us that we can change ourselves. But how often can they provide us with examples to show that the accepted methods of accomplishing this are the right way? Not very often. Persons who succeed in radically changing their basic character are a rarity. Perhaps a different approach, a metaphysical approach, would have more success; an approach in which we change ourselves not by trying to make those changes in our character in the present, but by changing ourselves in the very cauldron in which our destiny was first concocted in the past. The way to do this is by concentrating on first effecting changes in our day-to-day luck, starting with the little things, and gradually working our way into things of ever greater importance. Every stroke of luck we experience will contribute to our intelligence, wisdom, and every other aspect of our character. In this way we can ". . . mend an ill game by causing a new shuffle," as the English philosopher Thomas Hobbes put it.

Improving our luck involves many paradoxical contradictions. I have just said that ". . . luck and wisdom . . . originate in a time and place over which we have no control at the time in which these things are apportioned." I have also said that we change ourselves by retreating into the past, to the time in which our fate was first decided, to effect changes there in the way in which our course through life was charted. So it would seem that we *do* have control "at the time in which these things are apportioned." But the incompatibility of the two notions is only apparent. For the time being, let us just accept the two contradictory facts that though our fate may be fixed and preordained, we have the power to change it.

The conventional methods advocated by many books on self-improvement are flawed for one major reason. Most of us already know that self-discipline, determination, single-mindedness, patience, frugality, respect for the rights of others, and so forth, will bring us a good life. But simply knowing these things will do us no good if we have not been blessed with these virtues. Besides, these virtues will generally rest upon a base of wisdom. Without wisdom, self-discipline becomes senseless self-flagellation; determination and single-mindedness become mulish obstinacy; patience, frugality, and the rest, become brutish servility.

So, since it is only wisdom that can bring us all good things in life, and since we cannot acquire wisdom because our very lack of this virtue prevents us from knowing where to look for it, we will concern ourselves mainly with matters of pure luck. At the same time, we will show the interconnection that exists between wisdom and luck. Because, although it is possible to be dumb but lucky, the general thing to expect is that if you are lucky you will not continue that way for very long, unless you acquire a bit of wisdom with each stroke of luck that befalls you.

As a prime illustration of this last principle, let us go to a case from antiquity, King Midas and his famous golden touch. As a reward for having taken good care of the satyr Silenus, whom his gardeners had found sleeping off a drunken binge in his gardens, the god Dionysus offered to grant King Midas any wish. Midas, without pausing to reflect how troublesome such a gift could be, chose the golden touch. For a short while, he had a great time of it, turning everything he touched into gold; but then he got hungry, and sitting down to eat realized that along with his gift had come a serious problem. Dionysus, having enjoyed his little joke, told him to go to the river Pactolus to free himself of his burdensome gift by washing himself in the river's waters. Midas did so, and that is the reason, say the ancient mythographers, that the sands of the Pactolus remain bright with gold to this day. Good fortune still went with Midas at the Pactolus. There he was adopted as a son by King Gordius, famous for his Gordian knot, and he inherited that king's rich kingdom upon his death.

What a fortunate man was Midas. He was already filthy rich to begin with. He was the son of a goddess; his magnificent rose gardens were famous throughout the ancient world; twice, he became a king; and, whatever annoyance it may have caused him, the golden touch must surely have left him with a substantial profit. Why are people like King Midas so fortunate? Why are some people born with good fortune while others are not? Why do some people have the golden touch, whereas everything others of us touch turns into fecal matter?

Asking the question at all may at first sight appear foolish. It is clear, certain self-righteous types will tell us, that a person who is fortunate is that way because all the steps he takes in life are oriented towards specific goals. Fortunate people are that way because they are organized, prudent, and wise. The only way to improve our lot in life, they say, is through hard work; constancy of purpose; serious dedication to personal betterment through study; an economical life style; wise and measured procedures in everything we do. Good luck, these people say, is found in the way of the trite old saying, attributed to someone whose name at present escapes me, "The harder I work, the luckier I get."

This answer, however, evades the main issue. It is nowhere recorded that King Midas was particularly gifted with any of these virtues. In fact, it appears that he was rather foolish all his life. And anyway, maybe you have already tried all of the above, and your luck still continues sour and bitter. Maybe every step you take in life, no matter how studied and prudent, still fetches you up against the contrary wind of misfortune. Maybe you have worked hard all your life, and the harder you worked, the worse became your luck. Or maybe you simply do not have the capacity for hard work. In which case it is time to consider that your ill fortune consists in the very fact that you were born without those virtues that make a person fortunate. You were born into misfortune. In plain language, to paraphrase the old expression, somebody up there doesn't like you.

The type of good luck that Midas enjoyed is that kind of luck which comes despite the choices a person makes. Eventually, however, there can be a choice so drastically wrong that there is no escape from the unfortunate consequences.

To illustrate, let us continue the story of Midas's life to the end. He was called upon to act as one of the judges in a musical contest between the gods Apollo and Pan; Apollo playing his lyre and Pan his pipes. The other judges, whatever their true feelings may have been, prudently voted for Apollo who was more to be feared than the easygoing Pan. But Midas foolishly cast his vote for Pan, showing, again, that his great good fortune was not entirely dependent on his good sense. Midas had learned nothing from his nearly disastrous experience with the golden touch.

Apollo punished him for his judicial error by making a pair of ass's ears sprout from his head.

Midas hid them under a Phrygian cap, and for a long time no one knew his secret except his barber, whom he swore to secrecy. But the barber felt that if he couldn't tell someone such a sensational secret he would surely burst. So one day, while walking on the edge of a marsh, the barber dug a hole in the moist earth and whispered into it, "Midas has ass's ears!" Then he covered the hole and slunk away, no doubt feeling a large measure of relief. Soon, a new plant grew out of that hole and it spread over the entire marsh. When the wind blew over this strange new growth a vast buzzing and whispering was stirred up, and the secret of Midas's ears was let out. For this new plant was the bulrush, and the message it whispered was, "Midas has ass's ears, Midas has ass's ears!"

Midas was so mortified to see his secret discovered that he poisoned himself, and died a miserable death.

King Midas was apparently not very wise, in the generally accepted sense of the word, but he was so fortunate in everything he did that his lack of wisdom was effectively supplanted by his good luck. The good fortune that Midas enjoyed for almost his entire life was the same kind of good luck that can befall a dog, and that has given rise to the common expression, "You lucky dog, you!"

The kind of luck that a dog can enjoy serves to demonstrate the independence of the quality of luck from the quality of wisdom. Let us examine the parallel lives of two dogs. One of these dogs is, let us say, a border collie. Vivacious and active, it is blessed at birth with the good fortune of belonging to a highly prized breed of dogs with that insatiable appetite for leaping and chasing after thrown objects, a trait that endears it to children and grown men alike.

The other dog is a mongrel mutt, born lazy and gluttonous, with a dull and coarse coat of short hair, with a tail curving shamelessly upward, exposing its private parts to full view at all times. A dog that cannot be trusted alone with any food left carelessly on the kitchen table. A dog that will just as soon defecate on the living room rug as not. A dog that, if you throw a frisbee for it to retrieve, will wait for it to hit the ground before picking it up and listlessly bringing it to you. If it doesn't just yawn and lie down to take a snooze, that is.

The first of these dogs will be cherished all its life by its owners. It will be carefully guarded against all the mischances that can befall dogs; it will eat better than do people in many third-world countries. If it gets sick it will be taken to a veterinarian where it will, perhaps, receive better medical treatment than many humans.

The life of the second dog, on the other hand, will always dangle from a thread. It may sometimes eat reasonably well off the scraps left over from the family meals. But the very nature of this dog's origins dictates that its owners will be slipshod people who may carelessly feed it chicken bones, or other such inappropriate food. If it gets sick as a consequence of this, it is unlikely that its owners will spend a dime on veterinary attention. If the family moves, it may abandon this worthless canine to its own devices: to end up on the street, where it will be run over by a car or get picked up by the dog catchers.

The first of these dogs is very fortunate. It is a smart dog. One might almost call it a wise dog. It would never befoul the living room rug or steal a roast chicken off the kitchen table. But is this really wisdom? What has this dog done during its life to earn its fortunate status? It is commonly accepted that dogs, being unable to speak, cannot think, and therefore cannot be wise. Dog lovers will be inclined to say, "This isn't true. Dogs can think; there are wise dogs and there are dumb dogs." But, if this is so, can a dumb dog be taught to be wise? Anyone who has ever had a dumb dog, I think, will say no. It is almost impossible to teach a dumb dog to be smart. Of course this is also true, to a very large degree, of humans, but human beings have a recourse that is not available to dogs.

The real question, however, is not whether a dog can be wise or not. For it can readily be seen that some dogs are smart, i.e., "wise," and that some are dumb. In these two examples of dumb and smart dogs, the interrelationship between luck and wisdom can be seen, and the question therein posed is whether the good life that is a natural consequence of wisdom is only the good luck that is also the consequence of wisdom. The answer seems to be, as has been indicated above, that good luck, though it can be a natural by-product of wisdom, is also something that can exist separately on its own; and that just as wisdom can produce good luck (though this is not always the case), so can good luck produce wisdom. (And, again, this is not necessarily always the case.) Therefore, the wise dog's wisdom is only the good luck it was born with, which impels it to make correct choices. It does not have a clue that it is acting wisely. Combining the examples of the unlucky dog and the lucky one with the example of Midas we can then see, also, that it is possible to be lucky but dumb, and therefore, by extension, intelligent but unlucky. And finally, that "luck," therefore, must necessarily be a very tangible quality, independent of hard work, wisdom, or constancy.

Most of us believe that we are smart enough to earn a living, but most of us also believe that our luck is lousy, and that it could stand a little improvement so we could thereby lead a better existence. How can we bring this about? How else, except by tackling fate herself at a time *before* our destiny was first concocted—at a time *before* the amount of wisdom and the amount of hard luck that would be our lot in life was decided upon. Here I will talk about the ways and means by which you can do this.

Begin by imagining that your life is like a tree. Your present station in life is the fruit of that tree, and the nature of that fruit will vary from one individual to another. Some people are like lemons, soured by the life we have led. Others are like withered, worm-eaten figs on the branches; or like rotting apples; or like mulberries, sweet, but small and insignificant. Some people are like mangos, which, though growing on a stout and sturdy tree, are squishy and insubstantial. A very few of us are like the golden apples of the Hesperides, and others yet are nothing more nor less than dingle berries, growing on the dingleberry tree.

To make changes in your life, therefore, you must change the nature of that fruit. If you are a mango or avocado type of person, you cannot too easily change your fruit to apples or pears. It can be done, but it is a very long and slow process. However, there is a large assortment of varieties of mangos and avocados. You should begin your task of improvement by trying to graduate to a more commercial variety of those fruits. But if you are a dingleberry and would like to be a peach or a nectarine, then your task is infinitely more difficult. Even here, nevertheless, there is still hope.

Chapter 3

Acquiring Wisdom by Improving Our Luck

If things frequently go wrong for us, if we seem to be cursed by bad luck, more often than not the reason can be found in our own defects. We are slipshod, lazy, disorganized, inclined to procrastinate. It certainly seems that if we wanted to, we could correct these defects and forge another destiny for ourselves. Why don't we want to? Why do we continue to be lazy, slipshod and disorganized, when we know that by making those changes we could eliminate a host of evils?

Part of the reason is because most humans have no desire to become another person. Of course the common, ordinary Joe Blow would love to improve his condition in life. But if he has to become another person in order for this to happen, he is not interested. If he should manage to shake off the bad habits of thought and behavior that make him what he is, he would go from being a poor but relatively easy-going Joe Blow, to becoming a grim and dour miser, a Joseph Blowe. This new person would no longer be himself; he would be someone entirely different. So why should Joe Blow care? This is the nub that makes changing ourselves one of the most difficult things in the world to do. That, and the fact that united to our bad habits is the binding force of the basic condition with which we were cast into being—with its physical representation is our genetic makeup—which, in the vast majority of mankind, will be a condition marked by a lack of strong willpower and common sense.

We must therefore concentrate on improving the lot in life of our present self, the person that we are. We do this by improving our day-to-day luck, which we can accomplish by a prudent and selective observance of superstitious practices. Having attained this improvement, establishing a stable base under our feet, changes in our character will naturally follow, with little or no conscious effort on our part. Just as in sewing, the point of the needle goes first through the cloth, to be followed by the thread. Luck is the sharp point of the needle that pulls a new thread into the fabric of our destiny. So then, striving to change ourselves without first improving our luck is much like trying to push the thread through the cloth without the needle.

If we manage to bring about this improvement in our luck, we will also have naturally acquired a bit of wisdom in the process. This enhancement of our wisdom will give us the ability to take better advantage of our improved luck. Therefore, luck and wisdom will complement each other; the more we acquire of the one, the more will the other follow. Otherwise, it would do us little good to improve our luck. Without the capacity to use each fortunate incident in life to lift ourselves into a higher position, all strokes of luck that we might effect would be short-lived.

Still, however, it is possible to live a long and happy life with luck, unaccompanied by any great degree of wisdom and talent. Contrariwise, all the persistence, dedication and single-mindedness in the world will be useless if we are not also blessed with a reasonable measure of good luck. We cannot succeed—lead a happy life—if we have talent but no luck whatsoever.

As a few short and random examples of this truth, we can look at the life of Vincent van Gogh, or Edgar Allan Poe, or Mozart, who each, despite their undeniable talent and genius, led a wretched existence and ended his days miserably. They had no luck at all. No doubt there have been thousands upon thousands of other persons of a like condition who would have been worthy of even greater admiration and veneration, but left not a jot of evidence of their passage through life for that same reason.

In juxtaposition to these unacclaimed-in-their-day geniuses, we have the examples of many modern-day popular idols who, without any talent worth memorializing, have amassed great fortunes and attained near-idolatrous worship. They have been very lucky. Lucky in that, although born without any marked degree of the usual virtues that accompany good fortune, they have been destined to enjoy a happy and prosperous life.

We must also bear in mind that often a stroke of good luck, unaccompanied by any talent or other merit, can actually be nothing more than a curse in disguise. In these cases the recipient's life is too inherently unfortunate to benefit from any random lucky occurrence. There are many people who are that way. Their misfortune is too deeply rooted in the very wellsprings of accursedness to be easily changed. In simple language, these people are cursed. In their endeavors to improve their luck, therefore, these people should also concentrate on ways to lift this curse, so that they may derive some sort of benefit from any strokes of luck they might occasionally experience.

In other words, there is a marked difference between good luck and good fortune. Strokes of luck come about through the natural effects of chance and probability, such as in winning a lottery. Good fortune and blessedness come about from having been endowed with these gifts from before the beginning of life. Moreover, fortunate people are not favored by any overt imbalance in the laws of chance. The fortunate person does not have any greater probability of winning a fifty-dollar football pool than anyone else.

The unfortunate person, therefore, sometimes enjoys strokes of luck because of the rigid application of the laws of chance and probability. The forces that administer those laws are sometimes obliged to allow the toss of a coin or the roll of a pair of dice to favor the unfortunate person over the fortunate one.

An adjustment can always be made later on. Many unfortunate people know this, having divined it instinctively, or having learned the fact through many hard knocks. They know that if you have been unfortunate all your life and suddenly experience a great stroke of good luck, a correction will not be long in coming.

It can be seen, then, that our basic fortune must necessarily be harder to improve than our luck. By improving our luck, however, we acquire the power to change our basic fortune and our destiny. Little strokes of luck become a tool that we can use to probe into the receptacle in which our destiny has been concocted. We have seen, in the examples of lucky and unlucky dogs, how fortune or misfortune can be our assigned lot in life. The dogs we spoke of had no hand at all in forging their individual destinies. Their fates were due entirely to matters outside their control. It is the same with us; an unseen power has assigned us our position in life before we were born. But unlike the dog, our intellectual capacity and our reasoning faculties give us the power to change that situation in its beginnings.

In order to effect radical changes in our life, we need to effect changes in its very roots; and to have the strength to do this, we must first bring about small changes in our present situation through strokes of luck. We cannot do this by any mathematical or physical procedure. So we will concentrate mostly on metaphysical considerations which help us attain this end.

To provide a basis for these metaphysical considerations, let us assume that the ruling force in life—our individual fate—is personified by the three malevolent old hags of Greek mythology, who, on their loom, spun out the destiny of men on Earth: Clotho, the spinner; Lachesis, who measured out the thread of each person's destiny; and Atropos, who it seems had the quite simple task of snipping the dangling end of that thread when the person's life came to an end—when Clotho had finished weaving it into her creation.

But it can be gathered that their jobs were not as simple as all that. The Fates must surely have been the very architects of the beginning of creation itself, and responsible today for the destiny and purpose of every particle of matter, living or not, in the universe, ruling also over chance and probability. The ancient Roman and Greek view of the Fates bears this out. For it seems that even their gods were subject to the whims of Fate. In Ovid's *Metamorphoses* we have Jupiter saying to the assembled gods and goddesses, who were complaining of certain injustices, "You too, are ruled by Fate, and that you may bear your lot more cheerfully, even I am beneath its sway."

We might also mention here that it was not without good cause that the Greeks settled on three for the number of the Fates. They had noticed that fate and destiny are composed of three conjoined and intermingled parts.

We will combine this notion of the three Fates with other ideas, to show several approaches to changing the original conditions in our contract with Destiny and with life, a contract that was drafted without our consensus, of course, because we were not yet born when its conditions were drawn up. We will look into various ways in which some of the sentences and paragraphs in that contract can be annulled and abrogated. Such as by learning from our dreams; learning to spot the significance of an occasional coincidence; paying heed to omens and to superstitious taboos and even the advisability of eating properly to thereby improve our luck. Taken all together, they boil down to learning the art of a subconscious divination of the future.

We will begin, first, with the subject of coincidence, with a superficial explanation of why coincidences occur, and how we can use them to change our reality and our luck. The late Arthur

Koestler, in *The Roots of Coincidence*, tried to explain why a coincidence is something that can naturally be expected. But his approach, unfortunately, was hindered by his natural reluctance to use primitive and anthropomorphic terms, which is the only way in which such things can be explained without lapsing into incomprehensible pseudo-scientific or psychological babble.

In accordance with the foregoing anthropomorphic view of fate, then, here is a similar, straightforward explanation of why coincidences occur. When the Fates plotted, eons ago, the billions of events that were to take place on Earth, it is natural to suppose that they would often tend to dispose of matters in lump packages, impelled by expediency and propinquity. The way in which one event, name, number, or occurrence can suggest another is well known to us. It applies equally to the Fates. Just as the names Tom and Dick, to us, must immediately be followed by Harry, so to the Fates must a typhoon scheduled in the Nicobar Islands be followed soon after by the scheduling of a hurricane in Nicaragua.

One name often appears to suggest another similar name to the Fates. Or perhaps they simply become confused and forgetful when they plot their events. Perhaps they run out of names and numbers, and repeat one they have already used before. Such as when they have a child named Jessica fall down a well, to be rescued after great publicity and nationwide expectancy, and then repeat the event several years later with a child named Jesse, also rescued after great nationwide interest and publicity.

Or such as when they have a mare named Silver Sally win a race at ten to one at Belmont and a horse named Solid Silver win its race at Turf Paradise the next day, also at ten to one.

In the final accounting, one must remember that place names, personal names, and the names of horses, are just as limited to the Fates as they are to us. That, in short, is what produces a coincidence. An extremely simplified explanation, true, for something so unfathomable and mysterious, but for our purposes this view should suffice.

Moreover, is it really so far-fetched to ascribe human tendencies, failings, and procedures to anything whatsoever in the universe? For where did we ourselves acquire these proclivities if not from the primeval cauldron of creation?

The acceptance of this explanation for coincidences can be of inestimable help to us in every walk of life. We can become attuned to the hidden machinations of fate and destiny, to a certain degree, by paying attention to things and events in various corners of the world. By watching for the likelihood of a replication of any given event, we can pick better times to buy stocks, trade in our car, or change jobs. This holds true even in things of the most minor importance.

Say, for example, you get up one morning and notice, as you are donning your underwear, that your shorts are so old they are beginning to resemble an old jock strap. You decide you will go out today and buy some new underwear. Then, as you are having breakfast, you see on the news that a Frenchman named Jacques Le Strappe has been fired as CEO of a securities underwriting firm. This should tell you that it is not a good day for you to leave the *security* of your home to go out and buy *underwear*.

Notice the subtle relationship in the above words. Everything in life and in the world is that way. The example provides a clue as to how we can use the relationships between words and events to divine a superficial construct of the future.

Except for this hypothetical example of the Frenchman Jacques Le Strappe, I find myself hard pressed to come up with specific examples of mundane coincidences to illustrate my points. Someone once asked Kant why he had not included some examples in his ponderous and incomprehensible *Critique of Pure*

Reason, to make his work easier to understand. He answered that to have done so would have made his book too long. I, on the other hand, don't include more examples because I can't think of any. I would love to make my book longer. But coincidences are usually very subtle and tenuous, and hard to remember.

An exception to this rule, however, is the race track, where the names and numbers of horses provide a rich breeding ground for coincidence. At one time I was an assiduous frequenter of race tracks, impelled as much by my desire to investigate and test my theories of luck and coincidence as upon my desire to make unearned profits. The race track has the added advantage that when natural coincidences are not forthcoming we can manufacture our own. This involves practices somewhat akin to magic, I admit, but magic is itself based on my own theory of coincidence. In my ceaseless quest for the ultimate method of picking winning horses, I tried, at various times, several divinatory methods, among which the following two deserve mention because of the favorable results they produced.

The first of these methods involves rolling ten or so numbered golf balls (depending on the number of horses in the race being investigated) out of a receptacle and across a hardwood floor towards an upright strip of cardboard with one golf-ball-sized hole cut into it at floor level. The golf ball that goes through the hole will tend to correspond to the number of the horse that will win the race. This method produced excellent results for me for some time.

A second method had to do with placing a cat into a circular mesh cage made out of scraps of crab and crawfish traps, with several exits numbered from one to ten, using various cats that my little daughters would adopt from time to time. I would induce the cat to exit from the cage through the numbered gate corresponding to the number of the horse scheduled to win its race, subtly threatening it with dire consequences if it failed me. If the cat should show an inclination to curl up and go to sleep inside the cage, I would prompt it to make a speedy exit with a few drops of icy water. With one of these cats I found that a good way to accomplish this was by suddenly thrusting a world globe towards its face. For some reason that particular cat was terrified of it and would almost tear the flimsy cage apart in its efforts to escape. (I had to engage in this activity somewhat furtively, by the way, because of opposition from my daughters.)

Aside from these slightly harsh measures, I must assure cat lovers that no substantial mistreatment of the cat was involved, and that I rewarded the successful cats handsomely with the choicest bits of fish, shrimp, and chicken livers, and by allowing them to sleep in my bed.

The first cat that I used this way, a vagrant female that my daughters had named Precious, picked winners with an amazing consistency for several weeks. But with subsequent felines I was not so successful. Does this mean that Precious was a specially gifted cat? I don't think so. Over the years I have tried many other divinatory methods and I've noticed something peculiar about all of them: they produce results only at the outset. Then, something seems to build up a resistance and the method loses its efficacy.

An unbeliever would say, simply, that the laws of probability take over, and in a way, of course, that is true. Another way to look at the matter, however, is to consider that the powers that guard the arcane are initially caught unawares, and then, having recovered from the surprise, manage to hastily reform their lines of resistance, to thereby preserve the tapestry of time and life, with its inherent probabilities intact.

Using a set of golf balls to represent the horses in a race does not comprise "sympathetic magic," as Sir James Frazer, in his famous *The Golden Bough*, would have described it. What we are doing is tossing an extra thread upon the loom of the Fates, prompting them to weave it into their creation. We are doing it within the context of a specific horse race, for which they have already constructed a random set. Quite often, then, they will tend to simply use the same set they have already used for the horse race, impelled by laziness, convenience, and propinquity. They will not want to be bothered to construct a separate random set for something for which they have already arranged a sequence. The same applies to the gate that the cat will choose to exit from the cage. Because the cat has even less free will than we do, it does what the Fates tell it to do.

More often than not, as I have said, a coincidence is so tenuous and subtle that it passes unnoticed. Nevertheless, successful and fortunate people, though they may not realize it, and though they may scoff at the very suggestion, are greatly influenced in their every move and action by a subconscious observance of the power of coincidence.

You and I, however, since we were not blessed with the natural-born ability to perceive these coincidences subconsciously, must learn to recognize them consciously. That is the difference between fortunate people and you and me. The first-named have a power that aids and protects them (presently, we will talk about what that power is). You and I do not. We have lost our connections to that benign power, or, more properly speaking, our connection to it has always been imperfect. It therefore behooves us to establish an alternative to this connection, to thereby provide ourselves with a reasonable facsimile of good fortune, which will in turn serve to help us improve that imperfect connection.

True good fortune does not come without several concomitant virtues, one of which is patience. I mention this because any benefits to be found in my proposed system will not come instantaneously, but only after a long period of patient dedication to the principles espoused herein.

So I hope the reader will not curse me if, after reading this book, he still does not immediately improve his financial situation, or gain a promotion in his work, or win the lottery, as it is more than likely he will not. I am sure, in any event, that my advice is sound, and that it will make the reader a better, happier person. And that the weight and force of the ill fortune he was born with will be significantly decreased.

Chapter 4

Coincidence and the Outcome of Horse Races

My experiments with golf balls, divinatory cats, and many other such methods, involve the purposeful fabrication of a coincidence. But where horse races are concerned, such resorts are often not necessary since this is a field in which the occurrence of coincidence can be as rich and lush as the growth in a tropical garden.

The race track, then, is a place in which the evidence for the legitimacy of my theories can be most readily seen. That is the reason I will be referring so frequently to horse races, even though I myself no longer go to the track very often. During my years as a more or less fully dedicated racing fan, I extracted a great deal of benefit from my theories at the track, so that I can now pass on certain secrets and procedures to anyone who cares to use them.

In the earlier part of my race-track years, I relied heavily on coincidence. Perhaps too heavily. But where horse races are concerned, too much is better than none at all. I have many fond memories of fantastic long shots that put cash in my pocket because I followed a hunch, based on a coincidence.

After some time of betting on the horses this way—such as betting on a mare named Sara Toga because of certain dealings I was having with people from New York at the time—I became a handicapper, and sagely followed the counsel of veteran race-goers, who advise such things as: never bet on a horse that has never gone the distance; never bet on a horse that hasn't raced within the last two weeks; never bet on a horse appearing for the first time at a track; never bet on a horse that is not being ridden by one of the top jockeys at a meet; never bet . . . and so forth.

But adhering to all those rules took more discipline than I was endowed with, and my bankroll suffered, besides the fact that observing these restrictions took all the fun out of going to the track. Then I began to combine coincidence and hunches with my newly acquired handicapping knowledge, and gradually I saw an improvement in my fortunes.

Here is one example of how this worked out: Ten or so years ago I was going through one of those long losing streaks that all racing fans experience with more or less chronic regularity. One of those periods in which it seems that a malevolent fate has singled us out for persecution, so that no matter how long and conscientiously we study a race, and no matter how thoroughly we examine every possible outcome, we invariably wind up betting on the wrong horse, even out of a very small range of choices.

It was at one of those small tracks where cheap horses, with their notorious inconsistency, can often wreak such havoc on all the rules and procedures of sensible handicapping.

One day I was standing on the apron, between the grandstand and the railing, as I glumly watched my choice once more come straggling in at the tail end of the pack. As the horses pounded across the finish line, a woman standing beside me—a somewhat bony woman dressed in a slinky black dress—exploded in a fit of jubilation. She had a ticket on the winner, of course. She had just known it was going to win, she told me. The horse's name was Fast Buck Phil and her father, a man who I gathered was always on the watch for a fast buck, was also named Phil. Besides, she said, the horse was number five, and five had always been her lucky number.

I tried to show an appropriate degree of joy at her good fortune and her acute horse sense. As she hurried off to the windows to cash her bet, I followed her absently with my gaze, wondering why she was dressed in black, as we often wonder about things that are none of our business. Maybe she was recently widowed, I speculated idly, and was dressed thus out of respect for the deceased, as she tried to assuage her grief by picking up some fast bucks at the track.

Then I turned my attention back to the *Racing Form*, and opened the pages to the next race. I had already long since made my choice in that race, but this time, as I scanned the entries once more, my attention was drawn to a long shot I had already discarded as one of the more likely losers. It came from a poor stable and was being ridden by one of the less successful jockeys at the meet; the horse was not recently raced, had no recent workouts, and was being raced at the wrong distance. On top of all that, it had lost its last race by ten lengths, and was now stepping up slightly in class. But its name was Carbony. The name is quite similar to carbon, which is black, and I had just been talking to a strange, bony woman dressed in carbon black.

I decided that such a curious coincidence was worth investing in. Especially when one took into account the inconsistency of the cheap horses that Carbony was racing against, and certain other details that I now noticed about the favorites, too long to go into here. So I laid down a hefty bet on Carbony to win, and finally broke my losing streak when it came in first at a gratifying twelve to one.

There have been numerous other such coincidences across the years, which have convinced me of the legitimacy of my beliefs. At Turf Paradise in Phoenix I once stood by the paddock as the horses were saddled, trying to spot the one in the best condition. Two men stood nearby, apparently not too concerned with the business at hand of examining the horses, since they were exchanging family news and gossip. One of them was telling the other that his wife had just talked on the phone with "Millie," a woman apparently known to both of them, and that

Millie had told his wife that the snow was still a foot deep back in Ohio. At that very moment a mare named Millie's Snowflake was being paraded before our eyes by the cold walker. A most curious coincidence. I quickly checked out the mare's Past Performances, and realized that her chances were not as bad as appeared at first glance. I made a cautiously small bet on Millie's Snowflake to win and once more saw my theories vindicated.

Later, I realized that my caution had exceeded my good sense. The mare was going off at excellent odds, and the coincidence was quite remarkable.

Another example, at the same track: As I stood in the middle of the floor, undecided as to whether I should choose the prudent course of passing the race or of going to the windows and placing a wild bet on whatever number popped into my mind, I suddenly noticed an acquaintance, a woman who always brought her baby with her to the track, agitatedly changing her baby's diaper, trying to finish the chore in time to watch the race. Her baby's name was Luke. I quickly hurried to the windows and laid down a few bucks on Leaky Luke to win. Another good investment.

At Jefferson Downs, in New Orleans, I once placed a winning bet on a horse named Stinger, largely because on that same day I had been stung by two or three hornets as I crawled around under the foredeck of a small boat. Actually, the incident with the hornets prompted me to take a close look at Stinger. This close look showed me that Stinger had not raced for several months, and that it did well after a long lay-off.

There were many other coincidences that I cashed in on during my years as a serious racing fan; from my first-ever bet at Sacramento Fairgrounds many years ago, when I collected a rich payoff on a filly named Stepping Emily, which I bet on because that day I had met a young lady named Emily, who walked with a curious, mincing little gait, to the last such bet that I recall, on a horse named Affy David, chosen because of certain legal difficulties that a close friend was experiencing at the time.

These days, I do not go to the track too frequently; and, when I do, I rely on coincidence only sparingly. The reason is because of what I suggested in the preceding chapter: The efficacy of any method that is used for delving into the arcane wanes with use, until it actually produces a negative effect, because of the tendency of the arcane to develop a resistance against such incursions. This holds true, however, only in regard to the use of that method by each individual. When a different person uses the method, it becomes an entirely different game.

The judicious use of hunch and coincidence gives us several advantages over the strait-laced handicapper. First of all it will give us many chances to hit upon some spectacular longshots that we would never dream of betting on if we were to follow all the rules propounded by expert handicappers. Second, we can bet on every race in a day's card, making every day that we go to the track an exciting one, thereby freeing ourselves from the deadly boredom that can beset the pure handicapper. And, most important of all of course, if used correctly and wisely, with courage and with confidence, it guarantees that we will wind up ahead in the long run.

Part of the method, if I may call it a method, consists in combining hunch and coincidence with the fundamentals of handicapping, without letting these handicapping principles constrict our intuitive knowledge, and, at the same time, without letting our hunches cancel out what little handicapping skill we may possess. Sometimes we can allow a strong hunch or coincidence to overrule our handicapping skill. There are also times when we should shrug aside what we feel is a hunch, and let our handicapping common sense prevail. The trick, of course, consists in learning to recognize a genuine hunch, or a strong and curious coincidence. Distinguishing between a genuine hunch and a false one is something which, at first sight, appears impossible to do, but this isn't so. It can often be done.

Along with the rules of handicapping, we should also combine and regulate our system with a close observance of various facts of the real world ("real" in the sense that we disregard the mysteries of coincidence and the legitimate basis for superstitious beliefs, as if they did not exist). I am referring to the tote board, the odds, and the irrefutable fact of the laws of chance and probability. By carefully monitoring ourselves this way, we can avoid deadly boredom at the track by placing harmless little two-dollar bets, while we bide our time, waiting for the strong hunch or coincidence that will lead us to make a memorable bet, to savor for the rest of our lives. The system I am going to talk about entails belief in a certain theory about the basic nature of reality. This theory consists of several components, and these components, in turn, imply various corollaries. One of these corollaries is that a coincidence is only the natural thing to expect. Another is that the same force that causes the simultaneous occurrence of two or more unrelated but similar happenings could very well have other unobserved and mysterious effects. These unknown and unobserved effects should be taken into consideration whenever we might feel inclined to shrug off the importance of superstitious caution.

The acceptance of these beliefs and theories will show why the horse racing fan should pay close attention to coincidence, and why, more than anyone else, he should carefully avoid transgressions against the world of superstition. I am proposing, in short, that there is a real force that lurks behind our superstitious fears, and that this force, which is the same one that brings about the occurrence of a coincidence, can sometimes bring about the dire effects that are believed to follow the breaking of a superstitious taboo. I hope to show here, then, that superstitious beliefs have a legitimate basis in this underlying reality, and I hope to convince the reader that they should all be accorded a certain degree of respect, or, at least, tolerance.

In fact, even if we don't share someone's particular belief, it is advisable to respect it, if only to avoid friction. I remember the occasion at Turf Paradise, in Phoenix, when I stood at the railing to watch a race with a casual acquaintance, a young fellow yet unlearned in the hard knocks of the horse racing world. He refused to tell me which horse he had bet on, evidently through a superstitious fear that this would sour his luck. As soon as the horses left the gate, however, I could immediately see which horse it was. His choice took the lead from the start—it was a mile and a sixteenth race—and the fellow went berserk with excitement. At the half, his horse was ahead by some seven lengths, and my companion was grinning from ear to ear, glancing at the tote board and whooping out things like, "Forty to one, man, Forty to one! Go, man! Go, go, go!"

But this horse (I don't recall its name) was a sprinter, and had shown this same tendency to take the lead in every one of its previous races, all at six furlongs or less, only to fade away in the stretch. For some reason its trainer had decided to try it out over a distance, perhaps in an effort to break it of this perverse habit.

With the intention of providing a gentle let-down for my friend who, in his inexperience, thought his horse had already won, I observed mildly, "He's still got a long way to go." I could see, at the three-quarters pole, that his horse was already tiring, and the rest of the pack, all tightly together, was, inexorably, gaining on him.

I have never seen such a look of hatred as the one he gave me when, in the stretch, his horse seemed to suddenly stand still, as the rest of the field swept past him. No doubt he had the superstitious belief that with my words I had brought about this incredible outcome, hexing his forty-to-one shot when it had already won the race.

I have no doubt, also, that this young man had picked his horse through a hunch, or because of some coincidence or other that he had noticed. I will therefore say here what I will perhaps repeat again, since it cannot be stressed enough: Most hunches are very unreliable.

The art of hunch-betting, of correctly picking the winner by following a hunch, entails the ability to grasp a certain feeling, a certain response, when we see the name of the horse in question in the *Racing Form*, or hear its name. It awakens an awareness, sometimes actually expressed in words. Sometimes, we ourselves, when we get that feeling, say to ourselves, "This horse is going to win the race." When you get that feeling about a horse, and say those words to yourself, it shows that you accept the fact, either consciously or subconsciously, that somewhere in the future the race is already over and done with and the results a bygone conclusion. It shows that you believe in predestination and the immutability of fate. Are we right if we believe this? For the time being, I will just answer, "Yes, and no."

There is one superstition in particular with which I will mainly concern myself: The belief, firmly rooted in every culture on Earth, that everything that occurs in the world comes in sets of twos and threes. The reason this superstition is so widespread is because its effects are so manifestly evident. In fact, the effects of this tendency are so marked that there are few people who will dare to disregard it. When we look carefully, we can see even the most hard-nosed of skeptics observing the superstition, in some way or other, although they will stubbornly refuse to acknowledge it. We can frequently see high-and-mighty heads of state, prominent politicians, and other great leaders of men and nations, adopting certain ponderous methods and procedures in government affairs because of the occurrence of events which has awakened in them the fear that the event might occur again.

Curious to observe, these same people, who most frequently allow themselves to be influenced by the belief that all things in the world come in twos and threes, are the ones who will most firmly reject the idea that there is any such real tendency in the world. They steadfastly affirm that the effect is only apparent. They will say they are only being judiciously cautious when, for example, they institute new rules and regulations (which can sometimes go to ludicrous extremes) to forestall the re-occurrence of any particular disaster.

It could therefore be argued that superstition is really nothing more than an exemplary caution. It's the type of caution which should advise the racing fan that if a heavy favorite named Lights of London has lost his race at Belmont, at odds of two-to-one, another horse named London Bells, going off at Aqueduct shortly after, at the same odds, is also very likely to lose.

In ancient times this propensity of fate to produce happenings in sets of twos and threes was well known, and no one had any reason to doubt the truth of it. The belief was universally held, from the lowliest of men to the loftiest.

Herodotus says, in his *Histories*, "The Egyptians, too, have made more use of omens and prognostics than any other nation. They keep written records of the observed results of any unusual phenomena, so that they come to expect a similar consequence to follow a similar occurrence in the future." Were the ancient Egyptians carrying this belief to an extreme? Maybe, maybe not. However, I think it was a mistake for them to keep written records.

Skeptical persons today tend to ask how we can possibly show that a coincidence is a normal and natural thing to expect. They tell us that the phenomenon is illusory—that for every supposed coincidence, there are a thousand "non-coincidences." In answer to this, many prominent investigators of these things have pointed out that for every coincidence that is noted, there are a hundred which pass *unnoticed*, because they did not affect anyone's life.

By accepting my own beliefs and theories, however unscientific and harebrained, as indisputable truths, I have managed to make many good bets at the track, some of them at fantastic odds, as high as seventy-to-one on a single horse. True, I don't come out ahead every day or every week. Not even every month. But neither do the best of handicappers. And I don't have to undergo the trepidation that these handicappers experience; betting large sums on a single horse every day that they go to the track, and often losing many hundreds of dollars before they see a winning day.

I have found that my methods work quite well at any track, but are especially effective at the smaller ones. At those little race tracks which constitute the boondocks of the racing world—Atokad Park, Delta Downs, Boise Race Track, La Mesa Park—where the percentage of winning favorites may be as low as twenty-eight percent (at major tracks an acceptable percentage is usually about thirty-three) we will often find that it is just as easy to pick a winner by throwing a dart at the *Racing Form*, as by conventional handicapping methods. Even at the best tracks, as a matter of fact, we can find that most races are unplayable, because, with ten horses or more in the race, there will be five or six which stand an equal chance of winning, and the odds on any one of them will be less than five-to-one.

In these cases, the only thing our handicapping knowledge can tell us is that we should refrain from betting. Post position, speed, pace, weight, recentness of last outing, lifetime earnings, age, class—they all balance out; so that the horse with the best post position is outclassed by the horse unfavorably spotted, and the horse that has the best speed rating is overshadowed by the one most recently raced, and so forth. The majority of races, unfortunately, are of this type. The track's racing secretary cards them that way to preserve the basic nature and purpose of a horse race.

What do we do in such a situation? It seems that the sensible thing would be to pass on the race. But we've come to the track to bet on the races, not to just sit there and watch them run. In a field of the type described above, it would appear that luck is the only factor that could guide one to the winner. And so it is. Here is where the person who knows how to take advantage of a legitimate hunch or coincidence can make up for the absence of line and/or his imperfect skill as a handicapper. In later chapters I will present some insights into how this can be done—how you can sometimes grasp the answer to unsolvable problems seemingly out of thin air, to produce rich payoffs, not only at the race track but in every aspect of life.

Chapter 5

Lapsus Linguae *and Coincidence*

We have seen from the foregoing that a coincidence should be no cause for wonder and astonishment, unless we are astonished only to see at first hand the mysterious hand of fate. If we pour a bagful of marbles into a funnel, we are not astonished to see each and every one of those marbles emerge in its turn from the tiny mouth of the funnel, where each of its companions has also passed. This would seem like a remarkable coincidence if we didn't know that each marble must of necessity eventually find egress at the same point.

That, in essence, is what a coincidence is. Everything in the world has its origins at the same point in time and space. Herman Melville's "mightiest whale" is descended from the microscopic bacteria with which it traverses the same path to eventual entropy, the same as every other particle of matter in the universe. If two or more entities happen to be traveling the same road, it's nothing to marvel at if they occasionally bump into each other.

In *The Roots of Coincidence* Arthur Koestler cites the Cambridge Physicist, Adrian Dobbs, who speculated that what we call foreknowledge of the future could consist of messages that we receive by means of "psitrons," particles of matter which operate in a second time dimension. These particles of matter would act as messengers, bringing us intimations of the future from this second time dimension, where multiple probabilities exist as "compresent dispositional factors, which incline or pre-dispose the future to occur in certain specific ways."

When the matter of divining the future is presented in that manner, however, the racing fan, along with everyone else trying to gain a true vision of the future, loses interest. This would mean that when we divine the winner of a horse race, we would only be receiving the forecast of a probabilistic state, not the true future. We are not interested in probabilistic states. Anyone can take a guess at a probabilistic state. We want the sure thing, the definite winner of a horse race, or the true outcome of any other event in the future.

Nevertheless, a great deal can be inferred by the thoughtful racing fan or any other delver into the arcane from Dr. Dobbs' psitrons. One of the conclusions that could be drawn therefrom is that the tapestry of fate is not immutable. The personified fates are constantly patching and mending their tapestry. The little Dutch boy with his finger in the dike had nothing on the Fates. They have to ceaselessly stick their fingers into trillions upon trillions of leaks and fissures in the receptacle of destiny. Nothing is too small, or petty, or insignificant to be unworthy of their attention, from the beat of a fly's wing to the winner of a horse race at Boondock Downs.

The Fates created a slew of racehorses at the beginning of creation, spaced out over hundreds of years (at this writing I believe there are about 160,000 registered thoroughbreds in the *Racing Forms* computer banks), and inevitably they sometimes allowed themselves to be ruled by a sort of logical expediency when they decided which horse would win which race. If two horses, one named Bed of Cash and the other Making the Cash, were destined to run the same day at the same track, then we might expect that either one of them will stand a greater chance than usual of winning. (As a matter of record, both of these horses won their race, and a horse named Works Like Cash came in second behind Making the Cash.)

We can compare this tendency to our own human inclination to be influenced by a subliminal or repetitive message. In the case of the Fates, this human frailty is not necessarily an imperfection. It only seems so to us because in our imperfection its effects on us can often be deleterious. Frequently, the Fates committed what in a human being would be a *lapsus linguae*, accidentally duplicating a horse. More often than not, of course, the creation of two similarly-named horses is conscious and intentional, because they are limited by the number of available names just as much as we are.

The Fates will sometimes single out two or more horses for special treatment when their names have a certain affinity, like Marie Helene, Medieval Mary, Mademoiselle Fu, and My Nadia. These maiden fillies came in ninth, tenth, eleventh, and twelfth on May 14, 1986, at Belmont. In this outcome we can see that the Fates made a conscious effort to resist the temptation to bring them in first, second, third, and fourth, but still left them all carelessly lumped together at the tail end of the pack.

A remarkable example of how the Fates are not immune to the influence suggested by a name, is the well-known history of the immortal Man O' War. What was the name of the horse to which they assigned the honor of inflicting the only loss which Man O' War ever suffered? It was the longshot Upset, as every serious racing fan knows. This shows that the Fates share our human inclination towards irony, and probably enjoy a perverse joke every now and then.

Since long before the days of Kleoitas, who the historian Pausanias tells us invented the starting mechanism for the horse races at the Greek Olympics, humans have restlessly striven to learn about the future, resorting to oracles, even the cruder practices of sheep's entrails and other such unpleasant methods. For many centuries ancient Greek and Egyptian diviners, astrologers, and oracles often achieved astonishing results. Ancient histories are full of instances where a soothsayer or an oracle accurately foretold events to come in stark detail. In Plutarch's *Life of Lysander*, he tells of how that general was killed by the banks of a stream in a battle with the Thebans. Shortly after the battle some soldiers were discussing the circumstances of their general's death and mentioned how he fell by the banks of the stream known to them as the Hoplites. When he heard the name of the stream for the first time, a friend of the general's exclaimed in amazement that an oracle had recently given Lysander the following warning: "Beware the sound of the rushing Hoplites and the Earth-born dragon who cunningly strikes from behind." (The enemy soldier who struck down Lysander, by the way, had the figure of a dragon emblazoned on his shield.) Unfortunately for Lysander, he and most of the Spartan troops had been unaware of the name by which the stream was known in the region.

If the reader can contain his impatience to hear more about specific cases of coincidences involving horse races, I would also like to repeat the well-known case of the oracle which was given to Croesus, and which prompted him to initiate his disastrous war against Persia. "If you go to war against Cyrus," the oracle had said, "you will thereby destroy a great kingdom." So Croesus went to war and, sure enough, destroyed a great kingdom—his own.

These irrelevant anecdotes from antiquity serve to illustrate the manner in which the future is revealed to man. Notice that in every case in which startlingly true predictions were made by the ancient oracles, they were always couched in obscure and ambiguous terms. This is the only way in which fate and destiny allow their secrets to be revealed. The Greek myths are full of examples of what happens to those who predict the future too accurately and reveal divine secrets. The famous seer Phineus was blinded; Ocyrhoe, the lovely red-headed daughter of Cheiron the centaur, was turned into a mare (of course, she was already half-equine to begin with). We should not expect, therefore, to receive the prediction for the outcome of a race in clear, unequivocal words.

At one time there were dozens, perhaps hundreds, of oracles of more or less great importance all over the Greek world. People routinely traveled enormous distances to consult them and they seem to have been amazingly accurate in their pronouncements. Among the most famous were the Delphic oracle, and the oracle of Zeus Ammon, which was in what is today known as Siwa Oasis, in the middle of the Libyan desert. It's a place difficult to travel to even today, and yet Athenian and Spartan statesmen routinely made the immense journey from Greece to consult it.

Over the centuries the ancients gradually abandoned their oracles. One by one they fell into disuse and neglect. Why did they abandon them if, as I say, they were so truthful and accurate? It's evident that all the oracles had fallen into disrepute and were no longer dependable in their pronouncements. This only bears out what I have said earlier: All devices and methods to divine the future work well only at the outset.

Today, any such device will very rapidly become useless, especially if it's used for a selfish purpose like picking winners in horse races. In ancient times, devices lasted considerably longer, mostly because the nature of time was different in those days. Over the centuries, it has changed subtly, affected by man's technological advances and tampering. Perhaps they also lasted longer because the priests who officiated at the oracles discouraged people from utilizing them for puerile and petty purposes. Plutarch, in his essay, "Why Oracles Are Silent," records these words of the Cynic, Planetiades: "You ask why this oracle here [at Delphi] has not also fallen silent. It is indeed a wonder that it has not, harried as it is now with the shocking and blasphemous questions which people put to the gods. . . . Some beg for information on treasure troves, or about legacies, or about illegal marriages."

All this suggests that the ancient oracles, accurate as they were, may not have been well suited to provide us with the outcome of a horse race.

Another reason the ancient oracles were so accurate is that the people of those times were closer to the origins of creation than we are today. They had not retreated as much as we have from the sources of the esoteric knowledge which gave them so many insights into the workings of fate and destiny. This was especially true in Egypt, but since the Western world has inherited its civilization mostly from the ancient Grecian culture, very little of Egyptian knowledge and secrets has filtered down to us. One feature of their knowledge which is still known and much used is tarot cards; but tarot cards, useful as they are for other purposes, are peculiarly unsuited for predicting the outcome of a horse race.

Divining the outcome of a horse race, whether we do it by noticing a coincidence or by some method such as a divining cat, should be classified as a paranormal phenomenon. If we start from the premise of my theory, with its various components, it can then be readily understood why science, so far, has been unable to provide a rational explanation for these phenomena. Many investigators have made determined efforts to prove their existence, trying to find physical laws on which to base their theories. But, of course, no physical causes will ever be found, certainly no cause contained in the laws of physics as they are known today. So, since they cannot find these causes, scientists dismiss the phenomena in question as illusory.

In antiquity, most people accepted the existence of paranormal phenomena, and no one tried to probe into their causes with measuring or recording devices. But today, when a remarkable incident of this kind occurs, it is likely that scientists and investigators of every stripe will converge upon the location of the occurrence to delve, probe, and investigate from every possible angle, in efforts to find a physical explanation. Of course they don't find one. What they do find, quite often, is that the person to whom the incident occurred will finally confess that he or she achieved the effect in question by means of hidden strings, or other sleight of hand. Sometimes the physical manner by which the trickery was accomplished is of a no less remarkable nature than a paranormal phenomenon. But the investigators will usually accept it as the legitimate explanation.

I remember reading an article once about the lengths to which counterfeiters will go to falsify money. Some crooks, this article said, will even go so far as to split a twenty-dollar bill with a razor blade into two halves (so that each complete face of the bill is on one half) and paste each half on a one dollar bill, thereby creating two twenties. At the time I read the article I accepted it at face value and didn't pause to consider what a remarkable feat this would be. But I invite anyone to give that task a try. It is manifestly impossible. Similarly, the people who have experienced poltergeist phenomena and later admitted—perhaps when harried beyond endurance by investigators determined to prove that it was all a fraud—that they had provoked the occurrences themselves by physical means, are no less difficult to believe, when looked at with a sober mind.

Rather than believe that these persons simply changed their story because they were unable to withstand the pressures of their conscience, and of the investigators, we can consider that the same mysterious force that produces a coincidence—our personified fates—has stepped in and *rearranged* the occurrence (rearranged the past), in order to preserve the fabric of reality. Possibly, in centuries to come, the Fates will furnish the appropriate physical causes to correspond to the unexplained phenomena, but only when they can no longer hide the fact that these phenomena truly exist.

Originally, a great many of the events on Earth, which are today unpredictable, were as predictable as the orbits of the planets. Everything was created in a sequential and readable fashion, just as it would have been completely readable to predict that Upset would defeat the undefeated Man O' War, if human events had still been following the same pattern with which they were originally cast into being. Many of these events still remain in that original pattern. But as time progresses, it becomes increasingly difficult to find any coherence in the design.

We can still spot the occasional coincidence of a horse scheduled to win a race, whose name is suggestive of an event in our life; or a number in our affairs which coincides with the post number of a horse scheduled to win; or a winning horse's name which corresponds to some national or local event, and other such oddities. But these lucky occurrences become increasingly rare. More and more obscure and unused methods to divine the future become necessary.

For those readers who might share these beliefs, but feel slightly uncomfortable with them because of their apparently childish nature, here is a story. I recall that when I was a child in the fourth grade, and said to my teacher that the continents had once been a solid land mass and had drifted apart, as could quite obviously be seen by looking at a world map, she gave me a little condescending sort of simper, and said that no, I was mistaken. It only looked that way. Now, I see that the theory of continental drift is a respected scientific hypothesis.

No doubt many children, all over the world, knew this fact, though in their childish innocence they mistakenly thought that the continents were floating on the oceans, like huge lily pads.

Some day, perhaps, scientists will discover that all I have said here is true, and they will invest our theories with a mantle of respectability. They will, of course, bore deeper into the physical and philosophical strata of the universe to fix its bases, just as they have determined the movement of the continents to be in a deep-seated viscous zone within the Earth, and not on the surface of the oceans.

But wherever the foundation of these theories may be, the end result is the same. We are not primarily concerned with the exact explanation of these things, fascinating as that explanation may be. At present, we are only interested in applying the knowledge to pick a winning horse or two at the track—that and trying to figure the winning odds on life in general.

Chapter 6

Walking up the Stairs Can Change Your Luck

I have postulated that many superstitions are simply the residues of a survival mechanism, inherited from our remote ancestors, and that they should be respected.

Why do I insist that the horse racing fan, more than anyone else, should religiously observe all superstitious taboos? One reason, of course, is that betting on horse races is an endeavor which requires the greatest of luck in order to be consistently successful. We have all seen skilled morning-line experts and program handicappers who seem to produce excellent predictions throughout a racing season.

But what degree of success do they enjoy when they actually place a bet on their choice? I have seen very good handicappers pick a horse in each of ten races, correctly hit upon four or five out of ten, but place bets only on three or four of the losers, mistakenly choosing them as the best bets of the day. Legendary Black Cat McComb, of New Orleans, once picked ten out of ten for the Jefferson Downs program, but failed to bet on a single one of them.

Most of us have experienced the same misfortune. Time and again we will pick the two best horses in a race, study them carefully, finally choose one of them to bet on, and invariably, the one we discard comes in first and our choice fails us miserably. As I write these lines I am still smarting from having decided, some days ago at the simulcast races from Aqueduct, in favor of Noble Napper, against To B. Noble. To B. Noble came in first at fifty to one. There was absolutely no way a serious handicapper could have picked this horse. In the only other race in his career he had been eased. He was from a poor stable, of very poor pedigree, had no recent workouts; he was being ridden by an apprentice jockey, and he appeared dull and listless in the post parade. So I cannot blame my lack of handicapping skill for failing to pick this duplicated horse; only my lousy luck. I maintain, therefore, that in order to avoid contamination from those sources whence all bad luck originates, the horse racing fan should carefully avoid any action which might conceivably taint his aura. I know that many hundreds of thousands of racing fans all over the world, most of them of above average perception and intelligence, will agree with me.

As to the logic behind a superstitious belief or practice, why should there have to be any logic whatever behind it? This could be a reasonable expectation for a scientist engaged in an endeavor governed by known physical laws, but not for the horse racing fan. Besides, we can advance a reasonable hypothesis as to why there could be validity in any superstition. We have but to refer to our anthropomorphic view of fate and destiny. According to that view, we can say that unlucky acts are unlucky because that is the way they entered into creation and the entire scheme of things. Perhaps an insignificant act or occurrence can sometimes trigger the response it was assigned to set off at the beginning of creation. Just as the Fates often wove their tapestry following a human inclination to imbue it with a seeming logic, they also frequently followed no logic at all, or else worked according to obscure, non-human impulses.

The only rationale necessary to explain why some insignificant action could trigger an unfortunate occurrence to the person incautious enough to produce it, would be that fate and destiny arranged it that way. Just as they arranged that salt should have the effect that it does on the human palate, so could they have arranged that whoever should spill some would have bad luck, and that a person could save himself from these bad consequences if he would only toss a bit of it over his left shoulder.

This is all that would be necessary for the consequences of spilling salt to endure to our time. Many of these capricious decrees no longer preserve their effects. Of others, perhaps only tenuous residues of their original force still remain, diluted as they have been amongst the teeming throngs of contemporary humanity. Many of them, however, are still in effect, and much of their force is directed towards horse-racing fans.

Superstitious beliefs and behavior are something we have inherited from our very remote ancestors, who, being closer to the origins of creation, were aware, in a dim unconscious way, of the sequels and consequences which had been attached by the three Fates to every conceivable act and occurrence in the world.

However, without ceding any ground in the matter of whether superstition is a rational attitude or not, I must agree that it can be a destructive force when carried to extremes. A too-rigorous observance of superstitious beliefs can work to enslave us, constrain our actions and complicate our lives. In his essay, *On Superstition*, Plutarch spoke out against superstition as an emotion growing out of deluded reasoning. "So unhappy superstition," he said, "through an excessive anxiety to avoid everything that appears terrifying, unwittingly makes itself the victim of every sort of misery." The Greek word for superstition is derived from "fear of divinity," so perhaps Plutarch was mostly referring to an irrational fear of fate and destiny.

But a healthy respect for superstitious beliefs, such as I recommend, has nothing to do with fear. We should not fear fate. We should however try to understand it and avoid pitfalls, just as a sailor learns to respect the sea to avoid any foolish mistakes that will put him and his vessel in jeopardy. We should keep in mind that the polar bear that fails to observe the polar bear superstition of covering its nose will starve.

I am perhaps not the most qualified person to preach against carrying superstition to excess. I once threw away a mutuel ticket worth $220 in my haste to get rid of some others that were losers. I have the superstition, shared by millions of other horse-racing fans, that a losing ticket will contaminate my aura and sour my luck. At one time I used to contentedly munch peanuts while I watched my horses run and this helped ease some of the pain when they came straggling in at the tail end of the pack. But then I was told that eating peanuts at the track was unlucky, and I have gone peanut-less ever since; even away from the track, just to be on the safe side, thereby depriving myself, perhaps unnecessarily, of a nutritious snack food. And to be doubly safe, I have included popcorn and Cracker Jacks in the interdiction.

In summation: All unlucky actions are unlucky because the Fates decided it that way at the beginning of time. And, also, even though the exact nature of the unlucky act and its consequences have evolved over the ages, in tandem with the evolution of Man himself, the unlucky consequences still apply, though in a subtly changed form. Evidence for all this can be seen in the antiquity of many of our well-known superstitions. Take the common superstition of crossing the fingers. In Greek mythology we can see that it was known and used even by the gods themselves.

This superstition, by the way, is seldom applied in its correct form. Crossing the fingers should actually not be used to make something happen, but rather to *prevent* something from happening. This is illustrated in the Greek myth centering on the birth of Hercules. When the goddess Hera knew that Alcmene, Hercules' mother, was about to have her child, she sent the goddess of childbirth, Eileithyia, to delay his birth. Hera hated

Hercules' guts all his life, and even before he was born, because he was the illegitimate son of her husband, Zeus, you see.

The way in which Eileithyia attempted to carry out Hera's request was by sitting in front of Alcmene's home, holding her arms, legs, and fingers, tightly crossed while Alcmene labored mightily within the house. But Alcmene's slave girl, Galanthis, spotted the goddess in this suspicious posture, and immediately guessed what she was up to. She sidled up to the goddess and said, "You must go inside and congratulate my mistress. She has just given birth to a fine baby boy." The goddess sprang to her feet in shocked surprise, uncrossing her arms, legs, and fingers, and Hercules was immediately born.

The myth goes on to say that Hera—or perhaps it was Eileithyia herself—changed Galanthis into a weasel, for interfering in divine matters.

But this myth does not even begin to show how utterly ancient the origins of this particular superstition are. Because, quite possibly, it was inherited by Homo sapiens from his remote ancestors, the primeval protozoa from which he is descended. These primal life forms would have practiced our equivalent of crossing the fingers to prevent themselves from dividing in two, becoming two separate entities instead of one, and thereby, to all practical purposes, passing into another reality (we will have much to say about multiple realities later on). The secret was perhaps accidentally rediscovered in prehistoric times. Perhaps by one of our cavewoman ancestors, who realized that by crossing her legs she could prevent a pregnancy.

Today, crossing the legs is seldom used unless it is for the specific purpose indicated above. The reason, of course, is that we cannot walk around with our legs crossed. Especially not at the race track. So we cross our fingers instead.

As I have mentioned, the superstition is often misapplied. If you are at the race track and are watching a race in which the horse you have bet on is in the middle of the pack, crossing the fingers can be a big mistake. Because crossing the fingers only works towards preserving a status quo. Crossing your fingers, therefore, will only cause your horse to stay in the middle of the pack all the way. It is interesting to note that in this regard the primal protozoa from which we are descended had more sense than we do.

To prevent something from happening, there is an even more efficacious procedure, by the way, than simply crossing the fingers. It consists in hooking both index fingers and pulling tightly in opposite directions. In Central America, and no doubt in many other countries, the practice is well known. More than once in Honduras I have observed idle vagrants amuse themselves by doing this as they directed their attention to a dog attempting to defecate, thereby causing that canine considerable distress.

Make sure, therefore, that you apply the procedure correctly at the race track. Next time you're at the track, and your horse gains the lead, try that little trick, while concentrating intently on it and this should help it hold its lead all the way to the finish. This procedure is especially well suited with those horses that habitually gain the early lead only to tire and fade away in the stretch.

We can suggest a purely physical cause to explain how crossed or hooked fingers could affect a dog or a horse. Some animals perhaps have the ability to detect the waves of force from the mysterious field thus generated. It would appear that this force field is also generated by the Earth's tectonic plates when they strain against each other in the moments before an earthquake. In China it has been divulged in recent years that earthquakes there have been predicted by the behavior of domestic animals—dogs, pigs, and other livestock—which seem to experience distress of some sort just before an earthquake strikes.

Why would this supposed force be generated only by hooked or crossed fingers and the Earth's tectonic plates, you might ask, and not by the millions of other instances of unrelieved pressure, which abound all around us? In the case of hooked or crossed fingers it could be because the pressure is combined with mental energy which is directed toward a specific object or end. In the case of the Earth's tectonic plates, subjected to millions upon millions of tons of pressure beneath the Earth, and further combined with magnetic and gravitational fields, who can say what unknown effects could be thus released?

In these speculations it is well to keep in mind Arthur Koestler's observation, on how, in all of our theories upon non-physical phenomena, we invariably wind up postulating physical causes. So, in order to steer clear of this quite understandable inclination, let this physical theory about crossed fingers and the Earth's tectonic plates be our only concession to physical causes for paranormal phenomena. Let us keep in mind that no physical explanation is necessary.

Our remote ancestors, as we have said, were in closer contact to the origins of superstitious beliefs. They were closer in time, even though the difference between four billion years and four billion, ten thousand years may seem insignificant. But this small time difference put them much closer, spiritually, to the primitive life forms from which we are descended. And, just as important, they were relatively uncontaminated by modern thought and science. They knew and they understood, more clearly than we ever can, that certain things were bad luck and that certain actions could bring good luck, and that no physical, rational, or logical explanation was necessary.

Sir James Frazer, in *The Golden Bough*, contemptuously attributes all superstitious practices to "a childish belief in sympathetic magic," or that "like produces like," that primitive man in ". . . one great disastrous fallacy, a mistaken conception of the association of ideas . . ." erroneously believed, for example, that pouring water out of a vessel onto the ground would induce rain. Frazer failed to consider that some superstitions may have originated because of real effects observed by humans across many millennia, with the knowledge passed down from one generation to the next.

Primitive man, living in close alliance with nature, could see the tenuous connections forming the most improbable of relationships. The Malay crocodile hunter mentioned by Frazer, who would not remove bones from his curry because it meant that his quarry would spit out the sharp-pointed baited stick before it could snag in his throat, knew instinctively how fate and destiny work. He knew about the power of coincidence. He had observed that things happen in twos and threes, and he saw no sense in tempting Fate—in providing Fate with the excuse to have the crocodile spit out the baited stick, prompted by his own actions of removing bones from his curry. He was simply playing it safe, in the same way that the racing fan plays it safe by eliminating peanuts from his diet.

We could not expect Sir James Frazer, smugly confident in the superiority of his European intellect, to pause and ask himself if perhaps the Malay crocodile hunter could be right, that when he studiously avoided removing bones from his curry as he waited by his baited line, it was because he knew of the way in which all things in existence are related to each other. Other superstitious beliefs held by primitive peoples can also have a very real use: they can serve either to break a chain of continuity—to jar us into a different reality—or else to maintain a status quo.

The superstition observed by the Malay crocodile hunter, by the way, and other similar superstitions observed all over the world, are related to the very important worldwide belief that all things tend to come in twos and threes. Recently I observed a most striking incidence of this kind, which has perhaps passed unnoticed by the rest of the world. It involved gas explosions resulting in a great loss of life in three widely separated localities, all bearing a very similar name: Rio Piedras, Puerto Rico; Arroyo de Piedras, Colombia; and Guadalajara, Mexico. The name of the first-named city means rocky river; the second means rocky creek; and Guadalajara is the Spanish corruption of *Wad il Rashad*, which is Arabic for rocky river.

At first glance, it might appear to make sense if we took care to scrupulously observe every superstitious taboo in the world. But at second glance it can immediately be seen that this wouldn't be wise. If we began to observe every superstitious taboo in the world we would quickly reach a point in which we wouldn't know whether to go to the bathroom or go blind, as the vulgar thought goes. In short, it would not be wise to saddle ourselves with knowledge on superstitious taboos other than those we are familiar with. Because once we acquire knowledge of them, then they begin to affect us; whereas as long as we are innocent of their existence, we are safe. This is true only to a certain degree, however. There are some things that will produce bad consequences whether we are ignorant of them or not. Just as in jurisprudence, ignorance of a law will not save us from the consequences of violating it.

When we acquire knowledge of a superstition to which we have previously been immune it will begin to affect us, because by acquiring knowledge of it we thereby establish a connection with its origins, and the Fates will thereafter take care to include us in the consequences incurred when we violate that particular taboo.

In Claude Levi-Strauss' *The Raw and the Cooked*, for example, there is a reference to a belief held by the Warao Indians of South America. When a Warao tribesman noses his dugout into the bank in front of his hut with a string of fish, it is bad luck for him to carry the fish up to his house. He leaves them in the dugout and lets his wife carry them up, because otherwise it would sour his luck as a fisherman. But if this belief of the Waraos has a solid basis, does this mean that a fisherman in, let us say, the Louisiana bayous will possibly bring bad luck upon himself if he carries his own fish out of his boat into his house? It might, if he lets his knowledge of the superstition affect him to the point where his awareness of it forms a connection to that source where it is stored in the bad-luck data banks of the Fates.

For the same reason, though eating peanuts is generally an innocuous pastime, we should refrain from doing so while at a race track. Stated in other words, the effects of most superstitions are confined to specific geographical areas, and according to race, religion, and occupational pursuits. Because, in juxtaposition to the exotic examples of the Malay crocodile hunter and the Warao Indians, we have the common European superstition of spilled salt, the number thirteen, and walking under a ladder, which would only cause the Malay crocodile hunter and the Warao Indian to shrug their shoulders in complete indifference. But the evil consequences attached to the violation of superstitious taboos are transmissible from one land and from one race to another. And, just as some races are more susceptible to certain diseases than are others, so are naturally superstitious people more vulnerable than others to the dire effects incurred from the violation of any superstitious taboo whatever, once they have acquired knowledge of it.

Let me explain why these effects are so especially strong in the horse-racing world. Mainly, it is because so many people concentrate so intently—we might almost say fiercely—on the problem of discovering which horse will win a race. Inevitably, this intensity of concentration spills over into the realm of the occult, with many people striving to pick winners, when their handicapping skills fail them, by pure divination of the future. Those of us who thus persistently assault the gates of the arcane will thereby find that the powers that guard those gates will direct all their spite and venom against us. This spite and venom, by the way, will gradually dissipate once we have retreated from the picket lines of the track and its betting windows. The principal danger that we face is usually only that of going broke.

The product of this resistance which the arcane offers to our efforts to divine the outcome of a horse race will often take the form of bad luck, pure and simple. It is up to us, then, to take evasive action and subtract ourselves from the bad situations in which fate and destiny contrive to place us when they protect their secrets.

Sometimes, when we run into long stretches of bad luck at the track, it's hard not to believe that those three old hags, the Fates, have singled us out for bad treatment, simply out of vicious, sadistic spite. But the Fates are completely impersonal. An individual's personal fate is rarely of any overpowering concern to them, other than the natural one of maintaining their preordained stream of events flowing in an orderly manner. The Fates are impersonal and efficient to the point of ruthlessness.

As they preside over their universal drama—weaving, patching, sewing, covering up, making changes, corrections, amendments—they will casually push you here, place you there, yank your thread ruthlessly out of the tapestry to put it somewhere else. They don't care where you wind up, as long as their own work remains pleasing to their eyes. If you don't like the way they are treating you—if you don't like your position in that tapestry and the color of your thread of fate—it's possible to wriggle out of their grasp, and squirm into another reality where things are better for you.

Some superstitious actions are one of the ways in which we can thus squirm out of the malignant grasp of the Fates. Let us take the belief some people have, that if they have been taking the escalator at the track, they can change their luck by walking up the stairs instead. I happen to believe that they can be right. Suppose those three ugly old bags, the Fates, have decreed that you should go to the track on such and such a day, take the escalator to the balcony, sit in seat number 3A, buy a bag of peanuts, and bet on horse number three in the first race, number five in the second, number four in the third, etc., and that all these horses are destined to run a miserable race and you are destined to finally go home miserably broke and disgusted. But you, in your desperate twistings and turnings, thrashing about for some good luck, decide to walk up the stairs instead of taking the escalator. And you've always had such lousy luck when you sat in seat number 3A that you decide to sit in number 4B. And you've recently been told that eating peanuts at the track is bad luck, so you abstain. Having thus broken the chain of events that the Fates had planned for you, you notice that there is a longshot filly named Manchu Princess running in the first race and, through a curious coincidence, last night you saw an old-time movie, *The Drums of Fu Manchu*. You lay down a small bet on her, and she comes in first at forty-to-one.

You were able to change your luck by squirming out of the grip of fate, much as a little fish will slip out of a fisherman's fingers as he removes it from the net. If it's a small fish, the fisherman doesn't care, and he lets it go. In the same way, the Fates don't really care when you slip out of their fingers, as long as it remains easier for them to simply change other aspects of their creation to allow for the change. In other words, we have free will as long as it doesn't cause them any inconvenience.

As for Manchu Princess, the Fates had scheduled her to win simply because the name had happened to come to their attention when they scheduled the airing of the movie, *Drums of Fu Manchu*. To preserve the appearance of randomness, they might also have shuffled her around to come in last, as she was supposed to. But on this occasion they didn't bother. A great deal of the randomness in everything on Earth and in the universe is effected with the purpose of keeping secret the workings of fate. For the natural propensity of all things was originally for like and like to cluster together.

There are many people who never bother themselves or worry about anything that might bring them bad luck. They usually regard superstition as the silliest of human frailties. The persons who feel this way are more often than not among the most fortunate of people—wealthy, descended from the most comfortably established families, community leaders. Doesn't this show that they are right in their opinion on superstition? They seem to have achieved the greatest heights of good fortune without it. But regarded in the proper manner, this evidence only indicates that these people were born into such good fortune that they have never felt the need to bother about superstition, just as some people have never needed to see a dentist.

Also, there are many superstitions which are simply never regarded as such. Many of these privileged people have habits and customs so deeply ingrained that they should rightfully be classed as superstition. These people feel a great annoyance, far beyond the importance that these customs should have, if, upon occasion, they are forced to forego them.

In the book, *Meet General Grant*, it is said that whenever Grant would realize he had forgotten something after leaving his home in the morning, he would never simply turn around and go back for it. He would walk around the block instead. In her book, *Knock on Wood*, Carole Potter lists the aversion to turning back as a superstition, but it's doubtful that General Grant regarded it as such. He would probably have maintained that he simply hated to turn back.

If General and President Ulysses S. Grant could indulge this little foible, how can anyone look down on you and me because we believe certain numbers are unlucky; or that if we have to step off a tiered walkway at the race track, always on the same foot, it's bad luck; or that walking up the stairs or taking the escalator can have an effect on our luck; or that sitting in a certain seat will bring us bad luck, and that to keep losing mutuel tickets in our pocket will bring us more of the same? The reason we have these and other similar beliefs is because successive hard knocks have taught us to look in the unlikeliest places for the source of our misfortune.

Moreover, those privileged people we have mentioned above are not immune to a sudden and devastating reversal of fortune, and with it a possible change in their attitude towards superstition. There are numerous examples that could be extracted from the daily news of politicians, financiers, and entertainers (the most conspicuous examples, in recent years, have been some piously self-righteous televangelists), who have been brought tumbling down from their lofty pedestals.

Take any one of these persons. Deprive him of his money; send him to prison for two or three years; afflict him with a serious illness; have his wife and his family desert him, and perhaps you will soon see him as apprehensive, uneasy, and superstitious as any poor bugger at the race track who has just bet his last two dollars on a horse of dubious prospects. And I have no doubt that a lofty personage or two, who might chance to be reading these lines will, figuratively speaking, look nervously over his shoulder and knock on wood.

Chapter 7

Getting Your Fair Share of Good Fortune

Many investigators of paranormal phenomena have believed that the universe is progressing toward some kind of order, in which all similar things tend more and more to cluster together. Amongst the people who appeared to think that way were Paul Kammerer (whose biography was written by Arthur Koestler), Robert Harvie, Carl Jung, Arthur Koestler himself, and many others who have been prominent in scientific circles. They arrived at that conclusion because they thought they could easily observe a clustering effect in all experiments involving coincidences, card-guessing games, psychokinesis and, in general, any effect which goes against probability and chance.

My own theories, however, postulate the exact opposite, as I have already indicated. The fates are steadily at work eliminating as many coincidences and clustering effects as they can from the notice of Man. Proof of this can be seen in the fact that omens were much more common in ancient times than they are today. For many years I have preserved the racing program from Golden Gate Fields on the sixteenth of April of 1986, because it illustrates my point. If the nine races on that program had been held two or three thousand years ago, the following horses would have been the winners in their respective races:

1. Mar Della
2. Seabreeze Whisper
3. Ritzie Pirate
4. Capricorn Sun
5. Fleet Reflection
6. Special to Us (or possibly: Oh How Right)
7. Flying Rosario

8. Flying Admiral
9. Take it Home

The first three names have a naval connotation; the fourth can also be vaguely associated with maritime matters (latitude); the fifth can be associated with a naval fleet; for the sixth, nothing can be found with a sea theme, so we simply choose one that harmonizes with the others; the seventh is related to the eighth, Flying Admiral, which returns again to a naval topic; for the ninth, we pick Take it Home, which presumably would refer to the loot we would be taking home after betting on all those winners.

In reality, however, these were the actual winners of those races:

1. A Lotta Moolah
2. Clean As a Whistle
3. Boutiquos
4. Galawac
5. Exciting V.
6. Bargain Fun
7. Lady Don
8. Double Deficit
9. End Gun

The first set were a group of names that the Fates would have been inclined to choose because it made their job so much easier. Having once chosen Mar Della ("mar" is Spanish for sea) in the first race, they would then have followed their original impulse and continued with names which reminded them of the sea, admirals, or degrees of latitude. But, with the advent of Man's penchant for divining the winning horses in races, the Fates have been forced to scramble the orders of finish to preserve their secrets. They have not always been completely diligent in this task, and by keeping a sharp eye out for those instances in which they have been lax in their duties, we can often stumble upon profitable situations, not only at the race track, but in all walks of life.

This example illustrates the subjective nature of reality. That is to say, it shows that the Fates often arrange things with you, personally, in mind. The reason I say this is because that day at Golden Gate Fields, following a strong, false hunch, I bet almost all my cash ("a lotta moolah") on Mar Della to win, and my few remaining dollars on Seabreeze Whisper in the second. A Lotta Moolah, of course, won over my horse, and when my horse in the second race also lost, this left me "Clean As a Whistle." This shows the human-like nature of the Fates: they enjoy a perverse joke every now and then.

But let us leave the race track for a moment and look at the business of establishing the methods whereby we effect more permanent changes in our condition and status in life. Gratifying as it may be to put quick racetrack cash in our pockets, this alone will not permanently improve our fortune. There is often a somewhat ephemeral quality about racetrack profits. We will be returning to the track here and there throughout this book, but mainly for purposes of using it as a laboratory for the testing of my theories on luck and reality.

Moreover, in recent years, something has been bothering me more and more. Do horses really enjoy running, as apologists for the sport of kings tell us? I think it likely that the whole matter for horses is an unmitigated ordeal, that if they enjoy running they would far rather be doing it on a wide open meadow with nothing on their backs. Humans who run the hundred-yard dash or the marathon would probably look for some other way to glory if they had to run with a monkey on their backs, flogging them savagely with a whip.

Something else: when we win a pile of cash at the track on a long shot, that money has come from the pockets and purses of people less fortunate than ourselves, who could probably ill afford to lose it. Admittedly, allowing this thought to spoil our fun is perhaps carrying charity and morality to a slight extreme. But the thought is by way of bringing up the following consideration: The amount of good and bad fortune distributed through any given mass of humanity must necessarily be a fixed constant, governed by inalterable laws, and forming a bell-shaped curve if it were to be plotted on a chart. Not because I say so, but because this is the conclusion that must be drawn from the work of every mathematician and economist who has ever lived. If a great many people in this aforementioned mass of humanity were to improve their luck, and thereby change their lives and their destinies, this would seem to entail a change in the distribution of good and bad fortune, and a consequent change in the shape of that inalterable curve. But this is not really the case.

To understand how this can be, let us consider the following points:

1. Any change or improvement in our fortune can only come at the cost of an equal amount of ill luck or misfortune in the lives of our friends and neighbors, to thereby maintain the balance of each of those elements existing amongst humanity.

2. An ameliorating factor in this dismal truth is that this fixed constant of good and bad fortune is subject to a variation in degree; that is to say, though the amounts of each must always remain in the same proportion to each other, the *degree* of each may nevertheless be mutually variable.

Referring to the first point, if one million people were to believe, accept, and put into practice the precepts I am proposing and thereby increase their chances of winning the lottery by a thousandfold, this is not a gross violation of the laws of chance and probability. Because, they will have increased their chances only at the expense of a consequent decrease in the chances of the general population.

The second point provides us with an overpowering practical reason for generous and charitable behavior towards our fellows as we pursue the apparently selfish goal of personal betterment. Since the parabolic curve of human fortune and misfortune cannot be altered (unless we were to first alter the laws of chance and probability), it therefore becomes easier to accomplish our goal of achieving good fortune if at the same time we strive to maintain the integrity of this curve by returning some of that good fortune to the common pool.

This is one example of how a superstition can have its logical, practical, and humanitarian foundations.

In a preceding chapter, we agreed that in order to make changes in our life we should not begin by trying to change our selves. Because the way we are actually represents the firm grip that the Fates have on our destiny, and this grip cannot be easily broken. We should begin by effecting changes in our reality. When I speak of making changes in our reality, I don't mean that we change anything in our extant reality. What we really do is exchange one reality for another. At the same time, when the changes we make in our lives are profound enough, we are also obliging the Fates to repair and reweave parts of their tapestry. One way in which we manage to do this is by learning to post an agent—a fifth columnist, so to speak—in those metaphysical regions where the rules of our existence are laid out.

All of us, by the way, are born with this metaphorical agent in place in the roots of destiny. This is the power of which I spoke earlier, which aids the fortunate and the powerful. The only difference from one person to another is the quality of each person's connection to this agent. This secret agent could be what the earliest Egyptians—three or four thousand years before our era—called the *neter,* a word whose meaning, like many other ancient Egyptian words, is no longer known with any certainty. It has been variously translated as power, force, strong, fortify, protect, etc. But Wallis Budge says, in his translation of the *Book of the Dead* that:

> "...no one knows exactly what meaning the ancient Egyptians attached to the word. The truth is that the exact meaning of the word was lost at a very early period of Egyptian history, and even the Coptic [the liturgical Egyptian language of the Coptic Church] does not help us to recover it."

My suggested interpretation of the word would certainly agree with its translation as "power," and "protect." A good connection to our roots in creation would afford us the *power* to *protect* ourselves against disasters in life.

When we have maintained a good link with our "secret agent," its ability to communicate to us the imminence of disagreeable occurrences and impending dangers can sometimes take spectacular turns, as when we experience an unexplained urge to cancel a trip on a flight doomed to end in tragedy. Sometimes, also, this agent saves us from disaster even against our conscious volition, such as when we lose our luggage, or air ticket or passport, and are forced to cancel that same flight. This secret agent—what the ancient Egyptians pragmatically called the *neter*—is, in fact, what we commonly call our guardian angel.

Fortunate people maintain a close contact with their *neter.* They have been blessed with the ability to subconsciously realize that if they nurture and protect their connection to this agent, it will in turn protect them. Unfortunate people, on the other hand, are those who have blithely blundered haphazardly into life without the faintest inkling that something important for their continued welfare has been omitted from their constitutional makeup, that they have been cast into the world with only rudimentary links to the origins of their destiny. The person with these imperfect links is like a caged exotic bird that escapes its prison and flies off unthinkingly into an environment in which it cannot possibly survive, and out of which it is incapable of escaping to return to its cage for food.

Fortune and misfortune, therefore, are nothing more nor less than a good or a bad connection to the wellsprings of wisdom and secret knowledge. When we strive to improve our luck we are trying to improve our communication system with our *neter*, or guardian angel. We are trying to reestablish links that have been purposely and maliciously severed by the powers that have made us what we are. And by reestablishing those links we are gaining the power and the ability to lead a fuller and happier life.

When we pause to think deeply about the implications of this goal, it becomes evident what a daunting task it must therefore be to change our destiny. Let us only consider the billions of people now living in abject poverty, misery, and degradation, who will *continue* to live in abject poverty, misery, and degradation. Very, very few of them will experience any significant change in their destiny. Looking at this fact with dispassionate eyes we can see that this is because such a situation is a firm and fixed pattern, ordained thus by destiny, and *maintained* thus by destiny, through the simple expedient of obstructing, or totally severing, the links of the greater mass of humanity with their *neters*. These links are reestablished very rarely because in doing so we are acting in defiance and against the will of destiny.

This should not frighten us. We must remember that when we refer to the "will of destiny," we are only speaking metaphorically. The *will* of destiny is only a figment of our imagination (for which we shouldn't give a fig) which serves to represent to us the more or less inalterable condition of our life. Our superstition should be only of a selective nature. Our superstition should in no way impede us in our struggle to improve ourselves or to make the Fates reweave that part of their tapestry which represents our life. The fact that it is such a difficult task does not mean we should not try.

Now, what sort of changes can we hope to produce in this tapestry of life? Can we oblige fate to cast us forth into the world with the intellectual equipment to become brain surgeons? Can we force destiny to give us a more affluent and intelligent set of parents so that we ourselves will be born with a better start? Whether we can or cannot, it seems obvious that this could not be accomplished in one fell swoop. Usually, we can only cause very tiny and almost imperceptible revisions in our destiny. We do this by changing our reality, which we are able to accomplish because we have captured fleeting glimpses of the future smuggled out to us by our *neter*.

When this occurs, we take evasive action. We unconsciously swerve, bob, zig, zag, and sidestep unfavorable events in the reality we are inhabiting at the moment. This transports us into another reality, where those events are absent. Sometimes these occasional visions of the future come to us in the form of a hunch, or omen, or coincidence. But more often we receive obscure impulses which propel us in the right direction. Active, intelligent, forceful, and fortunate persons make many such changes of reality in a single day. Lazy, stupid, and unfortunate persons may remain in a single reality for days on end.

Each little change we make in our present contributes to that ultimate victory we seek over destiny, the one that will transform the fruit of our tree from dingleberries into golden apples. We are striving to change not only the fruit, but the nature of the tree itself. Lay this book down for a moment and take a look at a tree in your yard. Think about how you could make that yew, or willow, or dingleberry tree produce luscious fruit of some kind. When you realize how impossible this is, you should see why it is so difficult to change ourselves through the conventional methods advocated by many books on self-improvement—so difficult it can almost be termed impossible. Just as a dingleberry tree, as it is plain to see, will not produce golden apples.

From the foregoing it can be seen that, to a very large extent, changing our luck, our life, our wisdom means, in effect, that we must cultivate our ability to *foresee* impending events. Perhaps dismissal from your job is looming over your head. Perhaps the industry in which you labor is facing drastic economic difficulties in the very near future. Or perhaps a member of your family will shortly fall prey to a serious illness. In many of these cases, you would but need to be observant to foresee the event. In many other cases the clue is deeply hidden in the treacherous byways of life, and you are caught unawares when it occurs. You buy a house, maybe, the week before you are fired; you buy a new car the week before the company with which you work goes bank-rupt; you go on an expensive vacation during the same month that your mate is stricken with a devastating illness. . . .

The lucky, more fortunate person does not blunder into these pitfalls. He does not consciously know these disasters are about to occur, but something within his subconscious warns him, and he warily steers clear of the trap. In these instances there can be two different reasons for the fortunate person's good fortune. Either he has been blessed from birth with a good connection to his *neter* and the consequent power to subconsciously perceive impending events, which is to say he is naturally fortunate, or he has discovered a way to establish that connection, after the fact. He has repaired those congenitally imperfect connections to the origins of his destiny, consciously receiving and deciphering those encoded messages advising him of impending events that will touch upon his life.

In the first case, these messages come to him in the form of obscure and subconscious urges, unrecognizable impulses, that steer him away from those pathways which would lead to disaster, grief, and misfortune. In the second case, he has learned to obey omens, to heed the power of coincidence, and to observe superstitious taboos.

Often, of course, the disasters mentioned above could have been divined by simple observation. These are instances in which you could have easily received signals, not from your guardian angel, but from the reality around you by just opening your eyes. We should not expect good luck to completely supplant our common sense. If you are slated to be fired in the very near future, and if you are caught totally unawares when it occurs, you have not been very observant. If you were completely ignorant of the possibility that the industry in which you labor could experience a drastic slow-down, here again you could at least have received tiny indications by reading the business pages of your newspaper.

In many other things, close study and deep thought can reveal the possibilities of things such as changes in government, changes in society, climatic changes, and so forth. These things are often quite easy to foresee, and in fact, sometimes the impending event is glaringly evident. We should make the greatest effort we are capable of to let our decisions be guided by a careful consideration of the facts.

But, if we are deficient in sobriety of thought and common sense, because it is our preordained destiny to be that way, then we must depend on our luck.

There are many things for which no facts are available. Should you drive fifteen miles to visit a business establishment where you can save a couple of dollars on the price of that under-wear you decided you simply have to buy today, Jacques Le Strappe's problems notwithstanding? You have no way of know-ing that half-way there a truck loaded with plastic tubing will lose half its load in your path and cause you an accident. But perhaps, if you are a *lucky* person, along the way you suddenly, for no rea-son, choose another route, and thereby avoid the accident. Only your luck has impelled you to take the safe route; a subtle, sub-conscious impulse has guided you.

A careful cultivation of our connections to our *neter* guaran-tees that we will more consistently receive these messages. Just as the proper antenna will ensure the clear and ungarbled reception of radio signals, so will an efficient metaphysical communications system make it easier to receive those signals that impel us to make the correct choices.

How do we go about doing this? A full explanation of the procedure would take an entire separate volume. It would be a metaphysical technical manual, with many pages to explain the reasons for each of the steps that must be taken, with many claus-es, regulations and requirements. Here, I only have space for a few general hints, some of them having to do with the obser-vance of superstitious taboos and related subjects, and for one principal subclause: Whatever method we adopt to carry out a rehabilitation of our *neter*—a reestablishment of full communica-tions—it must be followed with great reserve and a certain degree of secrecy. And until some semblance of communication is estab-lished, we must carry out the task entirely on our own, without any help whatsoever from our *neter*, since it is isolated from our self until the said communications are enabled.

Far from receiving help from any occult source, we will only encounter opposition. It seems quite evident, when we stop to think about it, that the arcane has the ability to actively evade scrutiny. Its very nature dictates that it must necessarily, actively strive to remain hidden and invisible. It is like those camouflaged creatures of nature that blend in with their environment, assuming mottled and speckled shapes to deceive the eye. Sometimes, when we carefully scan the bottom of a pool of clear water, we can spot a fish, or stingray, or other creature quietly resting on the bottom. As long as it does not realize it has been seen, it will remain quiet. But if we try to approach closer for a better look, it will scoot swiftly away in a cloud of mud and silt.

The secrets of destiny are infinitely more well-disguised and hidden. When we spot the nebulous, shrouded shape of one of these secrets, we should pretend that we don't see it, so that it will not scurry out of our reach and grasp. The key is to look at your destiny without being seen by the Fates.

Chapter 8

Some Divining Methods to Spy on the Fates

When we have gone through a long spell at the race track without experiencing a profitable hunch or coincidence, and when all our handicapping skill seems to go sour, then it's time to look for other ways. Then it's time to resort to those other measures I have already talked about, consisting of pure divination of the future.

But the inherent unpredictability of horse races, coupled with the awe in which most people hold all unknown and mysterious forces, such as those which represent fate and destiny, will prompt many to ask, "How can we ever hope to succeed at this?"

How can lowly man, and the even lowlier representatives of humanity who hang around race tracks—whom we might call *Homo sapiens race-trackensis*—hope to thwart the Fates by looking into the future with enough consistency to make it pay off for him? How can mere man ever hope to outwit the Fates? Admittedly, it appears, at first sight, to be an outrageously presumptuous and foolhardy endeavor, possibly an even blasphemous and dangerous one.

But take a look at the cockroach, the flea, mosquito, the tick, and many other lowly species which have been nothing but a torment and a headache to humans for generations. Can we completely frustrate and eradicate these pests? So far, evidence indicates that we can't. And it is the same situation *vis-a-vis* humans and the Fates. Just as we are unable to free ourselves definitively from the annoyance of cockroaches, so are the Fates unable to completely defend themselves from man's incursions into their domain. Man can only strive to build better and better houses, designed to keep cockroaches out; but at the least neglect, a cockroach can slip in, perhaps loaded with progeny, to proliferate freely in the pantries and cupboards. The Fates have the same problem. They may constantly labor to disguise and conceal the future, but once we have understood that this is exactly what they do, it becomes easier for us to make frequent end runs around the barriers they erect and see what is going on behind them.

But there are limitations. We must be content, as long as our main interest is horse races, to capture only a very occasional bit of information. In centuries to come, science will pursue the problem in more disinterested ways, and eventually it will be solved. Unfortunately, as I have already hinted, when that day comes horse races will disappear. In antiquity, when seers and oracles were much more accurate than are the methods we use today, there appears to have been a tacit agreement amongst these diviners to refrain from prognosticating the outcome of horse races. Nowhere in ancient literature can we find any reference to someone consulting the Delphic oracle as to the outcome of a horse race at the Olympics.

Let us return to our problem. Now that we know the Fates deliberately scramble the results of a horse race, we can evolve various little stratagems to frustrate their purpose. All of these stratagems are actually a single method, in different guises, and they all consist of simple divination of the future. Each one of them can work equally well, their efficacy depending on the affinity which each individual may feel for any one of them.

Amongst the many such methods that I have seen people use, I can mention: a ball and pendulum; Tarot cards; ordinary playing cards; post numbers in a hat, or box; the names of the horses in a hat, or box; numbered golf balls; a crystal ball; tea-leaves; animal entrails; a Gypsy fortune-teller; a talking crow; darts thrown at the *Racing Form*; etc. I myself, have used them all (except for the animal entrails and the talking crow), with varying degrees of success.

All these divining methods would have a certain legitimacy because of the basic nature of fate and destiny, as we have explained it. In recent times quantum theory has also tentatively suggested that there could be some validity to the ancient philosophy of the oneness of all matter, which tells us that all things in the universe speak one language; the tea leaves on the bottom of a glass, the blurry images in a crystal ball, the pattern of a randomly spread deck of cards—they all follow the same universal design, in a language which diviners and fortune-tellers are able to interpret into human language. In accordance with this belief, we can say, for example, that if we give a bottle a slight tap with a hammer the resulting network of cracks will contain the entire past, present, and future of the universe, which would only require the proper diviner to interpret it. The story to be extracted from this network of cracks would be on many different levels, from the petty to the grandiose, depending on the caliber of the diviner, and his goals.

There is another thing that must be realized about horses picked by any divining method. First of all, of course, not all of the horses picked this way will be actual winners. Second, a large proportion of them will be horses that turn out to be heavy favorites in the betting. If you normally do not speculate on favorites, should you relax your rules if the favorite was singled out by, let us say, a prognosticating cat? It should depend on how much faith you place in your divining method.

When Precious (may she rest in peace) was picking winners for me at New Orleans Fairgrounds, I had such confidence in her picks that I would even bet on her favorites going off at as low as ninety cents to the dollar. It isn't necessary to point out here that as a general rule betting on horses going off at that kind of price guarantees that you will eventually wind up in the red. Don't try to convince yourself that you are such a good handicapper that you can pick out enough of these low-priced horses to come out ahead. A bit of reflection and rational thought will show you that you can't. Go through the charts for an entire season of racing at any track and add up the winners and the losers which went off at that price. You will usually find that if you had bet on every one of them you would have lost money. To make a profit you would have had to pick more than one winner out of every two. No handicapper that I know of can do this. But, if a solid favorite of this type is also backed up by a strong hunch, coincidence, or divining method, then it is quite possibly a good bet.

When your divining method singles out a very unlikely long shot, and you carefully examine its Past Performances, don't expect to find something about it to indicate that it should be a favorite. Expect only to find something about it, in conjunction with something about the top contenders, to indicate that its chances are not really as remote as they seem. Check to see if it is not subtly dropping down in class in some way. Take, for example, a maiden filly, running in a five-thousand-dollar maiden race for fillies. Maybe its last race, in which it finished eighth or ninth, was for a thirty-five-hundred-dollar claiming price, so it would appear to be stepping up in class. But perhaps, if you look carefully, you will notice that this last race was in open company, and against previous winners to boot, so that it is actually stepping back down into the class it belongs in. Or maybe it's a sprinter, running today in a sprint race, and it performed poorly in its last race or two because it was at a route distance.

Don't neglect to check its pedigree carefully, paying attention not only to the sire, but also to the dam's sire. If it's a Kentucky-bred horse running against Idaho breds, or Arizona breds, or whatever, this could also be a possible indication of superior class. Of course, good blood-lines alone don't guarantee that a horse is of superior class. But sometimes, an excellent horse, because of errors in its training, or for many other reasons, will perform far below its capacity in its first two or three races. The trainer, if he knows his business, will have noticed that he has a horse of superior quality; he will correct the errors and then enter the horse, seemingly without logic, in a higher class.

We must keep in mind that if fate and destiny have scheduled a horse to win a race, they have taken care to prepare it properly. They have ensured that the horse is of good stock, that it has a good trainer, and a good jockey, and that it is in good condition on the day of the race. Some readers might say that the fact that the best horse is the most likely to win a race is so obvious that it is superfluous to bring the personified Fates into the matter. But, though true that when an eighty-to-one longshot wins a race, it's because there was a real, physical reason; that reason can actually be a post-facto reason, non-existent until after human eyes have probed into it. Also, we should try to remember that the hand of fate is present, not only when the strange and unusual happens, but in the ordinary and commonplace as well.

Regardless of what you find in a horse's Past Performances, since you went to the trouble of using a divining method to single it out, it makes sense to bet on it, no matter what. You are examining it carefully only to determine how much you should risk. At small tracks, the bettor doesn't have much leeway in this regard. Usually, if the horse in question is a real long shot—forty-to-one or over—he can choose between betting the minimum two dollars, or up to a maximum of twenty dollars. If it is at anything like ten-to-one and the field is large, then a large bet won't alter the odds too drastically.

The golf ball method of divining the winner of a race, which I mentioned earlier, was so consistently successful for me that perhaps I should describe it in greater detail. Here is the way it should be done: If there are ten horses in a race, take a marking pen and number ten golf balls from one to ten. Put them all in a bucket or other receptacle. Take a piece of stiff cardboard, about four or five feet long and about fifteen inches wide. Cut a small hole at the bottom and in the middle, just large enough for a golf ball to pass through. You will prop it up by inserting each end in a wooden support, so that you can stand it upright in a corner, with the hole flush on the floor.

From a distance of about ten feet, preferably on a hard surface such as a hardwood floor, you will now roll the bucketful of golf balls towards the hole in the cardboard. (You will be doing this at home of course, not the racetrack.) Repeat this procedure until at least three balls have passed through the hole. The numbers on the golf balls will be the program numbers of the horses to consider. Then, of course, you will study the horses thus eliminated, and determine how foolhardy it might be to bet against them. This will guide you in your decision as to how much you can bet on your long shot.

When you roll those golf balls you are doing so within the context of the race being investigated, and the numbers will have a strong tendency to agree with the numbers of the winning horses. What we are doing is interposing our own threads across the fixed threads in the Fates' design. We are "plying the shuttle of free will between given threads" of fate's tapestry, stretched across the loom of destiny. Remember, the Fates do not want to bother to construct another random set for something for which they have already orchestrated a sequence. Here we have the reason why a secretive, unobtrusive approach is the best way to carry out your prognosticative operations. Avoid any actions that will invest your procedures with any appearance of importance and prompt the Fates to construct a separate random set.

When we deceive the Fates in this manner, we are utilizing a method that they themselves have provided us with. Let us take an example from nature as a parallel. Some birds, when a predator, such as a coyote, approaches the nest where they are nestling a brood of chicks, are able to draw him away from their nest by feigning an injury, flapping awkwardly on the ground. Invariably, the coyote will follow the hen, drooling with anticipation as he thinks he is about to catch her. But once the hen has drawn the coyote away from her defenseless chicks, she will suddenly recuperate from her supposed ailment, and fly blithely off. For century after century, the coyote has been thus deceived. Why do they never discover the deception, and, seeing a bird go flapping off in this manner, immediately guess that there are some tender chicks near by? It is not primarily, as some people might promptly say, because the coyote is stupid. Rather, it is because they are so close to Mother Nature that a certain aspect of their intellect is incapable of making the necessary closure to arrive at the inevitable deductions that a human intellect would. In this fact, then, we can see that Mother Nature herself (personified by the three Fates) is also incapable of making certain deductions. In other words, despite the vast and awesome intellect of the authors of creation, we can sometimes achieve the equivalent of deceiving them, much as the pea-brained fowl has continued to deceive the cunning coyote across thousands of years.

We should not expect to achieve a consistent success with our divining methods, only an occasional hit upon a spectacular long shot every now and then. Nor should we expect to receive stark and unambiguous indications, equivalent to a divine voice telling us which horse to bet on, or how to proceed in any other matter whatsoever. We must extract our information from what are often the fuzziest and murkiest of indicators. In fact, clear and unambiguous messages are not to be trusted. This was true even in antiquity when it would appear that legitimately divine messages were as common as telegrams are today. For example, in his essay, "Why Oracles are Silent," Plutarch records this most curious story, which I feel has some relevance to our thesis. An Egyptian pilot named Thamus was becalmed off the island of Paxi, when he heard a divine voice calling across the water to him. "Thamus!" it said, "When you reach Palodes, tell the people there that the great God Pan is dead!" Thamus, stricken with wonder and puzzlement at what he had heard, decided that if the wind was blowing when he came opposite Palodes he would just sail on, and forget about it. But when his vessel reached Palodes the sea was calm and quiet, so he shouted out the message to the shore. And even before he had finished, ". . . there rose a great moan of sorrow and astonishment from a multitude of voices." The news spread quickly all over the Mediterranean and was given great credence during the first century of our era, according to Louise Ropes Loomis, in her translation of Plutarch. She says that Christians of the time accepted it as a sign of the passing of the pagan gods at the coming of Christ.

However, Robert Graves, in *The Greek Myths*, says that not everyone believed the news, and that Thamus apparently misheard the ceremonial lament of the Paxians, "The all-great Tammuz is dead!" ("*Tammuz pan-megas tethnece!*") Thamus must have felt like an ass, if he ever discovered his error.

The description I have given of the golf ball method will give the reader a general idea of how all the other methods should be used.

In this pursuit, as in nearly every other thing in life, the one rule which we must take care to observe scrupulously is moderation. For while it's true that we have free will and can meddle around with our destiny, the fact remains that if we deviate in a marked way from the path of destiny originally laid out for us, and do not have the corresponding strength of willpower to carry us through, we run the risk of being figuratively squashed, like so many bothersome cockroaches, if we become too great a nuisance in the pantries and cupboards of the Fates.

This is another way of stating that fact which has long been known by investigators of the paranormal: The more we use our paranormal faculties, the less effective they become. However, this is true only when we are using these faculties in a direct and conscious manner. Gypsy fortune-tellers appear to be exempt from this rule, because they seem to continue in their profession, with no visible impairment, even into an advanced age. This might be because they are not using their psychic gift for divining the outcome of horse races in a way calculated to directly benefit themselves, and they have no material stake in the outcome of their predictions. True, some fortune-tellers are more accurate than others and thereby garner a profitable reputation. Of those who are less accurate, most of them will still be able to hustle a living, and they do not attach too much importance to the accuracy of their predictions. With this attitude, they manage to preserve a fair share of their ability. They don't worry about it, or try too hard, and this is all to the good.

I once consulted a Gypsy fortune-teller in Louisiana, and asked her to give me a number to bet on in the races at New Orleans Fairgrounds. "Bet on number ten," she promptly answered me. So, much as I dislike outside post positions, I followed her advice and hit upon three longshot winners that day. The next day, bursting with enthusiasm, I told her of my good fortune and congratulated her on her accuracy. I saw her eyes light up with greed, and was immediately sorry I had failed to keep my success a secret. The very next day I ran into her at the track, and guessed that she had decided to cash in on her talent by betting on her lucky numbers herself. But when I asked her how she was doing, I could tell by her evasive answer and crestfallen demeanor that she wasn't doing too well. Which is another little bit of proof that professional fortune-tellers perform best when they have no direct interest in the outcome of their predictions.

The reason our psychic abilities wane with use is because of the tendency of the Fates to plug up those holes through which knowledge of the arcane leaks out into our conscious mind. That is the reason we should be circumspect in our endeavors to peer into the future, to avoid calling attention to ourselves. One way to do this is by changing our methods frequently. That way, before the Fates have noticed that we are intruding into their mysteries, peering into the future through little holes in their fabric, we have abandoned the peep-hole and moved on to another. As I have hinted, a happy, worry-free attitude is the best guarantee to keep our intuitive powers functioning. This, of course, is easier said than done. How can we be happy, and how can we help but worry, when we can see our scarce cash going down the drain? Bad luck feeds on itself and the more bets we lose, the more will bad luck follow, as we become increasingly frustrated and pained to see our money disappear. It's not enough to say to yourself, "Act happy, don't let it worry you." You might fool some people, but you can't fool yourself. If you are not feeling truly happy and carefree, you will not get a trustworthy hunch. In short, you must absolutely attain a frame of mind wherein the loss of a bet or two (or three, or four, or five) does not affect you too adversely. This frame of mind is very hard to achieve, which explains why we who use these methods often have long runs of very rotten luck.

As to why we are better able to outwit the Fates when we are happy, who can say? Maybe their essence thrives best in a sick and worried mind, whereas a happy and carefree environment repels them.

After all I have said here about the tendency of the arcane to hide its workings from our prying eyes, some people might ask if it isn't dangerous to persist in our efforts to unveil the future. If the Fates themselves oppose our endeavors to make a fast buck at the track by esoteric divining methods, isn't it blasphemous to persist? I can well understand the concern of those people.

According to Dante's *Inferno*, there is a special place in hell for seers and diviners. Here, their heads are turned around backwards as a punishment for trying to see forward into the future, and Dante says that the tears streaming down their faces, ". . . *Le natiche bagnava, per lo fesso*." ("The tears ran down their backs and down the cleft of their buttocks.") Pious Dante was obviously imbued with the ecclesiastical fervor of the times against what had become a proliferation of false diviners and fortune-tellers. But I think that such concerns are completely out of step with our times.

We routinely use electricity, atomic power, and the products of other forces which have shaped the world and the universe. We also use the oil which the Fates created hundreds of millions of years ago and stored beneath the ground—so deep beneath the ground that it would appear they did not wish us to use it. Do we worry about offending the Fates when we utilize this oil? No, we don't. By the same token then, though they may try to impede us, we have the inherent right, by virtue of the intelligence which they, or one of their creations endowed us with, to continue to pry and probe until eventually, if the human race does not destroy itself first, we will break the code of creation and become masters of the future.

A great many racing fans, though they often don't realize it, persist in their dogged endeavors to beat the races, not mainly through a desire to make money, but through a vague and consuming wish to break this code of creation. We feel a driving need to resolve the deepest mysteries of the unknown, to make ourselves free by raising ourselves above the human condition, and sharing with creation a knowledge of the future. It's a frustrating pursuit.

It seems that all we can accomplish is to chip off tiny pieces of the solid masonry which hides the future. Each time we pick a winning horse by means of a hunch, by correctly recognizing a coincidence, or by some divining method or other, the Fates doggedly repair the cracks and rents in their edifice, and change the rules of the game. Perhaps the best course is to content ourselves with thus chipping discreetly away and not attempt to make too great an inroad, to not attempt to penetrate deeper into the arcane than the present state of our knowledge will allow us to exploit. We must proceed, especially at the racetrack, as did that Greek god of whom an ancient mythographer said, "He studies the sciences, and bides his time."

Chapter 9

Time, The Fates, and Your Grandmother

I have mentioned changing our reality. This process of changing our reality could be considered in two different ways. We can assume that we are making changes in the reality we are actually in, adopting the position that there is only one reality, and that all changes in a person's life take place in that single reality. Or we can consider that every change taking place in a person's life and destiny entails the occupation of an entirely new reality.

We will dispose of the first view very briefly here. It should be obvious, once we have considered what this would entail, that this cannot possibly be the way it is. It would mean that the Fates would be continually snipping out threads and changing their colors, to account for every time that Joe Blow would change his mind about going to the bathroom and decide to go blind instead. They would quickly be worn to a frazzle. This consequence holds true even if we refuse to accept the allegorical view of the Fates and their tapestry. Changing our reality then, means exactly that: We change only our *own* reality, and not anyone else's.

To explain the process, let us envision a model of destiny and reality, just as the first cosmologists constructed their models of the universe, and as the first geographers envisioned the Earth. Among the first models of the world was a vast turtle, floating on the seas, with the Earth riding on its back. I will try to achieve a slightly higher level of sophistication than that in my own model of destiny and reality. This model of destiny, though superficial in concept and of primitive simplicity, will provide us with a starting point from which we may venture out in our search for an explanation of why our lives are what they are and how we can change them. We hope it will afford us an insight into why chance and probability function as they do, providing us a tool we can use to unveil the mysteries of the remote past and the future.

We will follow that dictum which the cosmologist E. R. Harrison of the University of Massachusetts at Amherst expressed thus: "The physicists have made their universe, and if you do not like it, you must make your own." We can do this because, as Professor Harrison further notes, physicists are not concerned with questions of mind and life. I concede that I could be mistaken as to causes, but the effects can still be the same. The ancient cosmologists were mistaken in their geocentric concept of the universe, which had the sun and the entire universe orbiting around the Earth; but this did not prevent them from correctly predicting eclipses of the sun and the moon. Similarly, I could be mistaken as to *why* we can change our luck and our destiny, but still be correct as to *how*. I could be mistaken as to why and how chance happens, but still be right about how we can manipulate it.

Why should it be necessary to explain how and why chance happens? How else could events of chance happen except in the chancy manner that they do? Doesn't the very nature of chance dictate that it must happen in a random and unpredictable manner?

In the early history of the human race, no doubt, most people could see no reason to formulate the laws that govern motion. The behavior of objects falling to the ground, or those forcibly propelled, could easily be predicted. Most people could see no reason to look deeper into the causes and laws that make a dropped object fall downward. How else could a dropped object fall? It was obvious that it could not fall up, or sideways. But Newton, and many others long before his time, saw in the fact of gravity a deep mystery that needed to be explained.

It could be that a similar mystery reposes in the laws of chance and probability. Possibly some day a scientist will come to the realization that in the very fact of their unpredictability rests evidence that a hidden force, with laws as definable as those of gravity and motion, governs the random nature of all events of chance. But until that day arrives, we should feel free to speculate freely upon the nature of this unknown force, and we should not feel ashamed or embarrassed to seek our own resolutions with whatever mental equipment is available to us.

I have begun by presuming this force to be administered by the Fates, as they were regarded in antiquity. In *Moby Dick*, Herman Melville said, speaking of necessity (fate) and free will, that:

> "—aye, chance, free will, and necessity—no wise incompatible—all interweavingly working together . . . free will still free to ply her shuttle between given threads; and chance, though restrained in its play within the right lines of necessity, and sideways in its motions directed by free will, though thus prescribed to by both, chance by turn rules either, and has the last featuring blow at events."

Melville's view of chance is off the mark in one important particular: Chance does not rule necessity, because chance is nothing more nor less than necessity itself, the strong fate. In human affairs, in which chance plays a large part, the Fates and their mother, Necessity, will not too easily relinquish their control to free will.

We may suppose that necessity came into being as a consequence of the same processes responsible for the proliferation of Earth's primordial life forms. Through those same processes, feeling lonely, perhaps (as good an explanation as any), she bore her three daughters, Clotho, Atropos, and Lachesis. Then, just as all voids must be filled (just as we ourselves will inevitably fill voids of leadership wherever we come across them, imposing our will on whatever leaderless and weak creatures drift across our path), she set her daughters to work on the tapestry of life.

The Fates began by organizing the basic materials, the primordial one-celled organisms from which the higher life forms, which would ultimately become the colorful and interesting threads that are human life, evolved. But since time does not have the same meaning for the Fates as it does for us, it can also be said that they organized the destiny of the higher life forms first, and that from this ultimate material the lower life forms—all the way back to the one-celled organisms—have evolved in what to us seems a backwards process.

In these speculations, by the way, I am not proposing that humanity occupies the central position in the final designs of fate. We must remember that eventually we too will evolve, not only into a higher form of humanity, but into an entirely different species, which will retain only the faintest knowledge of who and what its ancestors once were. This tapestry of life, then, could be only something which will serve as a backdrop for those other creatures that will follow us; or it could even be intended only as a soft and caressing material, something for the Fates and their mother to wipe themselves with, to be finally flushed away into the sewer system of the cosmos.

It is most likely that the Fates, perhaps prompted and advised by their mother, decided at the outset upon the design and pattern of this tapestry. Great piles of thread and yarn of varying colors were laid up. The Fates knew, aeons before we were born, how much thread of such and such a color they would need. They decided, before the thread was woven into the design, where it would go and what color it would be.

We can assume all this from simple analogy. Everything in our world must have a provenance in the roots of creation. When your wife, or your aunt, or your grandmother begins to knit or weave something, she does not begin until after she has decided what it is she is going to knit or weave. She decides on the color, the size, the pattern, and then she buys the amount of material it will take. We must assume that the weaving Fates have at least as much intelligence and forethought as your wife or grandmother. From all this, therefore, we can conclude that our individual destinies have been, to a large degree, decided upon since long before we were born. This is the reason it is so hard to change ourselves.

But the human spirit rebels at the thought that our destiny is thus unwaveringly marked out for us and that there is nothing we can do about it. Can this possibly be the way it is? What sense would it make to get out of bed in the morning? What sense would it make to lift a finger for anything whatsoever, even in matters of life and death? One answer to this, which should be plain to see, would be that we are *compelled* to do everything that we do by necessity. We can't remain in bed, and we can't resist the urge to lift a finger, because that is the way we have been programmed by destiny. We must. It is necessary.

But an escape from this horrible truth can be found in the concept of multiple realities, that old ploy done nearly to death by writers of fantasy fiction, but which nevertheless contains a core of legitimacy. To legitimize this concession to free will, we must also advance the additional hypothesis that time should not be viewed as an integral part of creation, as it seems to be held now. The speed of light, though it can be expressed as so many miles per second, does not actually have any relation to time, and though atomic decay can be measured in time, atoms do not really decay *in* time. Nor is there any such thing as a billionth of a second, however much physicists may continue to define events with such a term, and even though some computers appear to execute a billion operations in one second.

Time, in fact, has no physical reality, as can be seen in the fact that no one has ever isolated a particle of time (elsewhere, we may speak of particles of time, but these are not *physical* particles). If it has no physical reality, then we must naturally suppose that real time is not subject to the presently known laws of physics. However, whether time has a physical reality or not, there is surely a particle of time beyond which it cannot be further divided. This observation would resolve that ancient paradox of Achilles and the turtle.

This paradox, propounded by the philosopher Zeno in the third century B.C., shows that Achilles, the swiftest man of his time, could not have caught a turtle, fleeing as swiftly as only a turtle can from the pursuit. Zeno's example shows that as Achilles would advance two feet in his chase, the turtle would advance five-thousandths of a foot; Achilles would advance another two feet and the turtle would advance another thousandth, and so on, into the ten-thousandths, millionths, billionths of a foot into eternity. But this capricious division of distance into meaningless fractions can be effectively eliminated by substituting time for distance and using the ultimate particle of it in conjunction with distance moved per particle of time. It could then be demonstrated that Achilles would make quite short work of the turtle, quickly settling its hash.

Trying to tell physicists what time is may appear to be like trying to teach our grandmother to suck eggs, but let us remember that most physicists admit that no one knows exactly what time is.

I do not propose these two conjoined ideas on time and multiple realities merely as a conciliatory gesture to advocates of free will, but because they are necessary to explain away many other otherwise unexplainable inconsistencies and paradoxes inherent to the idea of determinism. In these two ideas we can reconcile the belief in free will with the notion that destiny is immutable.

The advocates of free will, by the way—the common, man-in-the-street believer in free will—will not make a similar concession to us. They insist that we have free will, and that our destiny is in our own hands, but they refuse to consider the possibility of multiple realities. To them, this is pure poppycock, not seeming to realize that if an individual could have acted in a different manner in the past, his present situation would be different; that everyone whose life was touched by his, would be living a different reality; and that, ergo, there would have to be another reality to accommodate this different behavior. Otherwise, how could that individual have behaved differently?

How often have we heard something like, "If Napoleon had refrained from taking a nap during the battle of Waterloo, Europe's borders would be different today." Or, "If the Moors had managed to maintain a foothold in Spain, that nation would be Muslim today instead of Catholic." Or, "If I had bet two hundred dollars on Midnight Oil instead of on Lampblack Hardy, how different my financial situation would be today!" But a bit of reflection will show that things *couldn't* be different. Not in *this* reality, which we inhabit here and now. And yet, if there is such a thing as free will, then surely we had the *option* of behaving differently in the past, of having bet on a different horse in the past, or of having refrained from going out to buy underwear, or whatever, to thereby change the present. Those multiple realities of which we speak provide us with that option and with an alternative to the fatalism that says, "It is written," or "What will be, will be."

These multiple realities exist in multitudinous numbers, equal to the number of living creatures on Earth. They are the stuff of which small changes in a person's life are made. There is a reality in which you did not lose that one hair off your head that you lost this morning. There is another reality in which you lost two hairs, instead of one. But, if you are fifty years old and still working at your ditch-digging job as a construction laborer, you may be fairly certain that there is not a reality in your life in which you are a wealthy industrialist. There *could* be, but it would be very far removed from your present reality.

Which is to say, in all those trillions of realities, the color of your thread remains essentially the same. This fact of minute changes in those countless trillions of realities is what provides destiny with the necessary flexibility to ensure that it will not have to continually be changing the design of its tapestry. Moreover, without those teeming realities this tapestry would be brittle and extremely fragile. It would split and crack every time a living creature exercised its supposedly free will.

This is the way, then, in which we effect small changes in our life. We do it by slipping into another reality, a reality that has always been there, requiring only a sufficient degree of forcefulness and intrepidity on the part of the invader. The realities that we discard survive only in the consciousness of the one living creature that inherits each abandoned reality.

Just as these other realities are completely unreal and invisible to us, so they are to the Fates themselves, even though they continue to preside over each and every one of those invisible realities. This last conclusion can be reached as a consequence of the obvious fact that there can only be one reality for the consciousness of each living entity, and the rule would necessarily have to apply to the Fates themselves.

In a manner of speaking, then, though we may doggedly flee from one reality to another, we cannot escape our fate. Because even though we may evade the clutches of fate in one reality, in the next one we will find the Fates with their rule still unbroken, stolidly presiding over every breath we take. The reality that we flee from remains absolutely unchanged, albeit it has become some other creature's reality, and not our own.

Hereafter, whenever I speak of making changes in our life, let it be understood that I am really speaking of exchanging our old reality for a new; a semantic distinction that may have greater or lesser importance, depending on the way each particular person may wish to regard it.

The way in which we accomplish greater changes—the equivalent of a dingleberry tree turning itself into a golden-apple tree—is by the same process, and the miraculous nature of the change is never (or extremely rarely) visible. However, the fifty-year-old ditch digger mentioned above would simply have to traverse an enormous expanse of realities to reach the one in which he is a wealthy industrialist. This would take time, something that the fifty-year-old ditch digger does not have a lot of, especially since after a long day's work of digging, all he wants to do is rest his weary bones, with the added handicap that hard, unpleasant, physical labor tends to benumb the intellect, leaving no inclination towards the frame of mind necessary for migration through realities.

There is another recourse available to the ditch digger, however, by which he could accomplish this change: by forcing the Fates to snip out portions of their tapestry, replacing threads and changing their color, something we may be sure they do not enjoy doing. Sometimes, however, they have no choice. Sometimes a person may effect a change in the reality he inhabits, rather than moving into a different reality. The person in question may do this because the condition he desires in his life does not exist in any accessible reality, or it may not exist in any reality at all, or it may occur simply through an accident because the Fates have failed to take the necessary precautions against it.

In these cases, then, the Fates find themselves obliged to make the corresponding changes in that person's extant reality. The result is something very close to a visible miracle; sometimes it is an outright miracle. The Fates heartily dislike having to do this, and for obvious reasons: miracles and an orderly universe cannot coexist side by side. A recent example of one such miracle can be seen in the case of Michael Jackson, who went from being a handsome young black male to becoming a white person of uncertain gender, for reasons and through mysterious processes that only he is aware of.

At this point I should perhaps remind both myself and the reader that the much mentioned tapestry of life is of course not really a tapestry. It is merely a convenient term which serves to express a more or less superficial vision of what life is, without lapsing into complete obscurity.

To continue with the metaphor even so, we can sometimes invade the factory in which the Fates labor on this tapestry, to take a peek at it—any portion of it, corresponding to the past or the future, and thereby foresee coming events. When we make a successful incursion into the past or the future in this manner, we do not return with a conscious knowledge of what we have seen. The knowledge remains buried, deep within recondite strata of our psyche, to manifest itself only in obscure impulses which we are not aware of, but which pushes us into the proper course to take in the pathways of life, opening the barred gates to another reality in accordance with our evasive action.

Is there any danger in this business of poking into the past and the future? In forcing the Fates to redo their work when we

are able to accomplish this? Isn't activity of this sort blasphemous?

There is nothing blasphemous about it, any more than there
is when we try to force the criminal to change his ways. For the
thief or the child molester to reform himself entails the same sort
of rebellion against the Fates that we have in mind here.

As to danger, there is always danger in everything we do in
life to advance ourselves. I would say to the reader, don't worry
about it too much. Still, a little circumspection should be
observed. If we believe that this business of multiple realities is
poppycock and try to change our situation in life by making the
change in the *same* reality we are inhabiting at the moment, there
is a churning of the contents in the cauldron of life, and the lives
of other living creatures are affected. Even if we believe that
changes are accomplished by migrating into another reality, we
should try to achieve changes only in the same small increments
as would be the case when observing strictly conventional beliefs
and methods.

If we do not follow this precaution, if we try to make drastic leaps across a vast expanse of realities, there would be great
danger, of course, just as there would be if we try to make drastic changes within our present reality without following the rules
of life.

As an example, say you are a lowly army private, and one day
you decide you have had enough of being ordered around. "All
right, enough of this stuff," you say. "My destiny is in my own
hands. From now on, I'm giving the orders around here. All I
need is just a bit of courage, decisiveness, and resolution." Adopt
an attitude like this, not only in the army but in anything in life,
and you are letting yourself in for serious difficulties. You will
find that you have forced the Fates to change your reality, not
into a reality in which you are a general instead of a private, but

one in which you are hauled off by the MPs to the military stockade, or to the psychiatric ward.

Remember, therefore, that moving into another reality or forcing the Fates to change an existing reality, does not necessarily mean an improvement in our destiny. Great care and selectivity must be exercised. Changes in our lot must be brought about gradually by first changing very small facts in our life, by moving into a more favorable reality, not into one that is worse. We cannot shrug off the fardels we bear in life without first doing this, anymore than a horse can suddenly decide it will no longer carry a rider on its back. For a horse that did this, the pet-food slaughter house would loom ominously in its very near future.

This brings us back to our ditch-digger, whom we left wiping the perspiration from his brow while he wished he had been born a wealthy man. How could he bring the change about? Very poor people (a class to which our hypothetical ditch-digger obviously belongs) mainly think that it can be done by magic. It can be seen that people who resort to magical spells, *santeria*, black and white magic and witchcraft generally belong to this class. These people, by the way, are not deficient in gray matter. Their brains are made of the same stuff as the brains of Einstein, Newton, Santayana, Kant, and Michael Jackson. It's just that in the daily conduct of their lives they are trudging over different pathways in those brains. They fail to realize, therefore, that the attainment of their goals by these methods is doomed to failure because they entail a change in their extant reality, which is equivalent to a miracle, however small and insignificant it may be, and which the Fates will always very actively resist.

For a long time during my life, I must admit, before I realized the grave error in this procedure, I steadfastly tried to improve my position in life by changing my extant reality. I kept trying to force the Fates to weave out a new destiny for me—trying to grab them by the short hair (which I understand means grabbing them by the short hair at the nape of their necks, not elsewhere), not realizing how hard this was, because, for one thing, we only have two hands, and there are three Fates. This illustrates the malignant cunning of the Fates. They planned it that way—giving us only two hands, I mean—for exactly that reason. While we may grab, say Clotho and Lachesis, by the short hair, Atropos can still rap us smartly over the knuckles with her shuttle to make us let go.

More than once during my younger years, as I was saying, I tried to improve my position in life by a procedure similar to (though not quite that extreme) the hypothetical case of the army private mentioned earlier. But gradually, over the years, I learned better ways. Slowly but surely, I have somewhat changed the hue and tint of my thread of life in the tapestry of the Fates, though I will refrain from stating the exact degree of the change in dollars and cents.

I will drop one small hint, however. There have been long periods in my life when I was obliged to wash down my beans and rice with generic beer, such was my degree of penury. Now I no longer drink beer, generic or otherwise; only good wine, perhaps not the best and finest of wines, but good wine, nevertheless, and I now eat beans only occasionally, to evoke certain fond memories of those bygone days. I attribute this change to my careful regard and observation of superstitious practices across the years, coupled with my long and steadily-sustained incursion into the realms of the arcane.

Chapter 10

How Arcane Knowledge Leaks Into Our Life

Let's make another short excursion to the race track, while we digest the contents of the preceding chapter.

At New Orleans Fairgrounds, I used to see a handsome, well-dressed woman who stood at the exit from the paddock to the track, pointing a camera-like apparatus at each horse as it passed by her on its way on to the track. I was never able to extract any information from her as to what her apparatus was, but I suspect it was some sort of galvanometer that measured the electrical field, or aura, emanating from each horse, and which, presumably, told her which horse was in the best condition.

This suggests that we could use any method akin to a dowser's witching rod to tell us which horse would win a race, and any success we achieved could be attributed to a subconscious awareness (from the horse's appearance) of which of those horses was in the best shape.

Condition, of course, is the single most important factor in determining which one of an evenly-matched field of horses will win a race. Sometimes we can spot a horse in top condition with just the naked eye-ball. But often the appearance a horse presents in the paddock can be very deceptive. Most racing fans have experienced the pain of deciding against betting on a horse because it looked listless and dull, only to see it go on to win the race. Many times, a horse that appears to be bursting with health and energy will refuse to run. I remember a striking example of a horse that appeared to be in the greatest of condition. It was at New Orleans Fairgrounds and the horse's name was Crazy Lea. As he pranced into the paddock I was immediately struck by its glowing, shiny coat, its alert demeanor, its flicking ears. Moreover, as it passed by me it turned its head and stared directly into my probing eyes!

"What are you trying to say to me, horse?" I silently asked, and as it pranced away, still craning its neck to look back at me, I decided that it must be saying, "Bet your shirt on me, Mac! I'm going to win this race."

I rushed to the windows and laid down twenty dollars on Crazy Lea to win. I think he came in about next to last. (In subsequent races I continued to bet on Crazy Lea, so convinced was I that it had tried to tell me something. But he never won a race. At least, not that I know of.)

So, even if we know about the importance of condition, the knowledge of this fact is not enough. Even if we could unerringly spot the horse which is in its peak form, it is still no guarantee that he won't get caught in a traffic jam, or that he won't fail to conserve his energy with the proper pace, or be disqualified for bumping another horse. In short, we could still do with some occult foreknowledge of the future.

In a previous chapter, I made reference to a divining method involving a talking crow. It is not a legitimate method, inasmuch as its results were inconclusive, but I would like to tell about it here, as an illustration of the desperation which some people feel in their quest for the ultimate secret, and also as a further reference to the importance of condition.

There was this fellow I knew while I was patronizing Louisiana Downs, in northern Louisiana. His children found a crow in a field one day, with a broken wing, and they took it home for a pet. He immediately appropriated it, patched up its broken wing, and began to teach it to talk. He intended to train it to fly to the stables, he said, to associate with the horses there, analyze the aura emanating from each horse (crows are equipped by nature to do this, he informed me), and then fly back to him and let him know which horse was going to win.

Whether he was truly serious about his project or not, I can't say. But I would guess that if crows can really do what he claimed they could, they would do it by sensing the tiny electrical and magnetic field that all horses (and other living creatures) emit, and which would be strongest in the horse in the best condition. The talking-crow method, therefore, can only be marginally classified as an occult method, since it has to do with determining the condition of a horse by physical means.

Since the efficacy of all methods to divine the future wanes with use, does this mean that since I've already tried all the methods, they won't work as well for anyone else? Most readers already know the answer to that one. They will know it instinctively, without needing to be told. Each time an individual uses one of these methods, it is an entirely new ball game. Despite the obvious answer to the question, it's possible that many serious investigators of the paranormal have never realized what a valuable clue it can be, to guide them to the correct interpretation of exactly what it is they are investigating.

It should be obvious to those investigators that the reason psychic abilities wane with use is because there is a force that actively intercedes to stop the leaking out of occult information. Just as any large corporation will act quickly to stop any leaking out of its business secrets, so do the Fates act to plug up any leaking out of their mysteries. Just as the security officials of a racetrack keep a sharp eye out for sharpsters and shady characters, so do the Fates keep a sharp eye out for intruders who might gain an advantage by peering into the future. But, while I certainly don't advocate that we use fraudulent means to succeed at the racetrack, I believe that inasmuch as this occult knowledge is concerned, we have every right to use it, if we can only discover how to do it.

Another small indication of the validity of the above statements is the well-known fact—skeptics would call it just a belief—that newcomers, or neophytes to a new sport or game in which success is determined to a significant extent by chance, frequently experience remarkable luck; "beginners luck," as it is called.

In keeping with my theory, this would be partly because the Fates are caught initially unawares by this newcomer, and they will tend to lag a little in their task of plugging up those holes through which arcane knowledge tends to seep into human consciousness. Another factor which complicates things for the Fates is that the newcomer, innocent of the tremendous difficulty in correctly guessing the outcome of a race, enters into the task with a completely relaxed mind, and those fissures, which the Fates will soon step in to caulk and seal, are quite open.

It follows, then, that our luck would improve if we were able to adopt the behavior of the neophyte race-goer, who attends the track for the first time, wide-eyed with wonder and excitement. This is a hard thing to do, but here is a clever little ploy, which is the next best thing, and which I have utilized occasionally, with good results.

I will invite a neophyte to the track, and then casually let him, or her pick a horse in the first two or three races. If the horse this person picks is one of the favorites, then the fact that the neophyte chooses it becomes an additional consideration in its favor. If it's a long shot, I will sometimes place a small bet on it without even bothering to check out its chances in the *Racing Form*.

The only requirement I look for is that the person in question not be desperately in need of cashing a bet. It's best if the neophyte is female, the happy-go-lucky type, feeling in particularly relaxed and happy circumstances at the time, and preferably between thirty-five and forty-five years of age. The only problem with this method resides in finding happy, available women in this age bracket. I, myself, find it increasingly difficult as I get along in years. But if the reader is a young male, he can no doubt find many eligible candidates by subscribing to lonely hearts clubs, where he will find there are many older women, desperately looking for younger men.

Once he has found one of these women, just the fact alone of being invited out by a younger man will make her quite happy, thereby fulfilling the second condition. If he treats her to a nice meal before taking her to the track, and pays for her mutuel tickets, this will make her even happier, reckless, and inclined to pick winning horses. I recommend, however, that the person trying this method confine himself to taking his date to a modest restaurant, and buying her only two-dollar tickets, because it is by no means guaranteed to pay off for him.

After the neophyte racing fan has attended the races for a day or two, his/her luck usually will peter out, often showing a negative trend that will offset any original good luck. We can say, therefore, that the Fates, at first caught unawares by this newcomer, quickly recuperate and take measures to plug up any filtering through of their knowledge into her conscious mind.

While on the subject of neophyte racing fans, these persons are easy to spot at the track. They are the ones who whoop and shout so exuberantly when their horses come in first, causing the losing patrons around them so much annoyance. When their luck starts going sour, they are the ones who fume and rage, and hurl invectives at the jockey, accusing him of holding back his horse. Both attitudes are extremely foolish.

I have already mentioned the reasons pertaining to the first. As to the second, if we think a sport is inherently crooked and larcenous, we should not be attending it. Huey Mahl, in his book on handicapping, *The Race is Pace*, has an excellent section demonstrating how the only sensible course for owners and trainers when they enter a race is to hope to snag any part of the purse they can. As for the jockeys, no other athlete is more inextricably geared to winning. On those rare occasions when jockeys have taken a bribe to lose a race, they usually did so because they felt they had no chance of winning anyway. Cases have even been known in which a jockey took a bribe, and then went on to win the race, taken by surprise by a horse that was in better condition than he had realized.

In short, it's not easy to fix a race, and at small tracks it's more often than not impracticable. True, sly trainers and hungry jockeys will always strive to conceal the true condition of their horses in order to set themselves up in a good betting situation. But if we are mostly looking for long shots and following our hunches, we should be safe from the havoc that such deceitful practices can wreak on the handicapper's bankroll.

Speaking of fixed races, possibly the first fixed race in recorded history is that famous chariot race between Pelops and Oenomaus (pronounced, more or less, "weenie-mouse"), from Greek mythology. King Oenomaus had a beautiful daughter named Hippodameia, whom everyone wanted to marry. But her father instituted a chariot race, run between himself and the suitor, as the condition each suitor had to pass through—and win—in order to have her hand. The penalty for losing the race was he also lost his head, which Oenomaus would then tack up on his city walls.

Pelops bribed Oenomaus' charioteer, Myrtilus, promising him that if he could somehow see to it that his king lost the race he would share his bride with him on his wedding night, and furthermore, give him one-third of the kingdom he was going to win from Oenomaus. So Myrtilus, no doubt drooling in anticipation, accordingly removed the linchpins from Oenomaus' chariot, and covered the holes over with wax.

Even with these precautions, the race almost ended disastrously for Pelops. Very close to the end of the hundred-mile racecourse from the river Alpheius to the Isthmus of Corinth, Oenomaus was steadily closing the gap, and was actually lifting his spear to transfix the terrified Pelops (who by this time was probably urinating in his britches from the fright), when the wheels finally came off his chariot. Oenomaus, thrown forward, was entangled in the reins and dragged to his death.

This legend from ancient times can serve as a valuable lesson to the race-goer. He should take notice that although Pelops' horses were two magical creatures given to him by the god Poseidon, he still took the additional precaution of fixing the race. He knew there's no such thing as a sure bet.

An additional lesson to be extracted from the story is that we should beware of lavish promises. After the race, when Pelops and Hippodameia went off on their honeymoon in the chariot pulled by the magical horses, which could actually race across the sea without wetting their hooves, Myrtilus tagged along. This must have puzzled Hippodameia considerably. When Pelops stopped on an island to look for drinking water Myrtilus tried to collect the first part of his reward. But Hippodameia went running to Pelops and complained that he had tried to violate her. Later, when the chariot resumed its journey across the sea, Pelops suddenly gave Myrtilus a kick in the behind, casting him into the sea that has ever after borne his name, the Myrtoan sea, to remind the world of his treacherous murder.

But let us get back to hunches and handicapping. How do we know how much handicapping is enough, and how much is too much? This is a hard question to answer. Only experience and a good many hard knocks can furnish us with the correct answer.

Of course, sometimes a hunch is only a subconscious message which we receive because our handicapping knowledge tells us that the favorite has been falsely favored by the crowd. Maybe it's a front runner, up against two or three other front-running speed horses. A "speed horse," for those readers who may not know, is a horse that often shows early speed, in the first quarter, or the first half, and habitually takes the early lead. Several horses with this running style in a race will often start a duel for the lead, tiring each other out and allowing a horse with an even pace—often a long shot—to overtake them in the stretch. This is especially likely to happen at a track with a long stretch run.

Maybe the favorite has been running too frequently, and is in need of a rest. In an instance of this sort, it would seem that only our intuition could advise us. For, how can we presume to know more than the trainer, who has evidently decided that his horse should run again? But, sometimes it's not that the trainer doesn't know his horse needs a rest. It can be that the owner—because he is in financial straits, or for a number of other reasons—has pressured the trainer to enter the horse, against his better judgment, in another race. Perhaps he's hoping that someone will claim it.

If you have studied your handicapping conscientiously, then, you will be doubly armed. You will sometimes receive a "hunch" which is a manifestation of your psychic ability, and at other times you will capture subconscious messages such as in the instance we are referring to now, in which a horse has passed its peak, and is in need of a rest. If there is the tiniest bit of visible evidence of this fact in the Past Performances, then your subconscious mind will snag that information, and feed it back to you in the form of a hunch.

But you should not consciously try to receive a hunch, nor look too intently for a coincidence. Let these things come to you in a free and easy manner. Trying too hard creates those conditions in your psyche in which that mysterious force of which we have been speaking all along finds it easiest to frustrate you.

Here is another hint: Psychic ability has its roots in courage. However, we mustn't define the word courage too narrowly. I myself am terrified of heights, for example, anything over five feet high. Yet I would venture to guess that mountain climbers do not necessarily have an edge on me in psychic ability. There are many different kinds of courage. At any rate, courage is what the successful bettor needs a lot of, if he is to succeed at the track. It takes a lot of courage to lay down two hundred dollars on a horse to win. If you feel a sudden fit of cowardice, just before placing a bet, the best course would be to go home, with the few bucks you have left still in your pocket. Better yet, would be to make sure, before you even leave your home, that you will have the necessary courage to make your bets without any trepidation. One way to assure yourself of this is to plan carefully on the amount you can safely lose, and if you don't trust your own willpower and strength of character, take only that amount to the track.

Psychic phenomena also occur when a subject is in an intense state of concentration and excitement, like the dice-rolling subjects who have been observed by investigators of the paranormal. It is not practical, however, nor decent, to try to achieve this mental state at a racetrack.

To sum up, here are some of the divining methods I have used at various times, and which I invite the reader to try. I have graded them according to the degree of success I have personally found in them, but they will not be equally successful for everyone. Some experimenters may achieve better success with those that I have found to be a failure, and have less luck with the ones that I think are good. It depends on each individual's affinity for a particular method. I have graded them as follows: excellent, very good, good, fair, poor, lousy.

1. Observance of coincidences—excellent.
2. Cat-in-cage—excellent.
3. Cracked bottle—good.
4. Tarot cards—poor.
5. Ordinary playing cards—good.
6. Crystal ball—good.
7. Following neophyte's choices—very good.
8. Numerology (date, number of racing day, etc.)—fair.
9. Numbered golf balls—very good.
10. Tea leaves—poor.
11. Fortune-teller—very good.
12. Flights of birds—poor.
13. Animal entrails (I've never used this method, but I would guess)—lousy.
14. Talking crow—inconclusive. In the only case I know of in which this method was tried, the crow never returned home when it was sent on its mission.

This list is by no means the limit of methods that can be used. The inventive horse racing fan, and of course anyone trying to coax better luck into his life, will find that the number of options is limited only by his imagination and resourcefulness. Use each method for only a short period of time—two or three racing days—and then pass on to another. Don't wait until the method starts going sour on you before you make the change. After you have used every method you can think of, then go back to the first one, and start the cycle again. Use the entire system sparingly, as you would any other precious resource which should not be squandered recklessly.

Chapter 11

Lightning Bolts and Winning the Lottery

This business of changing our reality, apparently against the wish and will of the Fates themselves, and especially this business of grabbing the Fates by the short hair and forcing them to weave out a new destiny for us, may provoke fear and nervousness in some readers. There is a suggestion of sacrilege and blasphemy in the notion—a superstition, perhaps, that we shouldn't be able to get away with it.

This is the kind of superstitious fear that we must shake off if we are to have any success at all in this endeavor of improving our luck. This kind of fear is the ultimate expression of baseless superstition, which, if we were to adhere to it, would render all other superstitions superfluous. This sort of piety, this unreasoning "fear of divinity," is the refuge of the very people who sneer and scoff at the superstitious, while failing to recognize the superstitious basis for their own fears. Our superstition, as I have already said, but which can bear repeating, should be of a very selective nature. We should nurture and observe only those superstitions that are useful to us.

The "fear of divinity" appears to be a superstition that does not contribute in any way to human survival. Why has it been instilled in the human soul? It seems highly likely that it is a superstition which, far from advancing the human condition, only serves as an additional handle that destiny can use to jerk human beings around with, to keep them in their assigned positions. Because, even though we will continue in the firm grip of fate whenever we slip into another reality, there is nevertheless a certain degree of opposition to this reality-hopping. Why should this be? That reality is already there, awaiting the living occupant who wishes to take it over.

There are several answers to this question. When the Fates see us wriggle and squirm, they don't know what we are up to. They will continue to exercise the necessary force to keep an individual within the proper lines of that individual's extant reality. Another thing we must remember is that the new reality we are trying to occupy already has an owner, who may not be willing or ready to relinquish it. Migrations into other realities operate the same as transactions in the stock market. Every time you sell a stock, there must be someone willing to buy it, and for every stock you buy there must be someone willing to sell it. It is the same with realities. The hostile takeover of a reality also works, sometimes, but with many disruptions.

I have compared each individual life to a tree, with its corresponding fruits. Now let us go to a different simile, no less accurate for purposes of studying ways in which we can effect changes in our roots and origins. To the Fates, in their great tapestry of life, these trees are represented by threads of varying lengths and colors, which they arrange in patterns as they weave on their eternal loom. The length of these threads and their coloring is dependent on the whims of the Fates. Some of us are blue, or red, or yellow; others are purple, green, magenta, crimson, violet—there is a vast assortment of shades, hues, tints and colors. Certain colors will abound in a given land or nation, and it could be said that the prolonged periods of prosperity or decline some nations go through have to do with the fact that when that people's threads were woven into the work, the brilliance of their color was subsequently overshadowed—or made to stand out even more—by the shade of the colors woven around them. This would be the reason, as Dante said in the *Inferno* (canto vii), that:

. . . una gente impera e l'altra langue,
seguendo lo giudicio di costei,
che e occulto, come in erba l'angue.

(. . . some nations rule while others languish
following the dictates of her will
which lies hidden like a snake in the grass.)

Although the tree image looms mightily in the imagination, and it may appear infinitely more difficult to change a tree than a thread; it is actually just as easy—or difficult—to change either one. But we will lay the idea of the tree aside, for now, and consider the problem involved in changing the color of our thread of fate, since it presents the illusion of being a much easier task than changing the fruit of a tree.

How can we go about changing the color of this thread of our fate? For, basically, this is what we need to do in order to change our life. Usually, we do not really change anything, of course. We merely transfer our consciousness to another reality in which our thread already has the desired color. There may appear to be a glaring discrepancy between what I am saying and what we have all observed in life. We all know of, or have heard of, people who have changed. We can read about such cases almost every month or so in our daily papers and other media. The former wrestler becomes a state governor; the former B grade movie actor becomes president of the United States; the gang member or dope peddler becomes a born-again Christian; the flaming liberal becomes a conservative; the dour conservative becomes a liberal; the professional car-thief becomes a respectable worker and family man.

We see these things happen in *our* reality. So, how can we say that they occur because the person in question has exchanged his reality for another? If that were the case, we wouldn't be seeing the change—would we?

There is a simple explanation for this: Let us remember that when we see anything happen to another person it is something that only we are experiencing, because the reality we experience is ours alone and no one else's. Another thing to remember is that when we effect changes in the color of our thread of fate we are doing so by establishing new origins to our existence; we are acquiring a new past.

Here, again, objections immediately arise. How can it be that we acquire a new past, when we exchange one reality for another, when we can remember the same past every day of our life? The simple answer to that is, of course, it's the same past. At first glance it might appear that it would be a great thing if we could retain a memory of our other pasts, so that we could keep track of our progress, and compare our past in one reality to another.

But just think of what this would entail. The average person migrates to another reality about 24,166 times in the course of his life. Even the aboriginal jungle dweller exchanges his reality about 3,768 times during his lifetime. (If space allows, I will explain how I have arrived at those figures.) In our own society, the common man-in-the-street migrates to a different reality an average of 12,000 times. In the more active elements of society, this figure can go as high as 164,456.

It can readily be seen that we could not too easily retain a memory of so many pasts. Moreover, the vast majority of our changes do not involve any radical change in our deep past. One of the reasons this is so is that we refuse to relinquish certain elements of our reality. We tend to migrate into realities in which certain fond memories are still present.

To use an example from my own experience: when I was very little, I once found a five-dollar bill. So now, I have no doubt, whenever I migrate into another reality, it will be one in which that memory is present. It was during the Great Depression years, when five dollars was a vast amount of money, especially to a ten-year old boy who had never held in his hands anything greater than a one-dollar bill, entrusted to him so that he could walk two miles to a grocery store to buy coffee and beans.

That five-dollar bill, incidentally, had been lost by a Chinese boy named Lam, a nephew of the rich landowner on whose cotton farm we lived. And that is perhaps the reason I have always had such a great liking for the Chinese people. Because Lam was responsible for the greatest era of prosperity, relatively speaking, that I have ever enjoyed in my life.

When I had already spent about half the money, by the way, poor Lam came around by our house, asking if anybody had found it. And curious to say, because I consider myself a very honest person, I felt no guilt, nor do I feel any even to this day, for earnestly promising Lam that if I found his five-dollar bill I would surely let him know, and then afterwards continuing blithely to spend the remaining money on nickel hotdogs, Milky Ways, Snickers, Cracker Jacks, Tootsie Rolls, marshmallows, and ice cream, without the tiniest quiver of my conscience, that I can recall, or any concern whatever for Lam's misfortune.

Today I could never act so shamelessly. I have what I consider actual proof of this: Some time ago I had a curious dream, in which somehow a winning lottery ticket had come into my hands, and rather than keeping it I returned it to the rightful owner. "Oh, yeah, sure," anyone might say. "That's easy to do in a dream." But would I actually do that in real life? I feel that I can confidently answer in the affirmative. What we do in our dreams is indicative of our true inclinations.

If Lam is still alive today, I hope he can forgive me. He should take into consideration that he was rich and I was very poor, and that I enjoyed his money far more than he ever could have. Moreover, I have repaid Lam and his ancestors and descendants many times over since then by stoutly defending the Chinese whenever I have heard them slandered.

But, what I intended to illustrate by the anecdote is the degree to which we tend to restrict our migrations to realities with the same past. Not the same past exactly, but a very similar past. I, for example, have refused to relinquish that past in which that five-dollar bill is present, although that past also includes other not-so-pleasant events and circumstances, such as the extreme poverty in which we lived. I would have done better, I know, to relinquish that past which includes the pleasant memories connected to that five-dollar bill, migrating to a reality that included a past in which we were so comfortably well off that I immediately began inquiries as to who had lost the five-dollar bill, and returned it to its owner.

But more often than not, we do not really have a choice. We naturally tend to migrate to contiguous realities, in which the changes are slight, at best.

Today, the equivalent of finding that five-dollar bill would be finding a garbage bag full of hundred dollar bills, or maybe winning a small lottery. Since I am dwelling so much upon the lottery in my speculations, and since the lottery itself constitutes a good example of the sort of odds that are ranged against us in our quest for a substantially better life, let us take a deeper look at what those odds really are.

In my investigation of these matters, in my diligent quest to bring to the reader a vivid image of what is entailed in odds of sixteen million-to-one (15,890,700 to be exact), such as in a lottery with fifty numbers, I once counted the number of beans—the kidney variety—in one pound. There were 747. This means that in a one-hundred-pound sack there would be 74,700 and it would therefore take something like 212 sacks of beans to constitute sixteen million. Now, suppose someone was to mark one of these beans—paint it white, maybe—and then pour out those 212 sacks of beans, including the marked one, into your living room.

Imagine yourself blindfolded, trying to draw that marked bean out of the pile, one bean at a time. Imagine yourself blindfolded drawing out one bean at a time for 152,795 years, in fact. Because if you were simulating a fifty-number lottery, played twice a week, in which you bought one ticket for each drawing, that's how long it would take you to draw out every bean in the pile. Of course you would have to be very unlucky if you did not find the white bean before you came to the very last one (assuming that you threw each bean away as you withdrew it and that no other beans were added to the pile). However, where the actual lottery is concerned, those beans, figuratively speaking, are returned to the pile after each drawing. Therefore you could pick two beans a week for two- or three-hundred thousand years before coming upon the white one, and before you could reasonably begin to complain of your bad luck if you did not come across it in those years.

But suppose that, being aware of the dismal odds against you when you buy only one ticket, you cleverly decide to buy thirty or forty tickets at every drawing. In this case, you could quite reasonably expect to win the lottery thirty or forty times sooner, unless you are very unlucky. That is to say, if you had begun to play the lottery when Cheops was building his pyramid, you could now be reasonably hopeful that you would be winning the lottery any day, or any decade, or any century now.

Another view of the odds, which most people are familiar with, compares the probability of winning the lottery with being struck by lightning. A commercial message on TV, intended to convince people not to speculate on the lottery, tells us that our chances of being struck by a lightning bolt (about 600,000 to one) are better than our chances of winning the lottery.

But this is a very inept comparison. If the chances of being struck by lightning are 600,000 to one, what exactly does this mean? The chances cannot be the same for everyone. There are many ways in which we can increase our chances of being struck by lightning. We can go out on an open lake or river in a small boat during a thunderstorm; we can take shelter under a lone tree in an open meadow; we can hold up a long metal object—fishing pole, golf club, driller's loading pole, surveyor's aluminum stadia rod—during lightning and thunder activity. Do any of these things long enough, and chances are strong that some day you will be blasted right out of your socks. Do any of these things long enough and you will perhaps be increasing your chances of being struck by lightning by a thousandfold.

In a similar fashion, there are things you can do, and ways in which to proceed, that will make your probability of winning the lottery much more likely than that of being struck by lightning. Maybe in those 152,795 years you could hit the jackpot three or four times. The laws of probability would be balanced out by the fact that many other people would play the lottery for many hundreds of thousands of years, and never win even once.

In fact, winning the lottery, using the same logic as is used by those who compare the chances of winning it to the chances of being struck by lightning, is very much lower than 600,000-to-one. Let us consider: There are about 5,200 people who have won the lottery in the United States. Subtract from the population of the country all children, babies, and others who do not participate, and we can come to the startling conclusion that the odds against winning the lottery are much, much lower than the forbidding figures that opponents of the lottery so frequently cite—a mere 25,000-to-one, instead of fifteen or twenty million. (We can arrive at this figure by dividing 5,200 into 130 million, which is half the population of the country, approximately the percentage of persons who play the lottery.)

Now, does this really mean that the odds against *you* are 25,000-to-one? No, not necessarily so. That is only what the odds are for those people who do win the lottery. The odds against *you* are still in the millions-to-one. They are in fact even higher than the figure dictated by the mathematics of probability (and if you are one of those people destined to never win the lottery because you never buy lottery tickets, then they are of course infinitesimal). The odds against you have been greatly increased to compensate for those winners who have caused the visible odds to so drastically decrease from sixteen million to twenty-five thousand.

I have mentioned that there are things you can do to improve your chances of winning the lottery. I am referring to procedures based on coincidence and other superstitious practices, which I feel give us a better shake, and which should be mentioned briefly here (although this isn't a book about how to win the lottery).

For example, on various occasions, encouraged by the excellent results I obtained with the cat Precious in regard to horse races—and because I have always been intrigued and fascinated by felines, though I do not necessarily love them—I have used cats for this purpose. What I have done is place numbered slips of paper inside a jar, drawing them out with the cat's paw. The drawback to this system is that it requires a considerable degree of cooperation from the cat. Nevertheless, I have seen some interesting results with this method, though I have also encountered problems with uncooperative cats, biting and scratching.

I have also used slugs, with some spectacular results. The slugs are placed inside a sealed, dry fish tank and allowed to crawl around inside it during the night. The next day, you examine the walls of the tank and sometimes numbers can be read, etched out in the slug's slime on the glass. Large banana slugs from the Northwest, up to six inches long, are the best species for this purpose. (They can be obtained, if the reader is interested in trying this method, from Olga Metcalf, in Houston, who breeds and sells various exotic pets.)

But you must be careful. Slugs have the capability of stretching their bodies to ten times their length and squeezing through the tiniest of openings. This happened once during my experiments and they escaped out of the fish tank and into my then wife's indoor plants and other sensitive areas, causing no small degree of friction in my household.

Other procedures, which I invite the reader to try, have to do with the flights of birds, pyramids, coincidences, observing certain rules in regard to the time and place for buying lottery tickets, dreams, etc. We will deal later on with more details on all this. I feel that I can offer some valuable advice in this business of winning the lottery, even though I have never won the lottery myself. If we want to give ourselves a fair shake, and improve our chances so that they are at least comparable to the aforementioned odds of 25,000-to-one, it is obvious that something out of the ordinary is required.

This isn't a book about how to win the lottery. However, if you, the reader will dwell long enough upon the things I am saying, and believe them, you could substantially decrease the odds against you. But, given the fact that these odds will nevertheless still remain very great, the benefits will most probably accrue to you, not with a lottery win, but in other forms.

Chapter 12

Is Daydreaming a Dangerous Enterprise?

Certain imperfections of thought tend to perpetuate the unpropitious color of our thread; that is to say, they tend to keep us tied to one continuous reality. One of these imperfections has to do with the habit of daydreaming, such as in making elaborate plans for disposing of our loot if we should ever come into a large amount of money. Daydreaming may appear to be a harmless pastime, but this is not always so. It can often become an insidious detriment to the attainment of our desires. Evidence for this view can be seen in the clichéd saying, "He would never have dared to dream . . . " Why do we use the word "dare" in this context? Is dreaming a dangerous enterprise?

I would venture to say that the expression originates from a subconscious knowledge that daydreaming is harmful, that the dream can be cannibalistic, feeding upon both itself and the dreamer.

From a prosaic point of view, of course, daydreaming is a sterile endeavor, producing nothing tangible aside from the momentary pleasure the daydreamer derives from the dream. Metaphysically regarded, it seems likely that our daydreams only serve to dissipate the energy that could be used to transfer our psyche into another reality. At the same time, they create a habitat that favors the continued presence of our self in the reality it is occupying. It is quite possible that they also serve another purpose. They may leave a metaphysical essence in the space around us, demarking our position to the Fates so that they can more easily keep track of our position in life.

When we daydream of winning the lottery, then, we are doing two things. We are furnishing the Fates with a convenient handle on our lives, and we are dissipating a force which would be better spent in helping us to migrate into a better reality.

But if we banish from our soul this most pleasant of diversions, what is left? If we ruthlessly stamp out our dreams of winning the lottery, for example, we would be depriving ourselves of one of the greatest pleasures and consolations that help us through our humdrum, barren lives. Since it is highly unlikely that we will ever win a lottery, the daydreams that we indulge in are most likely the only pleasure we will ever derive from it. Must we forego this innocent entertainment?

My answer to this, which I'm sure will make the reader very happy, is "no." Such extreme measures are not absolutely necessary. For this would render many a miserable life even more dreary. There are ways in which we can enhance our luck, including our chances of winning the lottery, and still keep our daydreams. We can have our cake, and eat it, too. We must, however, learn to do it in a devious way; daydreaming, not with specific events and objects in mind, but rather displacing these as much as possible. This is an important superstition, and many people unconsciously observe it. They know, without ever having been told, that when they daydream of winning the lottery on a specific day they are thereby minimizing the chances that such a thing will actually happen.

This may all sound like unadulterated superstition, and sure enough, that is what it is. But we have already established that there is a sound and logical basis for superstition. In various superstitious practices, mankind has found a way to conjure away the threats and dangers that lurk in the pathways of life. Superstitions serve a useful purpose.

Summing it up, daydreaming does two things. First, from a prosaic standpoint, it dilutes the force of the mental energy which should be going into the application of our willpower. It does this by diverting the force that should be channeled into the effort to change the tint and hue of our thread (perhaps this is Shakespeare's, ". . . native hue of resolution, *not* sicklied o'er with the pale cast of thought"). Second, as a corollary or secondary effect, it more firmly establishes our prevailing color, the color of the dreamer, the loser, the inconsequential and habitually ineffectual person.

All this brings up a question which provides us with some mild entertainment when reflected upon: Is the habitual daydreamer ineffectual, inconsequential, lazy, and slipshod *because* he wastes his time daydreaming, or is he a daydreamer as a consequence of these defects? The question has been asked before, of course, in other contexts (Does smoking marijuana result in a propensity to accidents and other missteps in life, or is it the other way around?), nevertheless it actually contains some profound elements, applicable to other metaphysical aspects of improving our luck.

Now, we have agreed that we do not want to give up our daydreams. We want to, "take the cash in hand," but we don't want to "waive the rest," in the words of Omar Khayyam (the cash in hand being our daydreams). Because, as I cannot help repeating, it is entirely too chancy that we would ever see the real thing, the real cash. We will continue to daydream then, of fabulous treasure. But we must not do it in such a way as to tinge ourselves too starkly with that common dreamer-of-winning-the-lottery color.

Clear evidence that daydreaming is not good for us, inasmuch as it affects our ability to acquire money and power, can be seen in every aspect of life. Looking at any gathering of affluent and successful people, we can usually see that they are not people given to daydreaming. Go to a convention of business executives, or to a stockholders' meeting, or to a gathering of the board of directors of a large corporation, and study the faces of the people attending. You will notice that they all present that same no-nonsense appearance of forceful determination, a frame of mind that tends to leave no room for daydreams.

Most lottery winners, by the way, seem to share this same disinclination to entertain vivid daydreams. In their case, it is because they seem, to a marked degree, to be persons of quite modest imagination. When these winners of sudden millions are asked what they now intend to do with their lives, many of them do not have an answer. A surprising number of them declare that they do not intend to quit their humdrum, monotonous jobs. In fact, one large winner—a janitorial worker, I think—in a Midwestern state, surprised his employers by showing up for work the next day. He was promptly sent packing, his employers perhaps reasoning that his loyalty to his job, under the circumstances, showed a disturbing lack of common sense.

Another winner seemed so devoid of imagination that he waited until the last day of the six-month expiration period before claiming his prize, declaring that he had almost decided not to claim it at all, because he could think of nothing that he needed the money for. This shows a remarkable lack of imagination. Although a more charitable judgment, I admit, is that this person was so happy in his life before winning the lottery that he felt no urge to change anything in it whatsoever. Which begs the question, of course, of why he bought a lottery ticket in the first place.

While on this subject of the lottery, a careful compilation of lottery winners throughout the country would show, I think, a curious fact: a disproportionate number of winners are older people. There are very few winners in the early twenties age-bracket. Machiavelli says, in his famous work: ". . . Fortune is a woman, and in order to be mastered she must be jogged and beaten . . . she submits more readily to boldness than to cold calculation.

Therefore, like a woman, she favors young men." But Machiavelli was speaking of something very different from what we are calling fortune. For it can be seen that fortune—pure luck—does not favor young men at all. In fact, it seems quite evident that fortune enjoys cuffing young people around, afflicting them with every vicissitude of misfortune before they enter into old age. And, in fortunate occurrences ruled by the laws of probability, she rather favors older persons. Later on I will explain why this is.

At any rate, the above indicates that most people who have won the lottery have indulged very sparingly in daydreams, the same as the people of wealth and power we have mentioned above. But we will not dwell too much on evidence of this sort, for this would carry us into psychological reasoning, with which we are at present not concerned. We are focusing, not on specific ways to develop willpower, but on ways to achieve that same end by first improving our luck.

Moralists may argue that it is frivolous to concentrate on trying to improve our luck instead of striving to overcome our bad habits. Pure luck is simply a matter of sheer chance, over which we have no power at all, they say, while changing our character is something entirely within our grasp. It has nothing to do with chance. It depends wholly upon our willpower, and our desire to effect these changes.

But these moralists fail to realize that it was chance that has cast us into the world in our present condition, with our present character traits, and that to change these conditions and character traits must therefore be no easier than it is to affect any other aspect of pure chance. Once we have accepted this truth it becomes easy to see that the way to accomplish these changes would have to be by the process of improving our luck, since it is our luck, whether good or bad, that keeps us to our assigned destiny.

I have said that daydreaming affects the color of our thread of fate and dilutes the force of our willpower. I've also said that our daydreams emanate an aura, which serves the Fates as a sort of handle, which they use to keep us in our prevailing reality. It is clear, then, that we need to change our way of daydreaming in such a way that it will not subtract force from our willpower or leave that distinctive aura around us.

Why should the Fates care about keeping us in a reality, the reader might justifiably ask, since we have already established that our migration into other realities does not concern them and that when we migrate into another reality we are not changing anything in the reality we are leaving or in the one we are moving into. I have given two reasons for this resistance in the preceding chapter.

One, the Fates resist our move because they don't know what we are trying to do when we struggle to leave the reality in which they have us. Two, the reality we are trying to move to already has an owner. But since the reader is apparently not satisfied with those reasons, I must try to provide others.

One answer could be that it is because when we leave one reality for another, we are leaving the Fates in our old reality jobless, with nothing to do but to monitor the actions of the husk we leave behind, which would probably be a very boring and unremunerated occupation.

But this is not a valid answer, because what happens to the Fates in that reality when we abandon it for another? Why, they simply pass into the cell of the new occupant of that reality. From there, they continue to manipulate the acts and actions of the husk we have left behind, to make them conform to the reality of the new occupant of that reality. They are, therefore, never left jobless. This is the reason, as I have mentioned elsewhere, that when we arrive at a new reality we find the Fates already there waiting for us, and that we do not really ever escape from their control. They have been present in our new reality all along, in a way, manipulating it from a certain distance. When we arrive at a different reality, therefore, we arrive there simultaneously with the Fates who transfer into our cell of reality from the cell of the creature who is leaving it.

So, the first two reasons I have provided will have to serve as an answer to the question. These answers may still seem vaguely unsatisfactory, but one would have to admit that they are much better than simply admitting that I don't know. Moreover, the aforesaid resistance can be further explained with one all-encompassing answer: It is because we do not really have free will.

The content and the nature of our daydreams, therefore, is the principal, perhaps the only, facet of our character that we should aspire to change in the here and now (that is, apart from improving our luck) before we achieve any significant change in our destiny. The change in our mode of daydreaming, as I indicated in previous pages, consists in displacing the time and specific object of the daydream. Other changes in our character will come by themselves, naturally following any other change that we manage to bring about.

These changes we have been talking about, don't they imply that we have the power to change the unchangeable? If we can change our fate and our destiny doesn't this mean that we can change the very nature of fate itself?

Yes, that is exactly what it means. Those little bits of thread with which the Fates and their mother have been amusing themselves will some day bring about their downfall. With the advances of science and technology we are every day acquiring weapons which place Man on a more equal footing in his struggle against them, although we do not generally regard this fact in that light.

The field of medicine is one area in which it can be seen that we are steadily advancing in our struggle with destiny. More and more, every year, we see illnesses vanquished. One of the most marvelous triumphs of humankind over disease, which has not been celebrated as much as it should be, is the complete eradication of smallpox, which entailed the extermination of an entire race of microbes, a most remarkable accomplishment when we consider the many trillions of places where the microbe could have hidden to escape its complete extermination. And every day we see medical dramas of heroic procedures to prolong human life, which sometimes work but very often do not, showing that the Fates, though we may often defeat them in some other aspect of life, still retain a more or less firm hold on the matter of life and death.

The ancient Greek and Roman view of the nature of human destiny, by the way, could perhaps furnish a valuable clue to modern-day physicists in their quest for a Grand Unified Theory. The three Fates and their mother, Necessity, total four, corresponding to the four forces that physicists have for so many decades labored to reduce into a single one, from which the four would have separated as the universe cooled.

Necessity, "the Strong fate," against which even the gods were powerless, would correspond to gravity, the strongest of the four forces. Because gravity, although it is very weak in small amounts of matter when compared to the other forces, is, in the final accounting, actually the strongest one. Similarly, Necessity appears very weak when she is considered in matters of small importance. The weak nuclear force (which is responsible for atomic decay, and therefore death) would correspond to Atropos, "the smallest and the meanest" of the Fates, and the one who reputedly snips the thread of our life. Clotho, the spinner, would be the strong nuclear force which holds atoms together. Lachesis, the measurer, would be the electromagnetic force. We could see the four of them together as the force that binds the trillions of living creatures on Earth into a cohesive whole (so that each creature's fate has its effect, seen or unseen, upon all other creatures on Earth), deriving their power and authority from their corresponding counterparts in the four physical forces that rule the cosmos.

Chapter 13

Why You Should Avoid Peacocks

The superstitious habits of unreasoning creatures serve, to a large degree, only to keep them on their preassigned pathways until the end of their days. These habits are usually looked upon as instinctive behavior. Only occasionally do their superstitious habits serve to actually transport them into another reality in which they have a longer life span. If they fail to observe those superstitious habits, however, if they rebel against their fate and against Nature, it can lead to great discomfort, hardship, and even a premature death for those creatures. The polar bear that fails to observe the polar bear superstition of covering its nose will often go hungry. The caterpillar that refuses to observe the caterpillar "superstition" of first chewing through the stem of the toxic leaf before it feeds, will die.

Human beings, on the other hand, have a much greater potential to not only prolong their days on Earth, but to make those days much happier and more fulfilling. Many of us, through a judicious observance of superstitious taboos, and through cunning and devious superstitious practices, have managed to wriggle out of the grip of fate, escaping from this determinism into another reality in which our predestined life span is longer.

This determinism consists, as it were, of subparagraphs and/or clauses embedded within certain other laws that hold the fabric of reality together and which constitute our contract with destiny. But, just as in worldly law a contract becomes void if it goes against established law, is immoral, or is blatantly prejudicial to one of the parties, so does our "contract" with fate become void when we decide to make an issue of the fact that it is manifestly unfair and that it has been drafted without our conscious consent.

141

The older person more frequently manages to squirm out of this unsocial contract with destiny. One reason for this is because of the changed nature of the older person's daydreams, or because he no longer daydreams at all. The withered, emaciated old man may continue to dream of winning the love of a beautiful woman (or in the case of an aged female of being loved by a handsome young movie star); he may continue to dream of becoming a world-famous athlete, or of acquiring a vast fortune. But these daydreams, and almost all others, acquire a different tinge with the melancholy of advancing age. The old man (or old woman), no longer emanates that distinctive aura that the Fates look for as they stand guard over our route through life.

Another reason, a corollary of the first, is that the Fates relax their vigilance over us as we grow older, just as we ourselves may relax our vigilance over our children as they mature. In our case, we watched carefully over our children when they were little because we loved them, and we exerted ourselves in guiding them through the proper pathways of life. We relax our vigilance when we feel we have done all we can for them, and that they have grown old enough to take care of themselves. The Fates, on the other hand, leave us increasingly on our own because they think they have fulfilled their function of keeping us from straying out of the path they have marked out for us, which is often a path filled with evils and misfortune. They think they have us safely in the bag.

The lottery and other games of chance are where we most frequently see evidence of this propensity for old people to seemingly wriggle out of the clutch of destiny. I have already suggested that a careful perusal of lottery records would show that there is a disproportionate number of winners of advanced age. Death, although we have said that it is something in which the Fates maintain their firmest grip on destiny, is also another area in which the tendency for the old to escape the bag of the Fates would be glaringly evident if it were not for the fact that death in very young people does not normally present itself in a manner such as to offer a basis for objective comparison.

However, in the many odd instances of great longevity—cases in which the very old person seems to cheat death for prolonged periods of time, such as living to the age of 100 or more—the fact that the very old person has evaded his normal destiny can be seen. In these cases the Fates have lost track of the aged person; they have forgotten about him. Atropos has somehow been distracted at the crucial moment, and has forgotten to snip the thread at the proper time, which therefore continues to dangle, uselessly and to no purpose, out of the tapestry.

Her sisters must also share some of the blame. They have neglected those details which combine to mark the span of human life. In spinning out the thread of life, Clotho has not used the proper material. Lachesis has not measured it out properly. Both of them have neglected to afflict that person with any of the habits, vices, and dietary proclivities which determine the accepted life span of humans.

Besides these instances of great age, there are many other strange cases in which people have miraculously cheated death. In the nineteenth century, we have the case of a miner who survived a bizarre accident with no discernible impairment. A heavy ramrod with which he was tamping a powder charge into a hole passed through his head from beneath the chin through the top of his head when the powder charge accidentally exploded. Then there was the frontiersman who was "killed" by Indians, and then scalped. But he survived to live to a hairless ripe old age.

In more recent times, we have more than one case of parachutists, whose parachute failed to open, plunging for thousands of feet, to bounce off the solid earth and walk wonderingly away with only minor bruises. In the early 1970s in Peru, a young girl walked away unscathed from an airplane crash in the Amazon jungle that demolished the aircraft and killed all of the other one hundred passengers.

There are thousands of other recorded cases of similar oddities, which show that the Fates are far from perfect in the performance of their duties. This suggests that there are undoubtedly ways in which we can promote these errors, and thereby exchange our preordained destiny for something more to our liking.

A miraculous escape from death, nevertheless, does not occur too commonly. Such an escape requires either a prodigious leap across a vast expanse of realities or a rare confluence of greatly divergent realities flowing close together. More usually to be seen are little changes, so imperceptible that often we still retain a foothold in the old reality, and hop back and forth for a while between the two, before we finally take definitive possession of the new reality. A great many realities can also be intermeshing, so that large groups of people who may sometimes come together will interact in each other's realities, each of them contributing to the other persons' realities and incorporating substance from them into his own. In other words, sometimes the persons you are interacting with will be real persons, although each of you will be in his own separate reality.

One way in which many persons in antiquity made a timely exit from one reality to another to thereby escape death was by paying heed to the stark warnings and auguries to be found in the flights of birds. Next to coincidence, this is still an excellent way, much neglected in this modern age, to foretell the future. There is a wealth of information to be gleaned from the calls and the flights of many species of wild birds, and even some domestic ones. The presidents and ministers of modern nations would do well to maintain diviners, just as statesmen of old did, who would advise them on this score.

In olden times, every army, every general, and every great statesman had their diviners, whose sole function was to watch for auguries of this sort. The diviner Zog seems to have done an excellent job for Hannibal for several years, until the inexorable hand of fate finally brought Hannibal up short.

Xenophon tells us, in his *Anabasis*, that Cyrus had a diviner named Silanos who accurately foretold to Cyrus that Artaxerxes would not present battle within ten days. This seemed so improbable to Cyrus, and an outcome so much to be desired, that he promised to pay Silanos 3000 darics if it came true. "If Artaxerxes will not fight within ten days," he told Silanos, "then he will not fight at all." As it turned out, Artaxerxes fought on the twelfth day, and Silanos collected a rich payoff on his prediction. One daric was equivalent to a soldier's wages for a full month.

Summarizing the foregoing, in the ancient world, before the third century, B.C., the divining art was more akin to a respected science, and the seers and oracles of those times were much more successful. Very rarely can we hear any voices from those times scoffing at the belief. Even wise Socrates was a firm believer. In fact, he advised Xenophon to consult the Delphic oracle before going on his famous trip to Persia. The advice was probably redundant. Xenophon would hardly so much as go to the bathroom without first consulting a seer.

To return to our birds: not all birds are useful for the purposes indicated above. The English sparrow, for example, is almost completely devoid of any prophetic content worth bothering with. So is the grackle, the robin, the chickadee, and other similar birds. Hawks and falcons, on the other hand, are very reliable, as are egrets, cranes, storks, and other such fowl. There is very little advice I can give on the manner in which the flights of birds should be interpreted. This is a gift, rather than an acquired science. The diviner who can receive messages from the flights of birds can do so because his sixth sense is attuned to the tenuous messages transmitted in the lift of a wing, the outstretched legs, the set of the tail. . . .

One bird that I earnestly advise the reader to avoid touching, even its fallen feathers, is the peacock. Even hearing its plaintive and melancholy wail can bring bad luck.

The ancient Greeks and other peoples of the Mediterranean were well aware that the peacock is a bird of ill omen. They claimed that the lovely blue ovals in its tail were the eyes of the giant, Argus Panoptes, who had a hundred eyes. Let me tell the story here, so that no one can accuse me of being remiss in my duty to instruct the reader on the reasons why all superstitions should be treated with respect, just as a child must be taught that all guns should be treated as if they were loaded.

They say that Zeus was once dallying with a mortal girl named Io, having sneaked off from Mount Olympus while his wife Hera was asleep. But when Hera woke up and noticed that he was gone, she rushed down to Earth to look for him, well knowing his penchant for slumming with lowly mortal females.

Zeus heard her coming, almost too late, but he did have time to hastily turn poor Io into a cow to conceal his act of adultery from Hera. Hera wasn't fooled, though she pretended to be. "My, my," she panted, all out of breath from her hurried rush to catch Zeus in the act, "what do we have here? What a lovely cow. Where did you get her?" Zeus shrugged. "It's just an old cow."

"Why, how can you say that?" Hera said. "It's a beautiful cow. Let me have her for my herd." Zeus couldn't say no, of course. So Hera had the cow driven off to join her herd. All the gods kept herds of cattle in those days, in various remote corners of the Earth. She set the giant Argus to watch over the cow, strictly enjoining him to always keep one of his eyes on it, to make sure Zeus would not be able to turn it back into a girl again.

Argus tied Io to a nearby olive tree, and faithfully carried out his charge. But Zeus sent the god Hermes to free her, which Hermes did by first lulling every one of Argus's eyes to sleep by playing on his flute, and telling him long boring stories. When the last of Argus's eyes finally closed, Hermes crushed him with a huge boulder and then cut off his head for good measure. Then he freed the girl, Io, who went galloping off to look for her father. Hera set a gadfly to torment and pursue her relentlessly, so that she galloped all the way to the Bosphorus, named thus in her memory (Bosphorus means Cow's Ford), because that's where she swam across into Asia Minor, to then continue on into Egypt, where it is said she finally regained her human shape.

Hera, deeply mourning the death of her pet giant Argus, had his eyes set into the tail of the peacock, to ever after remind the world of his foul murder. This is the reason the peacock is an unlucky fowl. It is a reminder to the world of more than one ancient crime.

Mythical or whatever, the belief in the bad luck associated with peacocks is therefore very ancient. As long as we can never be certain as to the true reasons, we should play it safe and accept the belief at face value. I, myself, have an instinctive aversion to peacocks. I sense a somber and moody quality emanating from those ancestral mansions with the expansive yards in which a peacock spreads its tail to the world and utters its querulous calls.

I have a friend who was once considering marriage with a pretty Chinese woman whose American name was Joan. He asked for my advice on the matter, seeking to reinforce the decision he had already made. He told me of the delicious Chinese dishes Joan could cook, and that he would never have to actually support her, because she had her own business—a barber shop—and only wanted to marry an American to regularize her presence in the country. Then he told me her Chinese name. It was Fong, or Fang, or Fung—he didn't know how to spell it—but she had told him that it meant peacock in Chinese. I immediately gave him my opinion. Despite my great partiality towards the Chinese, and especially pretty Chinese females, I told him: Stay away from peacocks in any form or shape whatsoever, no matter how pretty and culinarily delightful they may be.

He unhappily heeded my advice, and subsequent events proved that my instinct had not been wrong. Along the way to his final decision to accept my advice, incidentally, my friend experienced one unfortunate consequence. In the course of carrying out his courtship he had been forced to visit her barbershop, under the pretext of needing a haircut, far more frequently than was really necessary, and he constantly presented a skinhead appearance, which was not his preferred style. "Never ask a Chinese barber," he later confided to me, "for a light trim. They think it means to cut your hair until it covers your skull very lightly."

Returning to the matter of the abrogation of our involuntary contract with destiny, how should we set about doing this? What metaphysical courts of natural law can we resort to for declaratory relief? There is no simple answer, but the reflective observer can extract a clue from a superficial dissection of two parallel lives.

When the son of a bank president or senator, or owner of a multi-million dollar business, or what-have-you, graduates from college and goes on to become a prominent and illustrious member of society, it can be seen that he is only following the pathway marked out for him by fate and destiny. He walks this pathway with the grace and assurance born of the knowledge that the miseries that afflict the greater mass of humanity will never touch him. No doubt he will marry a fine young lady with a college education, the daughter of another well-known and prosperous family. This young man will never have any pressing need to greatly change his condition in life. The routes he takes, the endeavors he will engage in, will all be shortcuts and detours which quickly reemerge onto the pathway the Fates have chosen for him. He will have no need or desire to make any drastic changes.

The underprivileged son of a laborer, or dirt farmer, however, may not feel too content with his situation. He will chafe at not being able to go to college. He is beset with money problems. The threat of unemployment hangs constantly over his head. He worries about losing his car because he cannot meet the payments. He cannot marry a socialite, so he must be satisfied with marrying the barmaid, or waitress—even the call girl—that he met somewhere along the sordid byways of his miserable life.

In both of these cases, the immutability of destiny can be seen. And it can also be plainly seen that in the second case all the pathways (reality changes) this poor laborer's son should take to bring about a significant change in his situation must necessarily be very far removed from his primary one. If he tries to change his life by taking little pathways that branch out from his roadway of life, he will find that, more often than not, these little detours inevitably take him back to his original trail, just as they do for the banker's son. To bring about a *substantial* change, it almost seems as if he would have to abandon all pathways, to slog out across woods and fields until he came to another road or highway. Then he would have to unobtrusively blend into the traffic on this new roadway, hoping no one would notice that he did not belong there. Such an approach often works, but it can be risky.

It is curious to note that the banker's son should find it easy to change his condition, if he so wished. It seems he could easily go from being wealthy and respected to being among the most abject and pitiable of creatures. He could give away his money and every last scrap of his property; he could abuse his socialite wife until she deserted him; he could cause his parents to disown him; he could alienate, by these and other like actions, all his friends, and thus descend into the same strata as the laborer's son. But this happens just as infrequently as the reverse—the laborer's son becoming a wealthy banker—and although it may appear that this is because no one in his right mind would want to do this, it is actually only evidence of the immutability of destiny, of the opposition of the Fates to *any* change in the design of their works.

Pious Dante would have considered fate only as a manifestation of a Divine will, and he would have considered the willful descent of a wealthy person into poverty as a grave sin, as can be seen where he presents just such a person (the Spendthrift Arcolano of Siena) in the depths of Hell, fleeing naked through brush and thorns. But there is nothing sinful about our opposition to the evil in our lives, whatever may be the power that has assigned it to us. In fact, we should find much to admire in another of Dante's personages, Vanni Fucci, who from the vaulted recesses of the Inferno could still shout, with both fists figcocked heavenward, *"Togli Dio, ch'a te le squadro!"* ("Take that, God, I square them off for you!") Though of course we cannot condone such an insane goal as descent into poverty.

My point is, the fact that the will and desire towards this goal occurs as infrequently as the desire for the opposite condition is gratified, is proof that an active force rules over both conditions.

The Fates have destined that the laborer's son will be wretchedly poor all his life, and he cannot too easily change this. They have decreed that the wealthy young man will be prosperous and happy all his life; and he, too, cannot too easily decide otherwise.

However, easy or not, it can be done. To more fully understand what is entailed in bringing about a real and lasting change, let us return to the simile of our life as represented by a piece of thread. To change our situation in life we would have to change the color of this thread. It can be quickly seen that it is not easy. We can change our color from red to pink, or from blue to blue-green fairly easily. But it becomes obvious that there is a deep-dyed difference in color between the thread of fate of the thief or murderer, for example, and that of the statesman, bank president, or community leader.

It can also be seen, therefore, that in order to effect a substantial change it sometimes becomes necessary to pour a bottle of Clorox into the washtub of our life—into the washtub of our daydreams—to blanch and bleach away our original color, so that it will then be easier to tinge our thread of fate with the proper shade. But we should avoid a too conscious quest of this goal and pursue it in a more relaxed and oblique manner, because the more we concentrate our conscious attention towards the end of radically changing our position in life, the more do we build up a resistance against us.

Let us address once more the question of whether our intrusion into the world of the arcane and our interference in the designs of fate is blasphemous and dangerous. The people who believe that this is so are thereby sustaining that we are what we are mainly because that is the way destiny wants us to be. In this they are quite right. The Fates want us to stay as we are, as they have made us. But, is it therefore wrong for the thief, the pervert, the pool hall bum, to try to change themselves?

No, of course it isn't wrong. Just as it is the duty of citizens to oppose their government domestically when it is oppressive and insufferable, so is it mankind's duty to oppose the evil in fate and destiny. When we have become aware of this evil, and realize we do not have to put up with it, it then becomes our duty to awaken the consciousness of others to the wrongs that are being done them.

Generally speaking, the Fates find it easy to keep the squirming masses of impoverished humanity in their place. The great difficulty that we find in laying aside our bad character traits cold turkey is a powerful tool that serves destiny in good stead to keep us in our present position.

Here's how it works: Improving our luck means changing our reality. Changing our reality means changing our character. Changing our character means changing the color of our thread in the tapestry of life. Changing the color of our thread means changing its position on the tapestry. Changing its position can also lead to a consequent change in its color. The four things, then, are one and the same. It only boils down to the most efficient manner in which to accomplish it. We are advocating here that the easiest and most efficient way is by, first of all, improving our luck. One way to do this is by a careful, selective, and judicious observance of superstitious taboos and practices—such as avoiding peacocks.

Chapter 14

Not All Rabbits' Feet Are Lucky

An integral part of the framework of superstitious practices is the belief in magical enchantments and good-luck charms, ranging from the time-honored rabbit's foot or four-leaf clover, to more sophisticated items such as the image of Tubro, the Panamanian god of money, which Peg Bundy sold her husband's patrimony to buy.

How do these good-luck charms work? It seems indisputable to us that most of these charms really do work. Here we have an intriguing illustration of the malignant nature of bad luck and misfortune. Bad luck can be compared to a venomous reptile that strikes blindly at an inanimate object that is dropped within its striking range. A good-luck charm is just such an inanimate object, although we do not toss it out, but rather simply carry it with us, to absorb the venomous strikes of misfortune. It is therefore a metaphysical magnet, or lightning rod, that draws toward itself the elements of misfortune, while at the same time serving as an extra antenna that helps us capture signals from our *neter*. It is more efficacious for both these purposes if we consciously seek to establish a linkage via our good-luck charm with our *neter*.

Another valid description for what a good-luck charm does is that it acts as a sump or drain hole for misfortune through which the excess of bad luck with which we are cursed is discharged. This should indicate, to anyone who will give the matter some thought, that we should be careful when we socialize with a person who carries an efficacious good-luck charm, because the bad luck that is being shunted and drained away from that person will then look for some other resting place. In other words, bad luck is contagious.

Whatever the explanation, it appears that good-luck charms are efficacious even when they are accidentally or unknowingly carried by persons who have no belief in such things.

When the good-luck charm has absorbed as much evil as it can contain—when the metaphysical drain hole becomes clogged with the sludge and gunk of all that off-shunted misfortune—it loses its power to protect us. For this reason, persons who carry these charms should monitor them carefully, to gauge that moment in which they should be replaced. If you have been carrying a rabbit's foot, you can simply replace it with a new one, or you can substitute something entirely different. A small charm such as a rabbit's foot is probably only good for a year or so (unless you are cursed to an extraordinary degree by bad luck, in which case you probably need to replace it sooner). Something larger, such as a porcelain owl, on the other hand, can last you for many years.

All superstitious persons already know all this. But here is something else, which many of them may not have realized before. It stands to reason that if some things which you keep, either on your person or somewhere within your house, can protect you, there must surely be many other things which draw bad luck and evil fortune to you. I have found it prudent to periodically comb through all my small possessions, mementos and keepsakes, to throw out all those things which produce an instinctive feeling of annoyance and aversion. True, sometimes in an excessive zeal to protect myself I sometimes throw away things that I later wish I hadn't. Nevertheless, it is a good practice to follow.

Another fact that should be considered is the relative nature of good or bad luck, the fact that it must have a beginning base.

Very fortunate persons—those persons who were born into good fortune—will be wasting their time carrying a rabbit's foot. Their luck is already as good as it can get. They can therefore rightfully scoff and sneer at the belief; the person who finds himself in a deep chasm of misfortune can do likewise. The condemned murderer on his way to the electric chair needs something much more miraculous than a four-leaf clover to save him.

This is so obvious that it may seem facetious and inane to point these things out, but the observation springs from a kernel of profound importance: Our luck should be regarded as something that must be *nurtured*, just as a sensible person guards his physical health. You do not wait until you are hopelessly sick before trying to cure yourself. Just as there are many medications that produce excellent results in the early stages of a disease, but which are useless in its advanced stages, so are there good-luck charms and superstitious practices that are good only if you are not already in the depths of serious misfortune.

Put in other words, it is much easier to climb to a height of ten thousand feet if you have been living all your life at an altitude of nine thousand feet, than if you have been living at sea level.

The mystical properties of many herbs indicates that they should perhaps be used mainly as a means of improving our luck, an improvement which, though it would remain mostly unobservable, would consist largely in the fact that they would keep us free of specific illnesses and disease. No doubt herbal remedies of ancient times, many of which are still widely used today, had a solid base of legitimacy. Many excellent herbal remedies very often produced tangible and observable results. The problem was, and is, that these herbal remedies are too often used from an inappropriate base.

Something else that most people don't realize today is that many ancient herbal remedies—the plants that were used in biblical times, for example—no longer exist, having been hunted and uprooted into extinction. The plant that we know as mandrake today is not the same plant that existed two thousand years ago. The real mandrake, or mandragora, had roots in the exact shape and form of a tiny little man, as we can read in the old bestiaries. When it was pulled up, it would utter a heart-rending shriek, a trait, unfortunately, which did not save it from being uprooted to extinction. It was sought after as a cure for sterility in women; the high value in which it was held is illustrated in the biblical story of Rachel, who traded off the rights to her husband to Leah for a few roots which Leah's son, Reuben, had found in the fields (Genesis 30:15).

Despite its uselessness to the condemned murderer, as I have noted above, the value of a four-leaf clover as a good-luck charm should not be underestimated. I have never been able to find one, despite assiduous searches I have made every time I find myself in a field of clover. So I have had to content myself with rabbit's feet. I find that jackrabbit feet are the best for this purpose. If the reader should choose this option, however, he should take care that it is properly cured. Otherwise he can find himself unknowingly carrying a stinking rabbit's foot in his pocket, which can be very unlucky, even if it be only because he will be shunned by all who come near him.

This happened to me once. It was a most unfortunate occurrence, bearing out the conclusion that must be reached from the above observation: Not all rabbit's feet are lucky, something that I have amply documented. Moreover, I have found that in my case, in order for the foot to be lucky, it has to come from a wild rabbit that I have been personally involved with.

But even there, deviations can occur. I once lived for some time in Mesa, Arizona, a suburb of Phoenix. I remember how amazed I was after first arriving to see how jackrabbits swarmed all over some of the less densely populated areas of the city. What a heavenly vision such a profusion of jackrabbits would have been in the San Joaquin Valley in the 1930s, when my oldest brother and I would comb the barren cotton fields in the cold months of January and February, with a single-shot .22 rifle, forlornly hoping to spot a jackrabbit crouched between the rows. Sometimes we would walk for miles and for hours without finding one. Jackrabbits were ferociously persecuted in California during the Great Depression.

In Mesa, there was one large vacant lot in particular that I would drive past every day. There would always be five or six fat jackrabbits there, brazenly grazing beside the road. Every day, as I would drive past that location, I would wish that I could once more savor the unique flavor of stewed jackrabbit, served with refried beans, like my mother used to make. One day, succumbing to temptation, I pulled over to the side of the road, took my .22 rifle out of the trunk, and shot a jackrabbit, under the amazed eyes of passing motorists. This was almost in the back yard of the Fish and Game Commission, as a matter of fact, though I didn't know that at the time. Fortunately this did not cause me any problem. After shooting the rabbit I had to scoop it up and flee very quickly to skin and dress it in the safety of my apartment.

As I was dressing it, under the disapproving eyes of my youngest daughter, who happened to be visiting, the point of the knife touched a large boil on its leg that I had not noticed before. The jackrabbit was evidently diseased. It burst and sprayed a foul-smelling liquid all over my kitchen, also spattering on my daughter's dress.

Strange to say, the odor persisted for days, and even for weeks, despite my relentless scrubbing, washing, and deodorizing. That is to say, the odor became entirely subjective in quality, the very odor of bad luck. My daughter tells me that on certain occasions she still experiences that subjective odor, many years later. I have questioned her carefully as to the exact occasions when she has experienced the odor, and have established that something bad has happened to her very shortly thereafter.

I had to throw that rabbit away, of course, and I instinctively knew that its feet would not make very good lucky charms.

I have not held my present views on lucky charms and related subjects all my life, by the way. During my younger and brasher years I generally tended to scoff at such beliefs. The turning point in my attitude came many years ago, beginning with an incident in Bolivia. I was crossing the Altiplano one day, when I came upon an encampment of Gypsies returning to La Paz from a fair in a provincial city. It was a group of three or four families, centering around one old hag who had a tent with a cardboard sign in front that said, as nearly as I can recall, and in all black letters: "SELENA, QUEEN OF THE GYPSIES." I entered her tent, mainly for the purpose of entertainment, and asked her to tell me my fortune. "But don't tell me too much," I said to her, "I only have twenty pesos to spend."

Selena sensed the mockery in my words, and took deep offense. She then proceeded to announce various misfortunes in my near future. I was going to have legal difficulties with Bolivian authorities; I was going to lose my job; I was going to experience several years of nothing but bad luck. . . . Towards the end she gave me seven or eight curious beans, speckled with red, white, and black, and told me to plant them to conjure away the said bad luck.

My first impulse after I left her tent was to throw them away. But, I remembered Jack and his bean stalk and held on to them.

I didn't plant them because for the next year I led a somewhat disrupted existence and had no place to plant them. But about a year later I happened to be in Honduran Mosquitia and gave them to a Miskito named Ingbacne, who had been living in the same shack for many years with his family, and had plenty of space in his yard for such things. I was curious to see what could grow from such strange beans.

I continued with my life and my endeavors, which by the way, were cursed by bad luck for several years, just as that evil Gypsy woman had foretold. Then, one day, about five years later, I found myself in Honduran Mosquitia again, and I immediately went to visit Ingbacne. I asked him about the beans, and he pointed to a little stump protruding from the sandy ground near his shack. A little tree had grown from the beans, he told me, and it had produced some long, violet-colored pods, with very edible-looking beans. One of his little boys had tried to eat some of them one day and they had provoked a flaming rash around his mouth and a violent stomach ache. So he had cut the tree down recently, and was now using it for fire wood.

Strange to relate, the very month in which he had cut down that tree corresponded to the date on which I had begun to see a change in my luck. This tells me that Selena, Queen of the Gypsies, far from giving me a lucky charm in that handful of beans, had actually laid a curse on me, to punish me for my mockery.

Lucky charms have a wide range of applicability, and I have indicated the tentative reasons why they are effective. Magical enchantments, however, are something else again. Magic sometimes works because it tricks the Fates into giving legitimacy to a reality that conforms to a set of spurious facts with which we provide them. In other words, they can produce shifts in reality, sometimes of meaningful extent, but usually very minor, affecting minor aspects of life. But they are not too reliable when we try to apply them to higher ends. In fact, as far as magic is concerned, I believe that it can be counterproductive in many cases, and, far from producing beneficial results, can actually be detrimental.

These ill effects come about as the result of a reflexive reaction from the Fates in their efforts to preserve the integrity of their tapestry. In something such as the lottery, especially, or other things in which the laws of chance and probability are involved, it becomes plain to see that magic will not work if it violates these laws to a very large and noticeable degree. Where great odds are involved it would take a tremendous amount of magically-induced good luck to produce any appreciable effect. In fact, where the lottery is concerned, it would take such an enormous amount of good luck to win it, that even luck, as I think I have already made clear, becomes almost irrelevant.

It is this fact which appears to give the reason to those people who have across the centuries railed against the folly of superstitious beliefs. They can quite reasonably point to the fact that no one can show how any particular ill-omened action has ever resulted in any consistent degree of bad fortune, or vice versa. As an example in their favor: recently it was common to see buildings whose floor numbering skipped from twelve to fourteen, in deference to the superstitious. Lately, however, this custom is largely ignored, and we can't deny that the occupants of that ill-omened floor do not seem to suffer any greater degree of misfortune than anyone else.

Of late, also, we can see many athletes brazenly flaunting that same number on their jerseys (a number I try to avoid mentioning as much as possible, by the way, because I happen to believe the very thought of it brings me bad luck). And here, also, we can't deny that those athletes do not seem to suffer any ill consequences thereby. Many of them, in fact, seem to enjoy more than an average degree of success in their profession.

But the reason for this apparent inconsistency lies, again, in that inescapable fact of probability. Of course the number cannot have the same effect for everybody. It must be balanced out by an almost equally beneficial effect for another segment of humanity. If this were not so, then of course the effect would be so marked and evident that it would constitute a most intriguing and mysterious physical phenomenon.

All superstitions, in fact, should be looked upon much as any sensible person should look upon any medication that can sometimes produce undesirable side effects. There are some drugs that will have an adverse effect upon a small percentage of subjects. On a small percentage of others, they will bring about a marked improvement. On the larger mass of people, they will have no effect at all. It is the same way with most things, actions, and numbers that are reputed to be lucky or unlucky. The pernicious effects they produce apply only to a select group of humanity, and they are balanced out by the opposite effect on an equal number of people.

Of course there are no physical causes or reasons for this, or, at least, no causes and reasons that are presently visible. If the number in question evokes in some of us a vague sense of unease, it is because we have the subconscious knowledge that we belong to that group of people for whom it announces the imminence of impending evil. We should steer clear of it as much as we sensibly can. The same holds true for all other things and actions which are reputed to bring us bad luck. The position I am adopting here is exactly the same as the position adopted by the FDA in the case of a medication which has been proven to have pernicious effects, even if these side effects occur only rarely.

So I avoid the number thirteen like the plague. When I was working in engineering-related pursuits my aversion towards that number sometimes caused me problems. In the field of engineering that number must inevitably crop up here and there. Then I would be faced with the problem of explaining certain discrepancies to some nitpicking engineer—"Why did you call that correction twelve centimeters when it should be thirteen?" "Why did you use bench mark No. 112 when such-and-such is half a mile closer?"—questions of that sort, not easily answered.

Despite those problems, everything has turned out for the best. I no longer have to cope with engineers and their hard-nosed ways, engineers and their exasperating insistence that things must be exactly to such-and-such a measurement, insisting that things be measured down to a one-hundredth of a meter. If those engineers only knew that there are some structures in South America that I worked on that were built (at least in the part of them in which I intervened) entirely without the use of that aforementioned number.

People have known about the evil effects of that number for many centuries. Robert Graves tells us, in his introduction to *The Greek Myths*, that the evil connotation that the number holds for the superstitious stems from the fact that in pre-Hellenic Greece the sacred king was sacrificed during the thirteenth lunar month. But there is another way to look at the matter. Perhaps the sacred king was sacrificed during the thirteenth lunar month because dark and evil deeds tend to gravitate towards that number. The most compelling proof for the conjunction of evil and the number thirteen can be seen in the case of the cannibal Aztecs, the most bloodthirsty, cruel, and savage people who have ever existed on Earth, with their thirteen day weeks, and twenty-times-thirteen-days divinatory calendar, and their recurring fifty-two-year cycles, which were equivalent to our centuries, divided into four thirteen-year periods.

Those very people who hold the superstitious and all superstitions in contempt are often amongst the most superstitious people in the world. Nominally non-superstitious persons are usually the most fortunate and happy of people. They are rich and powerful. They are eminent statesmen, physicians, lawyers, captains of industry, scientists. Doesn't this prove that superstition is foolish, that only fools are superstitious? In the first place, as to the fact that only fools are superstitious, this is true to a large degree because it is mainly foolish people who have been cursed with the additional misfortune of being susceptible to the bad effects of unlucky things, actions, and numbers. It is not their superstitious beliefs that make them foolish. Rather, the greatest fool of all is the born fool who says, while his ragged family endures hardship, and as he waits for his decrepit old car to be repaired for the umpteenth time, "I don't believe in that stuff. I've walked under ladders all my life and nothing bad has ever happened to me."

Those of us who hold many things in superstitious dread are that way because we have been cursed from birth with defective connections to the roots of our origins. So we have learned to look in the most unlikely places for the source of our misfortunes. We learn to avoid certain numbers and certain actions. We toss spilled salt over our left shoulder; we never open an umbrella indoors; we do not whistle in a hallway; we never walk under a ladder; we do not sweep a floor after dark, or sweep our shoes off with a broom. In this way we substitute superstition—sometimes misguided, sometimes on target—for the good luck and good fortune that we were born without.

The blessed and the fortunate, on the other hand, do not need to look in strange places to avoid misfortune. They do not need to worry about the effects of the more common taboos such as unlucky numbers and so forth. Their misfortunes, when they do strike, come through other pathways, and those people, if they are truly blessed, instinctively know what to avoid.

For these reasons, when these people form a decision they are often influenced by reasons so unclear or fallacious that they can only be properly termed as superstition. Here is a hypothetical example, frequently seen. A person—let us call him O'Leary—occupies a top position with a manufacturing firm, which he ably guides through the mazes and pitfalls of the world of industry. Suddenly things start going wrong. Unexpected competition arises; the industry changes; inflation, deflation, business stagnation, or what have you, combine to run O'Leary's business through the wringer. His company suffers terrible losses. The accountants try to cook the books. With hard times come bankruptcy, litigation, and endless lawsuits. None of this was O'Leary's fault. His misfortune derives solely from the fact that his fate was tied to that of the manufacturing company that has gone down the tubes.

When the dust finally settles, O'Leary, reduced almost to poverty, begins to look for another job. But no one will hire him, although it has been well established that he was entirely faultless, that he was an energetic and capable manager. Apparently his association with a business that has gone belly-up becomes a serious impediment. Prospective employers are reluctant to hire someone associated with such a fiasco.

Moral considerations aside, perhaps they are right. Those prospective employers, however, will base their prejudice against O'Leary on anything except the true reason: O'Leary has become a very unlucky person, and can possibly contaminate, with his misfortunes, any other business in which he may become involved.

Similar cases can be seen in other branches of commerce and industry. In the Texas oil patches, the exploration divisions of many oil companies will subconsciously shy away from the geophysicist who has never been associated with a significant oil or gas find. In the world of sports we can see owners of ball clubs ruthlessly chewing up and spitting out coaches and trainers who fail to win games with teams that have been destined, "by the power that arranges these things," to be losers. Those owners know, in their subconscious, that the trainers and coaches involved are not so much incompetent as unlucky, but they fire them anyway.

Yet, all those people will steadfastly deny they are superstitious. They are seemingly unaware that many of their decisions are based on a *disguised* superstition.

The rest of us, however, in similar situations, might still make the same decision, but we will base it, frankly, on our superstition. We will be fearful of the bad luck that is lately hounding O'Leary. We will be prejudiced against the exploration geologist precisely because of his lack of good luck with other exploration companies. We will want to get rid of a coach perhaps for the simple reason that we once had bad luck with another person of a similar name.

In this manner we supplant our inherent poor judgment—our faulty connections to the nucleus of our reality—with superstition.

To further illustrate the relationship between bad luck and ill-omened occurrences and actions, let us return to our medical metaphor. Every illness has its particular symptoms, which to the layman often present the appearance of being something entirely removed from the illness itself. When we treat only the symptoms, we often thereby neglect their real causes, and only achieve a temporary relief. We should not, therefore, treat a disease by addressing only its symptoms. However, who can deny that by steering clear of its symptoms in the first place—even better, by avoiding their causes—we would thereby have averted the disease?

It is much the same with superstitious taboos. Walking under a ladder does not actually cause the bad luck that will follow. Rather, walking under the ladder is only a *symptom* of the bad luck which is in store for us. Therefore, it follows that we can prevent this bad luck by avoiding its various symptoms.

However, I will concede that there is this difference between the symptoms of a medical condition and the symptoms of bad luck: The symptoms of the first come after the illness itself, and are usually a manifestation of it, whereas the symptoms of the second are precursors of something in the future. Ladders, unlucky numbers, spilled salt; they all serve as markers with which that mysterious power, which we are equating with the three Fates, tags us so that we can be dealt with efficiently in the near future. If we consistently avoid those markers, we thereby make its task more difficult, and eventually we achieve a marked improvement in our luck. Just as by avoiding those things which can make us ill, we will stay clear of the symptoms which announce the onset of a serious malady.

As we have already pointed out, to a great many people those ill omens do not constitute the forebodings of bad luck, just as most people are immune to allergies and other ailments. But unless you are sure that you are one of those fortunate people, you should carefully avoid them yourself, avoid the symptoms of bad luck, and thereby prevent the illness itself. My fervent advice to the reader is, if any thing or event has been accompanied by unpleasant effects for you in the past, then pay heed, and avoid it in the future. Just as any sensible person will avoid a drug which has once possibly caused him harmful side effects.

However, we should not carry superstition to an extreme. Unwarranted superstitious fears are one of the greatest evils which have plagued humanity. Superstition has often been at the root of some of the greatest cruelties and inhumanities in history. A good rule of thumb is, if your superstitious beliefs may lead you to any act of stupidity, such as selfishness or cruelty, then it is time to lay your superstition aside, and consider that no system of beliefs can possibly justify such behavior. If a superstitious soldier is assigned to a squad already composed of twelve men, and sent out on a dangerous mission, he must, of course, swallow his superstition and go out to do his duty.

As to the unfortunate O'Leary, we should hire him and give the poor bugger a chance to shake off the misfortune dogging his footsteps, even though we might risk becoming contaminated by his bad luck. For yes, bad luck is contagious, just as are many medical conditions. But no feeling person will contend that medical personnel should stay away from contagiously sick people. Medical persons take reasonable precautions in these situations, and so should we, when succoring people cursed by misfortune. Moreover, if we should become contaminated by the bad luck hounding O'Leary, it would be offset by the chance that we, under similar circumstances, might also find the same compassion and understanding.

Chapter 15

Duplicated Horses and Identical Twins

To understand the proper manner to apply my theory of coincidence, we must remember that the Fates will usually have made a deliberate and conscious effort to effect randomness in the scheduling of their events just as the human operators of a lottery will strive for randomness. The randomness achieved by human agency, however, is still subordinate to the whims of fate.

This conscious effort of the Fates to effect randomness is why we so often meet with disappointment when we think we have spotted a sure-fire coincidence. Like when we notice that Apt To Do and Oughtado are running together in the same race, but they come in third and fourth. And that is why a horse named Norman's Promise could fail me so miserably on the same day that a fellow named Norman promised to do me a certain favor. An acquaintance with whom I discussed this particular race, by the way, told me that she had bet on the winner, a horse named Dance A Bunch, because the previous evening she had discovered a new night spot, with a band and a dance floor, and she had really "danced a bunch."

And come to think of it, the coincidence of Norman's Promise and the promise made to me by Norman was not a false coincidence, because Norman also subsequently failed to fulfill his promise, an outcome which I should have immediately deduced when I saw the outcome of the race.

As to the matter of betting on similarly-named horses, I don't claim the idea as exclusively mine. A fellow I knew at New Orleans Fairgrounds—a little Honduran named Gregorio, who confided to me that he sometimes used spell-casting to make his horses win—once told me that at one time in his career he had confined his bets exclusively to horses which bore a name very similar to another horse on the day's card, as long as the two horses were not named thus because of common blood lines, and if the odds were at least five- or six-to-one. But of late, he said, this secret no longer seemed to produce results, so he had moved on to other tricks and secrets.

Gregorio tried to convince me that there was a simple mathematical logic to the system of betting on one of two similarly-named horses, all esoteric considerations aside. Suppose, he said, that we separate two horses from a field of ten. If we were to bet on both of them, the net odds against us would be five-to-one. But, suppose we carefully handicap these two horses, and find that we can safely choose one of them over the other. We could then bet on this one horse and, in a manner of speaking, the net odds against us would still be five-to-one. Gregorio explained that although we would have eliminated one of the two horses, the remaining horse would have twice as much chance. When I pressed him to explain how this could be, he shrugged off the question and changed the subject.

I think the belief he was reluctant to express probably went somewhat along the simple lines of the theories I am propounding. The two horses represent a duplication. When the three Fates created two horses named, let us say, Lion's Rage and Raging Lion, they became slightly confused as to which was which, and thereby accidentally intertwined their separate destinies. At times, then, each horse becomes one aspect of two different entities and therefore has twice as much chance of winning.

In identical twins we can see the same effect. Cases are known in which a set of twins, orphaned at birth and adopted into different families, nevertheless led identical lives. Each adopted the same profession, suffered from the same illnesses, married at the same age, etc. In one remarkable instance, they each married women with the same first name, on the same day. Another recent case of identical twins, separated at infancy and adopted into different families, reported them running into each other at a volunteer fireman's party (both of them had become volunteer firemen), where the amazing resemblance between the two led some people to investigate their background and discover their relationship. What other explanation can be offered for such a coincidence, except the simplistic one which a horseplayer can advance? In keeping with this simplistic view we can say that the birth of identical twins is a slip committed by the Fates, who, annoyed at the birth of a double individual, could not be bothered to provide each of them with a separate fate.

Often (but not always!) we can therefore accept this view to place a bet on a horse which has apparently been duplicated, on the same theory by which a pair of horses coupled in the wagering offers a better chance of winning. In a field of ten horses, with two of them coupled as number "1" and "1A," with all other things being equal, the odds that one of them will come in first are obviously five-to-one. Horses coupled in the wagering have an additional edge, of course, in that one of them is often chosen to force the pace—the "rabbit"—so that its companion can come from behind to cop the race at the finish (sometimes the rabbit surprises even its own jockey and maintains the lead all the way to the wire). The rest of the pack has no way of knowing if the lead horse is actually going at a pace faster than it can sustain to the finish, and often, in trying to catch it, will tire itself out to no avail. This strategy doesn't always work, by a long shot, and the genuine advantage that such a pair of horses has is usually offset by the low odds at which they will go off.

A pair of "duplicated" horses, on the other hand can often be going off at fantastic odds. Few bettors will regard them as anything other than a mild curiosity. Many will not notice that there is a similarity between the names, One Jose and Native Joe, or that there is a sort of poetic affinity between Windy Valley, Blowing Sand, and Cup of Wind. Most handicappers will be engrossed in trying to separate the three or four main contenders, trying to decide whether Lord Catcher's lifetime earnings overshadow the fact that Change of Motion, with much lower earnings, has better recent speed ratings and workouts, or whether they are both outclassed by Frothy, which has the best pace rating and is more recently raced.

Sometimes, in these situations, a careful scrutiny of the "duplicated" horses will show that one of them is a sleeper: maybe he had trouble in his last race; maybe he has previously raced out of his class, or at the wrong distance; maybe, if you examine him carefully in the paddock or in the post parade, you will notice that he is feeling in great shape today. There might be a dozen other reasons which make him a good bet.

If one of the two horses in question happens to be the favorite, it pays, in the long run, to bet against it. The logic in this is easy to see (if you believe in my theories). Let us say that the two horses are named Prevailing Winds and Winds of Life. One is going off at two-to-one, and the other at eighteen-to-one. If fate and destiny have confused the two horses, then it is far better to risk your money on the one that will make your risk worthwhile. If the race is taking place at one of the smaller tracks, where the percentage of winning favorites is about twenty-eight percent, we would start off with a probability against us of almost four-to-one, if we bet on the favorite. With another horse of similar name confusing the issue, the odds against would be even higher.

Sometimes it helps to know why a particular horse is named as it is. Take a horse named Summer's Callin'. When we check those three little lines above its Past Performances, we can see that its sire was Summer Time Guy and its dam was Winds a Callin'. Then we can see, perhaps, that something or other, which we had at first considered a remarkable coincidence, is really nothing of the kind. On the other hand, it could be an even more remarkable coincidence than we had at first thought. For example, it could be running at a small track: let us say in Finger Lakes, New York, far away from its birthplace in California, and be entered in a race with another offspring of Summertime Guy named Summer's Glory. This would be remarkable, however, only if we knew that these two horses had come together through sheer happenstance, and not because they had been brought to Finger Lakes by the same owner.

At the better tracks, of course, we can frequently see as many as three or four entries by the same sire, and this does not necessarily constitute much of a coincidence. The high-class, well-bred stock will naturally tend to converge at these high stakes races.

Overriding everything else will be the fact that *you* feel it is a coincidence. If two similarly-named horses are present at a meet, and are running together for the second or third time, it can still be considered a strong coincidence, and if neither one of them has yet won a race in which the other was also running, then both of them would be strong prospects for a hunch bet.

Whether we do it to check for a coincidence or not, it pays to check out a horse's blood lines as thoroughly as we can, especially if it's a first-time starter. Following this practice, I was once able to place a very good bet on a first-time starter at New Orleans Fairgrounds when I noticed that, although it was from a poor stable, and had a mediocre sire, its dam was a Northern Dancer mare.

It also pays, if we are letting ourselves be guided by esoteric beliefs, to not neglect our education and our intellectual pursuits. An ignorant, unread person would never notice that the name of the Spendthrift Farm mare, Plumovent, is derived from the French for "feather in the wind," and would be unable to form any association between it and another mare named Dream Feather. Or, he would be blind to the fact that Ore D'Argent (by Silver Supreme out of Ortona) is a play of words involving both gold and silver. Or that Salud y Pesetas should be associated with Spain, and not Latin America.

I mention all these quibbling things only to emphasize the importance of being thorough, whether you are playing the horses by pure handicapping, or by heeding your intuition and the observance of coincidence.

At this point, we must stop to consider that when we allow ourselves to be influenced by the impression that a horse's name exercises on our subconscious, we are often, thereby, making the task of picking a winning horse all the more difficult. Whatever handicapping skill we have is sidetracked, as we succumb to our emotions and our prejudices, and try to rely solely on our intuition. When we do this, we are flouting the laws of chance and probability, and we will inevitably be crushed by failure.

These laws of chance and probability, by the way, are seldom looked at with the wonder and awe which they deserve. What is it that makes them work? What mysterious power makes them adhere so rigorously to the norm?

When we take the time to scrutinize the problem closely, we can see that there is something more to it than meets the eye. Just as primitive man never stops to question what it is that makes an object obey the laws of gravity, so modern man seldom pauses to consider that in the laws of chance and probability, we can see the workings of the mysterious hand of fate.

For it is the hand of fate, of course, that makes the laws of chance and probability work. Religious persons, at least, should have no problem with this. It is the living Fates who have dictated, at the beginning of creation, how many times each particular flipped coin will come down heads, and how many times it will come down tails. Skeptics may well ask, "So, what if there wasn't a living force that decided how many times a coin would come down heads and how many times it would come down tails? Wouldn't that coin still obey the laws of probability?" But this is the same as asserting that objects would still fall to the ground, even if there was no law of gravity. In other words, we must accept the fact that fate is inextricably bound with the laws of probability, that they are one and the same thing.

What does it mean then, when a coin comes down heads, say, ten times in a row? It simply means that somehow or other the Fates were distracted from their business at the time of creation, and the destiny of this particular coin momentarily escaped their attention. We may be sure that they will quickly step in and correct this anomaly.

We are told, by mathematicians and other men of science, that inanimate objects do not have a memory; that a flipped coin which has come down heads five times in a row (or ten times, or twenty times), still has a fifty percent chance of coming down heads on the next toss. They are right, but only in a certain constricted sense. Surely, a coin that has come down heads twenty times in a row has reached a precarious point in its streak. Anyone who would bet on it to come down heads again would be, let us not say a fool, but at least someone who makes a habit of bucking the odds. Simple proof of this is the obvious fact that coins will very rarely come down heads twenty times in a row. Mathematicians would be right, I repeat, when they say that the coin still has a fifty-fifty chance of coming down heads again, but only if we disregard the fact that there is a living force whose laws this coin has already evaded for an inordinate length of time.

At the racetrack, then, we should learn to recognize and respect the laws of chance and probability. We should learn to distinguish between what may be expected according to those laws, and what may be expected because of visible or invisible factors, man-made or otherwise. Then, having made the distinction, we should be careful not to buck those laws of probability. Because, even if we should meet with initial success, fate and destiny will inevitably step in to correct the imbalance. We can avoid the danger, which this tendency of the Fates to balance their books poses for us, by charting a proper course between cold-blooded handicapping practices and the use of our intuitive knowledge.

Chapter 16

Evasive Maneuvers in a Foreign Language

I have stated that lifting a finger, or not, depends upon the mandates of our destiny. But this statement should not be taken too literally. We can lift a finger on our own whenever it doesn't really matter one way or the other. For example, at this moment the reader can lift his right index finger if he wants to, simply at my suggestion.

That is to say, the control over human destiny by the Fates is not perfect. Every word that has entered the human language to catalogue human imperfections can be applied to the Fates. They can be forgetful, slipshod, and occasionally lazy. They can also be spiteful, cruel, vindictive, and grossly unfair. They are also stupid at times, since cruelty derives from stupidity, and nature is full of cruelty. We must conclude that the qualities of kindness, compassion, fairness, and reason have been developed mainly by virtue of human evolution—because man has, across the centuries, managed to subtract himself, more and more, from the control of the Fates.

Because of this imperfection in the functioning of destiny, therefore, every single instant of a living creature's life has not been filled with preordained actions and responses. There are gaps and *lacunae* in the destinies of all living creatures (and in the destiny of lifeless matter and plants, too, for that matter). We might say that the Fates have frequently availed themselves of the convenience of gestalt psychology to fill in many little gaps in animal behavior. A very effective trick, therefore, in our endeavors to squirm out of the grip of fate, is learning to recognize these gaps, so that instead of the normal gestalt closure that would be expected, we can often scurry away into a completely irrelevant and unexpected action.

This sort of behavior to a very large degree is what contributes to the success of wealthy, happy, and fortunate people. Successful people are seldom idle. They will never sit still, to stare blankly at a wall, or to stare unseeingly out of a window, for example. This sort of inactivity is almost always an empty period that has not been filled in by destiny. The person who does not resist the inclination to just sit and do nothing is making things easy for fate. When he finally does bestir himself out of inaction, chances are strong that he will continue exactly on the very same pathway that has already been marked out for him. We should do something, *anything*, so that this does not happen. Jump up and dance a little jig or tap dance, do a Tai Chi exercise, imitate the FTD florist commercial . . . do anything, but do not allow yourself to drift back into the same miserable stream of events that is probably your lot in life.

We must be careful not to do these things too often, however, because then they are no longer unpredictable, and we could then find that we are actually being impelled to do these things by the very power we are trying to evade.

When we have carried out one of these little actions, it is easy to imagine the breathless state of the Fates when they catch up with us again, after they have returned from whatever it is they do when they leave us on our own, and don't find us where they left us. Then is the time to execute another like action, while they are off balance.

There is one very effective little trick that we can avail ourselves of to sidetrack the Fates. But in setting it down here I must observe a certain reticence. Because it must be kept secret of course, and if I spell it out in specific detail then it will no longer be secret. The reader must decipher the exact meaning for himself.

It consists, in part, of thinking in a foreign language. I mean, in a language that is foreign to us, of course, a language in which we do not normally think. The task is easy for me because I have a smattering of many foreign languages: Greek, German, French, Chinese, Arabic, Italian, Quekchi, Mayan, Miskito, Achuara, in which I cannot too easily think (my knowledge in some of the above-mentioned languages extends to "hello" and "goodbye"). When I plan to carry out a little evasive act, therefore, I think in a medley of six or seven languages.

I can imagine the Fates going, "What, what, what? What did he say?" While they are puzzling it out, I am gone. I execute whatever it was I was planning to do, and I am back at my blank wall before they have figured it out. They never realize that I have been gone. This takes some very fast action, of course.

But what if we don't know any foreign languages? Then we use code, encryption, or doodles on a piece of paper to aid our thinking, without stating our thoughts in stark and clear language. But we should do all this, as I have already mentioned, only on certain select occasions, observing moderation. Otherwise, of course, it becomes our usual mode of thought and behavior, and the Fates will soon figure it out.

My former wife could never understand this explanation for certain of my actions, despite the long and patient expositions I would take the time to make. She was not of a scientific turn of mind. The tracks of escaped slugs in her bathroom, for example, was to her only something totally unacceptable, rather than an opportunity to delve deeply into the mysterious and hidden significance in the slimy trails. In vain would I point these things out to her, and remind her of the medicinal value of slug slime.

By taking the evasive actions I have indicated above, are we guaranteeing that our lot in life will change dramatically for the better? No, of course not. There is no guarantee of anything in life. The force of destiny is strong, and even when we subtract ourselves from its grip, more often than not we will be caught up again. However, persistence will frequently pay off. The Fates may become weary and disgusted with their chore of keeping in step with you, and finally allow you to pass into another reality. "The hell with it," they will say, "let the bugger go." Just as we ourselves will finally give up trying to teach an old dog a new trick, despite the more or less firm control we have over its life. If we persevere, if we unrestingly twist and squirm, if we doggedly struggle against the iron grip that holds us, we will surely experience some measure of success. At any rate, we should not allow ourselves to be led off unresistingly like chickens to the slaughter.

This is the largest concession anyone can possibly make to the believers in free will: I concede that we can make a difference by our energy and our determination. It is only the laziest and stupidest of humans who allows his *entire* life to be completely ruled by the mandates of destiny. Accordingly, the more abjectly lazy and stupid a person is, the more will destiny have filled his life with blank periods of inactivity. Just as the guards in a prisoner-of-war camp will not be greatly concerned with keeping a close watch on prisoners known to have surrendered eagerly, to escape from their duties, so will destiny not be greatly concerned with keeping any great degree of vigilance over those individuals whom she knows to be devoid of ambition. She can leave such persons staring at a blank wall, return half an hour later, and there she will find them, ready to be nudged along their preassigned pathways in life.

From the above it might appear I am saying that the teeming trillions of living creatures on Earth are ruled by Destiny as a single entity. But of course this isn't so. Destiny deals with only one person, or other living creature, at a time. Each of us has his separate destiny, and his personal fate.

Summing up, we may be mostly powerless against the mandates of destiny inasmuch as our principal pathway and ultimate end are concerned, but we have many choices. Even though, more often than not, we are like that chess player who has made a bad move at the beginning of the game. That chess player may still have many choices of moves. But none of them will save him from final mate. Fortunately, in our game of chess with the Fates, we are able to cheat, while they cannot. We can move their pieces when they aren't looking; we can take back bad moves we have made; we can sing, whistle, and yodel when they are pondering a move; we can stare fixedly at them to disturb their concentration, as Bobby Fisher is said to have done with his opponents. If we still find ourselves frustrated, we can pick up the board and pieces, fling them into their faces, and refuse to play anymore (which is what we do in some cases of suicide and incurable insanity).

Destiny has strewn our path with pitfalls, traps, and markers; the first two designed to keep us to the primary path she has plotted for us, and the markers to serve her as indicators of our position in this pathway of life. But when we learn to consistently avoid the one and the other, then we are well on the way to frustrating our destiny and carving out a new one. We do this by improving our shoddy communications with the dwelling place of our *neter* so that we may more consistently receive signals which guide us in the right direction. When we do this, we are enhancing our intelligence, which then contributes additionally to our luck and good fortune. Proof that all this is so is the following consideration: If animals cannot think, then the only difference in intelligence from one individual to another within a species—the only thing making one dog less inclined than another to walk into the street in front of a vehicle—would be a better connection to its roots; that is to say, it would be a luckier dog.

The ancient Egyptians (those living in the years before 2,200 B.C.) were perhaps aware of all this. That mysterious Egyptian word, *Ka*, which continues to puzzle Egyptologists, was possibly the Egyptian concept of the force that actively holds a person to his fate. Perhaps they knew that the *Ka* was the person's double (one of the modern, tentative interpretations of *Ka* is "double") in his cell of reality, which acts out that person's life on another plane, and by thus acting out his life, holds him to his preordained fate. Put in other words, the *Ka* would be the handle whereby the Fates maintain their grip on an individual, to jack him around as they wish. Which would mean, in turn, that the reason we can sometimes triumph over the Fates is because they have an imperfect awareness of our existence, since for them the most visible form of it would be manifested in the *Ka*.

We can conclude that the *Ka* is actually an ally of the Fates, collaborating with them to keep us to our preordained destiny. To a certain degree, however, this cooperation is only an outward show, much as small and weak nations have always allied themselves with a more powerful neighbor, because it is in their economic interest to do so, and because dire punishment awaits them if they do not.

One way in which we effect significant changes in our destiny, therefore, is by forcing ourselves to draw closer to our *Ka*, putting ourselves in a better position to do battle with it, and reversing the roles. Instead of the *Ka* running our life we force it to conform to our own desire of what our life should be. Drawing closer to the source of our misfortunes might appear foolish and dangerous. But it is plain to see that fate and its ally, our *Ka*, can handle us best at a distance. So by drawing closer we are only doing what a torpedo boat, for example, would do if it were attacking a battleship. It would draw close to its sides, where it is safe from the battleship's devastating superiority in firepower.

Drawing closer, moreover, puts us in a position to better receive warnings of the *Ka*'s future actions. It shortens the spiritual distance that our *neter* must cover in order to bring us vital information. In this way we can often avoid an injury, an auto accident, an ill-timed, ill-advised investment, the loss of a valued friendship, the loss of property, and so forth.

We must keep in mind that the *Ka* is the duplication of our fate. Drawing closer to our fate is not the same thing as drawing closer to the Fates. Moreover, when we evade the Fates we do it by metaphysical means, not by actually hiding under a basket. We can draw closer to our *Ka* without making ourselves more visible to the Fates, so, therefore, the things I have said before (about carrying out evasive actions to subtract ourselves from their control) still hold true.

If I have still not convinced the reader that we can evade our fate more easily by drawing closer to it rather than by trying to run and hide, let him remember the story of Jonah, fleeing across the sea to hide from his fate, but who, even within the belly of the whale, still remained in its grip.

Chapter 17

The Luck of the Baloney

A cautious attitude towards superstitious taboos, a subdued and curtailed way of daydreaming, a judicious use of magic and good-luck charms, drawing closer to your *Ka*—all these things have their importance. It can certainly do you no harm to give them all some careful consideration, especially if you have never given such things any thought before, and if your luck has been lousy all your life.

But let us suppose that you now begin to take these precautions, and your luck still continues the same. This shouldn't surprise and discourage you. A radical change in our destiny cannot be brought about so simply. You must remember that in trying to improve your luck you are trying to shake off the grip that a most insidious power has over your life. It isn't that you are so important. Your importance to this power is no greater than that of the bush or the tree that has been assigned its role in the lives of millions of insects, birds, and other life forms. Every creature, and every object has its purpose; even the lifeless stone on a pathway, destined to stub the toe of the barefoot boy running over it. Your importance consists only in the fact that, like the stone, you have been assigned your place, and you are expected to stay in it.

Everything you come into contact with is therefore a marker. All your actions, your movements, the trips you make, the jobs you take, the foods you eat, even your thoughts and moods, have the secondary purpose of revealing your presence and your situation in life. When we refuse to walk under a ladder, or to take a job at an address with an unlucky number, or when we throw away an unlucky object we have been keeping, we briefly subtract ourselves from observation and control. But the Fates will quickly find us again, and if we have enjoyed any great strokes of luck during those brief moments in which we were out of their grasp, they will quite nonchalantly take compensatory action, to bring us once more into the hopeless situation we were in before, or into an even worse one.

Extreme examples of this effect can be seen in some people who, through the vagaries of probability, win large lotteries and thereby acquire, not everlasting happiness, but an endless chain of aggravations and misfortunes: the very young man who immediately buys a new motorcycle, and promptly breaks his neck in an accident while riding it, to wind up paralyzed for the rest of his life; the young lottery winner who buys a one-hundred-thousand dollar automobile, has a bad accident, and spends the rest of his life fighting lawsuits; the old and ugly man who with his new-gotten riches finds a beautiful young woman to marry (because of that mysterious power money has to make old and ugly men attractive to young women) who soon poisons him so that she can inherit his money.

All this because those people experienced a tremendous stroke of good luck without first actually improving their luck. To effect a lasting change, the appropriate groundwork should first be laid; measures should be taken to ensure a solid foundation for good fortune.

One such measure has to do with our diet. Maybe something you are eating every day is causing you bad luck. Maybe that something is leaving its metaphysical mark upon you, because it is an item of diet that the Fates have arbitrarily decided to associate with poverty and misfortune within a given time and place. Before you dismiss this idea as pure baloney, consider that the foods we eat are one of the greatest factors in the quality of our life, which is to say, our luck.

And speaking of baloney, this is one item I have managed to single out as causing me nothing but bitterness and disappointment in all my endeavors and aspirations. For as long as I was brown-bagging baloney sandwiches to work, I knew nothing but exasperation, monotony, drudgery, and low wages. There were several other foods which were also to blame, and which I have gradually eliminated from my pantry. I refrain from naming them, because they do not carry the same effects for everyone. What can be one person's lucky food can be another person's poison, and vice versa.

I am speaking mainly of the metaphysical effects of different foods (lucky foods and unlucky foods), but even on a physical plane, the pernicious mental effect of some foods can be seen. Take a look, for example, at the mental constitution of the people in those lands where cassava is an important staple of the diet. Without exception, it can be seen that those people are distinguished by a marked mental sluggishness. This is due, in part, to the burdensome chore placed upon the metabolic system obliged to digest, assimilate, and pretend to like, the insipid and unappetizing taste of cassava. The brain, thus forced to endure this abuse of the palate and the body, and deprived of tastier fare, becomes dulled and unresponsive, just as a brain which presides over the functions of a body forced to endure monotonous, numbing labor for prolonged periods eventually becomes brutalized, losing all inclination towards intellectual pursuits.

This state of affairs with cassava eaters is so pronounced that I have no fear whatsoever of offending them, because it is extremely unlikely that a cassava eater will read these words. They are, by and large, people incapable of reading.

Before we occupy ourselves strictly with the metaphysical properties of different foods, let me make one more observation on the *physical* properties of food. Even a superficial study of the matter will show that most persons who eat sensibly enjoy good fortune in everything they attempt, and, conversely, people with slovenly dietary habits very often fare badly. Although it could be argued that people who eat sensibly are only demonstrating their good sense, and that this good sense is what guides them in all their actions. But if people who were not born with good sense would only eat sensibly this would be a step towards acquiring good sense, the first manifestation of which would be an improvement in their health, with a consequent improvement in their luck.

There is more than a grain of truth in the old saying, "We are what we eat." Food, perhaps even more than genes and heredity, makes a race and a people. Some nations and races, having established at an early time of their history an inclination towards the consumption of auspicious foods, have reaped more than their share of good fortune. Others, partaking just as liberally of foods stigmatized by fate and destiny, have harvested nothing but bitter poverty.

But even within a nation or race there will be deviations. You might belong to a racial group for whom the unmeasured consumption of cabbage, or oysters, or cassava, has brought poverty and misfortune, yet you might be exempt from those consequences. If your day-to-day luck has been bad throughout your life, I would recommend that you experiment with foods, keeping careful track of different items in your diet, to see upon which of them you can place the blame for your misfortunes, to thenceforth eliminate it from your fare.

Some foods are lucky or unlucky for reasons beyond our comprehension. Other foods, however, patently announce their inauspicious nature, such as horse meat, and cats and dogs. The Indians of the Argentine pampas, the Apaches, the Sioux, and other Plains Indians, all had a great liking for horseflesh. The

Plains Indians also ate their household dogs when other meat was unavailable. It cannot be said of these tribes that they have prospered. The French are another people who express their love of horses at the dinner table, and some day the bad luck that naturally attaches to this practice will catch up with them.

To feel revulsion at the very thought of eating horses, dogs, and cats, does not require any exceptional degree of perception. We have only to consider that these creatures were manifestly intended for another purpose; the horse, to ride, and other uses; the dog and the cat, as our amiable and trusting companions. The fact that eating these animals will bring us bad luck shows that, despite the picture we have painted of the Fates as ruthless, callous, uncaring, and stupidly cruel entities, there still appears to be the clear indication of a concept of justice somewhere within their system. This is only natural to expect. The Fates are images of that creature over whose cell of reality they preside. Our own inclination towards justice and humanitarian principles is what brings about this concept of justice in the powers that shape our lives.

Aside from the element of justice, there are often deeper reasons why eating certain foods is unlucky. Sometimes, careful inquiry may appear to show that the prejudice against eating any specific food arose in ancient times due to economic considerations. For example, Marvin Harris affirms in his book, *Of Cannibals and Kings*, that pork became a prohibited food in ancient Israel because the nature of the land did not lend itself to intensified pig farming. The raising of pigs would have contributed to an impoverishment of the population, he says, because it would have interfered intolerably with the cultivation of grain. Similarly, Harris says, the Mosaic prohibitions against eating horse and camel meat were also dictated by economic considerations. But, surely, even without these economic considerations, we would like to think that most thinking human beings would see the inherent evil in eating horses, cats, dogs, and camels. Nevertheless, even if we cannot see this evil, there is a price to pay if we ignore it: It will bring us bad luck.

Many other foods are unlucky even though they have nothing to do with insensitivity. A look at dietary habits across the globe shows a pattern of poverty and misfortune associated with specific foods, most of which are plants and grains. The reason for this is sometimes visible, if we only open our eyes, such as in the case of cassava, but more often it is completely invisible to our normal senses, and beyond human understanding. Sometimes, bad luck attaches to some of these foods only when they are cooked and prepared in certain ways. Tomatoes may be very unlucky (for certain racial groups), but only when stewed, for example.

Let me clarify what I mean by racial groups. A group of families who can all trace their descent to any specific individual of the past century, one who had a great liking for stewed tomatoes, let us say, and who ended his days on the gallows, can form a racial group whose only common characteristic, outwardly indistinguishable, is that they are descended from that aforementioned lover of stewed tomatoes. These people should be leery of eating stewed tomatoes, for there is something within us that is capable of much more astounding feats than the transmittal of purely genetic information.

Beans, shunned and ostracized by most Anglo-Saxons, are one of those foods which produce different effects according to race and region. At one time in history, beans were held in low regard in some regions of the Mediterranean. The Pythagoreans, in fact, expressly forbade their consumption. In Greece, whenever beans were planted, it was done with curses, the farmer hurling curses after each handful of beans that he sowed in his field, as a propitiatory rite towards the gods. As for the Egyptian attitude towards beans, ". . . they cannot even bear to look at them," Herodotus says.

The exact reason for this ancient prejudice against beans is not known today, but Peter Levi, a one-time Catholic priest who translated *Pausanias* and other classical works, thinks it may have been simply for the reason to be found in that modern ditty, which goes, "Beans, beans, the musical fruit . . ." The Pythagoreans, says Levi, citing Sextus Empiricus, were against beans because of the flatulence they produce, ". . . which interferes with the spiritual function." This notorious property of beans and the Pythagorean attitude towards them is what Herman Melville, in one of his rare crudities, was referring to when he has Ishmael say, ". . . for in this world, head winds are far more prevalent than winds from astern (that is, if you never violate the Pythagorean maxim). . . ."

Pausanias himself says that beans were prohibited in Pheneos because when the goddess Demeter came through that place she gave the inhabitants seeds for many other crops, including the lentil, but not beans.

It could be, however, that a large part of the prejudice against beans sprang from purely economic reasons. Despite their lowly status today, it is evident that beans can be an expensive crop to raise, when compared to the relative cost of growing most grains. The Aztecs, as Fray Diego Duran recorded in the sixteenth century, were forbidden to eat corn and beans together, except on one special day, which was called *Etzalcualiztli*, when everyone had dispensation to eat *etzalli*, which was beans cooked with kernels of corn. This was because beans were usually very scarce and expensive, affordable only to the richest citizens. So strict was this prohibition on eating corn and beans together, that a violation of the law was punishable by death, or so Duran believed. It is easy to imagine that anyone who violated this law would have been haunted by the fear of being found out—to have his crime revealed on the feast day of Tezcatlipoca, the all-seeing god with the burnished-gold mirror, when such things could be revealed—and that this fear would become a superstitious dread, which would inevitably bring bad luck to the guilty.

All these practical reasons aside, however, it still seems that the ancient prejudice against beans must have had some other reason—a metaphysical reason?—about which no one, even in those same times in which the prejudice was born, was entirely clear.

As to eating cats . . . surely there could be no economical reasons against it, we would say. Cats abound in the alleys of all cities. Cats can fatten themselves on mice and birds, and by scavenging in garbage cans. They are easy to catch, and reproduce quickly. Their meat, I have been told by someone who has eaten them, is tender and tasty (I must assure the reader that I have no firsthand knowledge of this). It seems that cat-haters, especially, could eat cats with absolutely no qualms of conscience about eating a creature that is an amiable companion of man. Some people might even propose that by eating them one could acquire a cat's occult abilities, in keeping with the age-old belief that the properties and abilities of some animals can be acquired by eating them. Such as in the example of Achilles, who was supposedly raised by Cheiron the Centaur on hummingbird tongues, to make him swift of foot, and lion and bear entrails to give him ferocious courage.

But very few people would dream of eating a cat. Not even a cat-hater who scoffs and sneers at my beliefs about lucky and unlucky foods. Why is this? It can only be because, though a person may profess total disbelief in my ideas, there remains a deep-seated, subconscious knowledge that I am right, that eating cats would be unlucky.

The Chinese, by the way, have been much maligned as a people who will eat anything, especially cats. But this is not true. The entire Chinese nation has paid for the sins of a few, the Cantonese, of whom the Chinese themselves say, "They will eat anything that flies except an airplane, and anything with four legs except a table." Though our own view of the Cantonese may be more charitable than that of their Chinese compatriots, we must admit that their critics are not too far off the mark. A recent article in the *Asian Times* told of a restaurant that had opened in Gwangzhou (Canton) which specialized in rats, cooked in a variety of recipes, some of which sounded very delicious and tempting. There is something about the idea of eating rats which suggests that it could be very lucky (although I cannot honestly bring myself to recommend it, no matter how bad your present luck may be). Therefore, perhaps the bad luck attendant upon eating cats is balanced out among the Cantonese by their taste for rats.

Anyway, I think there are better ways in which to take advantage of this arcane knowledge that cats possess besides eating them. In his book, *Catlore*, Desmond Morris derides the belief that cats have any occult powers whatever, and lists many reasons to support his position. Many of us, however, will not be convinced by his arguments. We have seen too much evidence to the contrary. Desmond Morris, moreover, claims that male felines do not purposely kill kittens. In this he is plainly mistaken. Other observers have abundantly verified that they do, indeed, kill kittens they have not sired (as Herodotus noted more than two thousand years ago) so that the female will quickly be ready to mate again.

The primary underlying reason that cats, and human beings too, for that matter, are endowed with occult abilities proceeds from the same set of circumstances that produces coincidence.

Everything on Earth and in the universe proceeds from the same matter. The material the Fates have used to weave a cat's random actions and the material they have used to construct a horse race, or a lottery (or anything else in life), is one and the same.

When the Fates began to weave out the destiny of man, well aware of the great propensity that the human race would have for probing into the future—its consuming passion for divination and for ferreting out the secrets of the occult—they took special care to purge the material with which it was made of any stray elements which might reveal these secrets. Despite this great care, however, it can be seen that they were not entirely successful, and that many a slip was made. This is the reason for the many famous seers and diviners who have existed across history.

Just as we ourselves will not worry about the presence of a dog, a cat, or any other animal when we are plotting or discussing a covert deed, the powers that have plotted and woven the destiny of man and all living creatures did not go to any great lengths to keep their workings secret from those animals. In the creation of cats, especially, the Fates failed to take into account the peculiar relationship that cats would have with man, and the connections that the cat maintains, much more so than other animals, with both the spiritual and the material world. For the domestic cat is an animal that walks a fine line between instinct and conscious intelligence. For this reason the human mind can often translate their random actions into occult knowledge. And the cat itself has the innate potential to unequivocally reveal its occult knowledge.

Unfortunately, the cat is also an egotistical, uncaring creature, with absolutely no interest in sharing its knowledge with us.

My attitude towards cats is, I suppose, somewhat ambivalent. Watching the antics of happy, healthy cats, it's easy for me to understand why so many people love them. Cats have a great capacity for astonishing us with occasional acts of sheer cleverness. We can see in their eyes unfathomable depths of wisdom and intelligence. At such moments we become convinced that cats, so intelligent and living in such close proximity to nature, their brains untrammeled by the mundane knowledge that encumbers the human psyche, must know many arcane mysteries. Looking into those huge, bright round eyes it's easy to believe that cats can see into the future, and that if they cared to they could tell us what numbers are coming up in the lottery.

Yet, how stupid and hateful cats can be. Scold them until you're blue in the face, and they are incapable of understanding what you want from them. Call to a cat to come to you, and it will only do so if it thinks there's something in it for him. Neglect to let a cat out of your house when it wants to leave, and it will spitefully urinate on your most cherished possessions. Try to use a cat's paw to draw lottery numbers out of a jar and instead of being grateful for the opportunity to make itself useful—for the opportunity to give something in return for its board and keep— it will bite and scratch your hand, the very hand that feeds it.

When not eating or sleeping, cats spend hours diligently licking their fur, thereby acquiring large hair balls in their stomach. Then they will vomit these up—cigar-shaped masses, coated with green slime—preferably while you sit at your dining room table enjoying your supper.

In this pastime of licking themselves they show a great predilection for their private parts, pointing one hind leg straight ceiling-ward as they perform the chore. Their readiness to engage in this disgusting habit has given rise to the phrase, much used in the South, "Quicker'n a cat can lick its rectum," referring to a task that can be performed with great celerity and dispatch. At such times it becomes easy to hate all cats.

The ancient Egyptians, Herodotus tells us, loved their cats so much that when a house would catch on fire the neighborhood people would quickly form a line around the house, not to pass buckets of water to put the fire out, but to rescue the cats inside. The inhabitants of a house where a cat had died would shave their eyebrows in mourning, and take the dead cat to Bubastis to be embalmed and buried in a sacred receptacle. This seems to me excessive grief for the death of a cat.

Nevertheless, though I am not a cat lover, neither do I hate them, and I must repeat again that we should never consider eating cats as a way to enhance our divinatory abilities. In short, eating cats would be a very unlucky thing to do. It is perhaps superfluous to be admonishing the reader on this point, since very few people will ever feel the desire to do so. I should instead be reminding the reader that there are other foods which are also unlucky, and that these foods, unlike cat, dog, and horse meat, which should be universally avoided by all humanity, and must be identified by each individual to whom the rule may apply.

Chapter 18

Foods That Make Us Wiser

The last chapter brought to mind a most curious experiment that was once carried out with flatworms. I forget now what the experimenters were endeavoring to prove. Whatever it was, they do not seem to have accomplished much, since nothing more has been heard from them. However, the experiment seems made to order for our topic, because it shows how our diet can influence our behavior, our psychological makeup, and ultimately, our destiny.

In this experiment, several dozen flatworms were placed on a metal plate, which was connected to a tiny electric current. The experimenters would turn on a light bulb that hung over the plate and immediately would follow this by flipping a switch to send the electric current through the plate. When the current hit the metal, the worms would naturally contract from the shock. This was done over and over again across several days, until the worms no longer waited for the current, but would contract as soon as the light was turned on. When they had learned this behavior, they were then killed, and chopped and ground into a sort of worm-meal. This meal was then fed to other flatworms, which knew nothing of the sheet of metal, the light bulb, and the electric shock.

A strange thing happened. After feeding for a time on this food these untrained planaria were found to have learned to contract as soon as the light was turned on, before they had even learned about the electric shock.

This example illustrates the importance that food has in our lives, besides its obvious function of keeping us alive. The food we eat shapes and sets our behavioral patterns; it makes us what we are, and keeps us that way. It is obvious that certain dietary excesses can even affect our mental stability. Indeed, this premise has even been accepted in a court of law, and we have a famous case in San Francisco, in which a man was acquitted of the charge of murder because he was able to prove that he had been driven to his murderous act through an excessive indulgence in Twinkies.

The physical consequences of dietary habits can be explained by the laws of physics and chemistry. But to explain the *metaphysical* effects of those same foods no scientific discipline will serve. A partial indication can be found in the old term, "happy-go-lucky." Happy people are lucky people. When we are eating properly and maintaining a good physical and mental health we will be happy and will consequently enjoy a heightened receptivity of arcane and occult knowledge, which, in the final analysis, is what good luck consists of.

But the full answer goes deeper than that. Why is it unlucky to eat peanuts at the race track? Why is lobster unlucky for Jews, but not for others? In both of these cases, guilty knowledge does its part. Jews know, ever since Moses told them, that those marine creatures that ". . . have not scales" are prohibited food. The guilt they feel upon eating a prohibited food marks them, so that destiny can easily find them and mete out the punishment they deserve.

In the case of the track patron, it is the same way. The fact alone of being at the track automatically includes him in that group of people who will experience adverse luck if they eat peanuts. Even if they are totally unaware of this superstition (thus, feeling no guilt or fear), it will still affect them. If we are strong enough, however, we can thumb our noses at these two, and at all other superstitions, with no ill effects. Most of us do not have this strength, so that once we learn of the ill effects associated with a particular superstitious taboo (or put ourselves in a position wherein we come under its effect in any other manner) we thereby enter into the lists of those who are affected by it.

Put into other language, the foods we eat are a labeling and filing system that destiny uses to keep track of us. But there are some types of surface on which her labels will not adhere. Just as the laws of physics and chemistry will thwart us when we attempt to bind certain substances together with certain types of glue, so is destiny baffled when she tries to attach her metaphysical labels onto certain very strong and assertive characters. The label will quickly come loose and drop off. Even so, I would recommend to those strong individuals who scoff at all superstition to beware. Even if the label will adhere to them only briefly, sometimes that is all the time that is necessary for disastrous misfortune to strike.

Combine the above view with the fact that humble foods are eaten by humble people—poor people—and that rich foods are eaten by the elite of humanity. What does all this tell us? It tells us plainly, if we look at the matter with unprejudiced eyes, that what we are determines what we eat, and that what we eat determines what we are, and that the two things are one and the same. Therefore, it makes sense that the first step in making changes in our luck and our destiny is to change our dietary habits. And if the reader should still persist in scoffing and asking why this should be, I can only point to the unanswerable riddle of the origin of the universe, with all its vast, unknowable mysteries, and further assert that some foods are lucky and others unlucky simply because that is the way it is. It is not something that must be taken on faith. We have the means at hand to prove that this is so. Go to the race track and gorge yourself on peanuts if you do not believe me.

We cannot, however, completely discount the possibility that the lucky and unlucky effects of different foods are also caused, to some degree, by some subtle chemical quality of those foods. It could well be that the seemingly metaphysical effects assigned by fate and destiny to various foods are of a well-defined physical quality, invisible to our present knowledge only because no one has yet looked for it, and that some people are susceptible and others are immune in just the same way that some people are allergic to any given substance while others are not. I have already mentioned that when we become aware of a definite physical effect which appears to have no physical cause, that cause must subsequently be made evident, or else that physical effect must be disguised, transposed, or otherwise made invisible.

Whether obeying physical causes or not, then, the lucky properties of specific foods would exist because they enhance our receptivity to subtle messages from our cell of reality. Unlucky foods, on the other hand, would deaden this receptivity, and instead of discreet and disguised messages from our subconscious, which guide us to the correct actions, we would receive only static and garbled information.

Pursuing this line of thought further, it becomes likely that there could be a food, as yet unknown, that could enhance our luck to such a spectacular degree that we could even divine the numbers in a coming lottery. But we must also thereby recognize that a food that could do this would be, literally, a food of the gods, and we should keep in mind the reason that Tantalus was punished in the way that he was in Hades. The ostensible reason was for trying to inveigle the gods into partaking of a cannibal feast. But another reason, just as important, was for stealing divine nectar and ambrosia from the Olympian banquet table to share with his low-life cronies back on Earth.

Therefore, if such a food exists, it would probably be advisable to use it with great caution. I have been, all along, advocating the need to sharpen our paranormal faculties. But this should be done with a full participation of all our normal senses, and not by any method which would sharpen only one edge of our consciousness, which is what we would be doing when we attain this goal by ingesting strange substances. This would be like honing an axe blade to such a keen edge that you could shave with it. You would thereby render it unfit for all practical uses. Likewise, if we could hone our paranormal senses to such a degree that we could divine the numbers in a lottery, we would run the danger of ruining the cutting edge of our consciousness for all other tasks of daily life.

But maybe this doesn't worry you. Maybe your life is so miserable, barren, and poverty-accursed that you say, "I wouldn't care. If I could only win the lottery, money would take care of any problem that might arise." Maybe you agree with Ross Perot, who said, "If I'm going to die anyway, I'd rather die trying to get cured." If that is the way you feel, I won't argue with you.

So let me point again to my model of destiny and reality. Perhaps therein lies a helpful clue. We inhabit the walls which surround the nucleus of the cell, where the Fates hang out and work upon the tapestry of life. We are like termites, constantly tunneling through the material in the interior of the wall, occasionally creating little holes in that wall through which we peek in on the Fates or through which we listen to their conversations. It seems likely then, that there could be certain foods we could eat which might be the equivalent of the termite's action of eating through the wall to peek into your living room.

I don't mean that this food would necessarily resemble wood, such as the termite eats. It could be that this food I am thinking of is entirely metaphorical in nature. Either way, I offer the above as food for thought.

Not far back I suggested that everything we do in life is only a mirror image of everything that goes on in the nucleus of the cell of our reality, that our life could possibly be nothing more nor less than the projection from another self in our cell of reality, our *Ka*, which is manipulated there to dictate our actions in life. Perhaps this belief was at the core of early Egyptian religion and it could be that someday an Egyptologist will discover the connection, wrapped, like a mummy, in the etymology of some as yet undeciphered word. We have already spoken of one of these words, the *neter*. An equal mystery surrounds the word *Ka*. Egyptologists today can only agree that it was one of the seven parts of which the Egyptians believed the whole man was composed. The other six parts were the *Khat*, the *Ba*, the *Khu*, the *Sekhem*, the *Ren*, and the *Khaibit*.

It is known that the *Khat* was a man's physical body. It is also generally agreed that a man's *Ba* was his eternal soul, that the *Ren* was his name on Earth, and that the *Khaibit* was his shadow. As for the *Sekhem* and the *Khu*, Egyptologists have done the best they could with these words and defined them as Spirit-shadow and Spirit-soul, which only separated from man upon death. The *Khaibit*, on the other hand, could apparently separate from the body while it was still living.

When we come to the word *Ka*, however, there is great perplexity. It has been variously translated as spirit, ghost, double, vital force, character, fate, etc. Conferences have been held, and many scholarly papers written on the meaning of the word *Ka*. But, "What the *Ka* really was has not yet been decided," says Wallis Budge.

Julian Jaynes, in *The Origin of Consciousness in the Breakdown of the Bicameral Mind*, advances the hypothesis that the *Ka* was the voice which the ancient Egyptians, the same as all people of ancient times, heard in their heads, just as schizophrenics do today, because the human brain in those times had not yet evolved into full consciousness. There is a great appeal in this theory, when we consider the incredibly stupid actions which can sometimes be seen in those ancient races (such as human sacrifice, for example), which suggest that those people were not entirely right in the head. Moreover, Julian Jaynes has some authority behind his theories, as a professor of psychology at Princeton University.

I, myself, have no such credentials, nor am I an Egyptologist, but nevertheless I feel that my own speculative theory as to what the *Ka* was merits a bit of serious thought. Let us consider: The Egyptian religion, when it finally dwindled away and disappeared from the heart of humankind, was already four thousand years old. It seems that such an ancient civilization, with "more monuments that beggar description," in the words of Herodotus, must surely have possessed some reservoir of profound knowledge, beyond the childish and primitive beliefs of the greater mass of the population. It could be that thousands of years before the construction of the pyramids there was a deep store of mystic knowledge that eventually was lost, diluted amongst a large population of inferior mentalities incapable of correctly grasping it, so that, finally, only the grossest elements of the knowledge survived.

Part of this mystic knowledge would have been a clear idea of what the *Ka* really was. I have suggested that the *Ka* is a man's double in his cell of reality, where his fate and his destiny are acted out, to be thereby projected onto our own physical plane. This interpretation of the word would concord with some statements in the *Egyptian Book of the Dead* about the *Ka*: "Thy *Ka* eateth bread with thee unceasingly forever. . . . Thy *Ka* is joined with thee in the great dwelling. . . . I do that which is pleasing to my *Ka*," and so forth.

In the Pyramid Texts dating back to 2,200 B.C., moreover, can be found the statement, referring to the dead, "They are masters of their *Ka*'s." Which could mean these very early Egyptians understood that upon death the human soul goes to the nucleus of the cell of its reality, taking charge of it, to thereafter dictate the terms of its subsequent life—to become a god, in effect. Which would be the reason that the hieroglyph for the word *Ka* was drawn upon a base which is otherwise reserved only for divinities.

In later centuries, the Egyptians believed that the *Ka* needed food, just as did the mortal body. When a man died, therefore, food was offered to it at the tomb of the deceased. If food was unavailable, the *Ka* could survive for some time off the paintings and pictures of food in the tomb, gaunt and unappetizing fare though this must have been for the *Ka*.

This belief, however, was no doubt a perversion of what the original priests and seers probably taught. While a person lives and eats, then of course his double in the mirror cell of reality also eats. But it is actually the *Ka* that keeps the person alive, by continuing to eat for as long as it is predestined that the body will continue to live, and not the other way around. Once the body dies, then of course the *Ka* no longer eats. But the unenlightened followers of the seers who originally discovered these truths did not entirely understand, preserving only the notion that the *Ka* needed food just as the body did.

Perhaps the earliest Egyptians, though not necessarily more intelligent than later generations, had a clearer view of the true meaning of life and death. This would be because in that early time of man's history man's brain had not yet developed to that point in which his comprehension of nature was obscured by intellectual rationalization, which in its infancy will inevitably be flawed. Being in closer touch with the origins of human intelligence, these earliest Egyptians could thereby perceive notions which later peoples could not. Possibly, great secrets were lost to humanity when the mind of the ancient Egyptian made the first leap from intelligent primitivism to incipient modern intelligence.

In a scroll known as the Westcar Papyrus, the following story can be read: Herutataf, son of the Pharaoh Khufu, told his father of a sage he had knowledge of, 110 years old, who could reattach a man's severed head and bring him back to life. Khufu had this sage, named Djeta, brought to his palace and prepared to have a prisoner's head stricken off so Djeta could then demonstrate his power by reattaching it.

Djeta excused himself from performing this act with a human being, but proposed to do it with a goose, instead. The goose was beheaded, and head and body were placed in opposite sides of the chamber. Then Djeta pronounced some magical words, and the goose began to move towards its head. The head also moved towards the body, and when they were close together the head and body joined. Then the goose stood up, cackled, and waddled away.

This story indicates the existence of a deep mystical knowledge, lost to later generations of ancient Egypt, who also lost the knowledge of what the *Ka*, the *Khu*, the *Sekhem*, and the *neter* really were.

Returning to the simile of the termites, we can derive a lesson, therefrom, and take care we do not harm the walls to the cell of our reality. For what happens to the termite when he begins to destroy the walls of the house he lives in? He thereby destroys himself because the houseowner will then decide to call the exterminators. But, despite the precarious existence that the termite leads because of this, it does not really need man and his house in order to survive. It can live in ways other than by chewing and devouring a house. In the long run, termites will most likely still be around long after the last human tribe has become extinct.

In this respect, man is to the Fates as the termite is to us. We will win out over the Fates in the end. It is only a matter of time and evolution. Our problem at present is that, although mankind has time on its side, you and I cannot wait. We want to discover a way to gain access to arcane knowledge right now. We want to uncover a way to unerringly read the designs of fate, so that we may more easily accomplish changes in the roots of our existence. We wish to find a way to utilize a knowledge that is still inaccessible and aeons away for the generality of mankind. We need to find a way to penetrate the nucleus of the cell of our reality, without being exterminated in the process.

It can be done. As long as we obey certain laws. The past, present, and future are laid out across the loom of the centuries. They exist in each of our individual cells of reality, and that information belongs to us by right. I do not believe that it is blasphemous, greedy, or irreverent if we try to collect some of that information now, before the Fates want to let us have it, which would be when we pass out of this world into the next, when it can no longer do us any good at all. We have a legitimate right to do it, if we can only figure out how. For, as Hobbes so aptly expressed it, speaking of the powers of sovereigns over their subjects, ". . . the right men have by Nature to protect themselves when none else will protect them, can by no Covenant be relinquished." (Leviathan, 21:114)

So, we have a right by nature to protect ourselves. We have the right to grapple with those three ugly old bags, the Fates, to wrench their secrets out of their grasp, to protect ourselves from the thousand vicissitudes they have in store for us. We have a right to spy on them, to intrude into their dominions, to pry into their mysteries, to eat good luck foods, and to make their secrets and their powers our own.

We will have to do it in a very special way, however, being careful not to chew too great a hole in the walls of our cell, so as not to provoke the Fates into resorting to their exterminating service, or into packing up their loom and their shuttles, to leave us marooned between realities, without one to call our own.

Chapter 19

Almost All Heads Are Unlucky Foods

I must say just a few more things about food as one of the more important determining factors in the shape and quality of our lives before I lay the subject aside. The fact that some foods can contribute to a life of serenity and happiness while other foods make it more likely that you will lead a life beset by ill winds and misfortune was a knowledge commonly disseminated among the seers of various ancient civilizations. Today, however, only the barest framework of the knowledge survives among primitive tribes, this bare framework comprising the elements from which the aforesaid seers deduced and developed their own, more complete, philosophy, thousands of years ago.

In primitive tribes, by the way, we have one striking example of people who have made the wrong moves in their desperate efforts to improve their fate. Why did the remote ancestors of Amazon tribesmen, to cite one example, ever decide to entomb themselves in the stifling atmosphere of the jungle? The jungle is among the most vile of habitats on Earth. Clouds of mosquitoes and almost countless varieties of gadflies, deerflies, horseflies, gnats, screw worm larvae, chiggers, ticks and other blood-sucking parasites make life in the jungle a living hell. It is hot and humid; rain pours almost continuously upon the sodden earth; food is scarce; poisonous snakes are a constant menace; the nights are long intervals of boredom with nowhere to go. . . . Why did human beings ever bury themselves in such a brutalizing environment? Surely, the first jungle dwellers must have had a very compelling reason for such a drastic and desperate choice.

Here is a possible explanation, based on speculation and pure hypothesis, but very possibly legitimate: The first jungle dwellers were people mercilessly hounded by fate and destiny who fled to the jungle attempting to hide from the Fates beneath the mortuary shroud of its green canopy.

From their prolonged subjection to misfortune, and in their writhings and squirmings to escape their destiny, those ancestors, quite intelligent compared to their present-day descendants, were no doubt aware that diet can constitute the chains and shackles of that destiny. They carried this knowledge with them into the jungle, as one more weapon with which to fight against their evil fate, and this would be the reason that primitive jungle inhabitants are the people among whom food taboos are most frequently seen; they have inherited remnants of the knowledge from the very first jungle dwellers. Those first jungle dwellers were on the right track, inasmuch as diet is concerned. If they had concentrated solely on changing their dietary habits, they might very well have succeeded and their descendants today would be successful and well-placed people in modern society.

But they committed the drastic error of first trying to hide from fate beneath the trees, and the very act of entombing themselves in the jungle compounded their ill fortune, forcing them to eat the very foods—cassava (or any of its equivalents) and monkeys, two of the unluckiest foods in the world—which have perpetuated their lowly position amongst the teeming tribes and races on Earth.

The disbeliever may ask: If the people we are speaking of above know all about lucky and unlucky foods, why do they continue to eat cassava and monkeys? There are three conjoined answers to this: First, the fact that the unlucky effects of cassava are of a universal nature make these effects harder to see, just as we cannot see a forest for the trees; second, what else can they eat? They are trapped in their sorry situation, with nowhere to turn; third, they turn a blind eye upon the problem, and try to compensate by avoiding other foods, which have an unlucky effect on only select individuals or small groups.

We tend to regard all dietary prohibitions among primitive peoples as superstitious taboos that make no practical sense. But the tribesman in the Amazon jungle knows the reason it is all right to eat tarantulas and palm beetle grubs, whereas he will not eat the tasty *shanja*. He knows this bird is unlucky food. Though this primitive tribesman will never bet on a horse or buy a lottery ticket, he knows that eating unlucky foods will increase the likelihood of being bitten by a snake, or make it easier for game to elude him, or for a tree branch to fall on his head, or for his wife to be unfaithful.

As noted earlier, some foods have these lucky or unlucky effects because the Fates have specifically assigned them this function. Their reasons for doing this are easy to see, once we have accepted that this is indeed what they do. These functions of lucky and unlucky foods are simply a convenient way for destiny to keep track of an individual's position on the pathway of life. They serve the same purpose as the color coding of the tiny wires in a telephone cable, or other such modern technology. When the Fates use a food to apportion us our desserts in life they are actually only using these foods as convenient tags in their filing system—as extensions in their document names. They serve the same purpose to them as do those superstitious markers that we mentioned earlier, i.e., they serve as identifiers and milestone markers on each individual's roadway of life.

We have seen, also, that bad luck may follow as a consequence of the guilt and fear we may sometimes feel when we eat something we know we should not, as in the example of the bean-eating Aztec, or as in the case of the modern Israelite who succumbs to temptation and sits down to a feast of Lobster Thermidor. This feeling of guilt serves either to mark us—the color-coding effect—or it serves to produce the bad luck and misfortune which is the assigned function of the unlucky food.

Guilt and fear. The first is invariably accompanied by the second. These two emotions combined are a powerful force which inevitably brings us trouble, exasperation, annoyance, sorrow, or outright grief and disaster.

What if we feel no guilt? What if an unlucky food may seem to us of the most innocent and innocuous nature? In that case, the other edge of the sword comes into play, and the bad luck accompanying that food will manifest itself in a hidden manner. The feeling of guilt, being absent, will not work towards bringing you your punishment, but punishment will reach you anyway, and in a more vengeful form. That food has marked and color-coded you so that you may receive what you have coming to you sometime in the near or distant future. No guilt can attach to eating fried bananas, but if it is an unlucky food for you, there will be no escaping the consequences.

A usually reliable test of a food's auspicious or inauspicious nature, by the way, is the intuitive feeling we have about that food. If someone tells you that something you have been eating all your life is unlucky, then, if that person is right, this truth will dawn upon you, either suddenly or gradually. If you continue to eat that food even when you have thus realized that it is harmful, you will feel guilt—guilt at eating something you know you should not—and you will feel fear of the consequences. In these cases, your bad luck will come quickly, and you will be more easily able to divine its origins.

Besides baloney, one food that I sedulously avoid, by the way, is toasted flour tortillas. Something bad will occur to me if I so much as see someone toasting a tortilla. When I lived with my wife and daughters, I strictly forbade them to toast flour tortillas, but I suspect that they engaged in the practice when I wasn't looking, permeating the entire house with the evil fumes. I don't blame them, however. It is quite understandable that they could see absolutely nothing harmful about a crisp golden brown tortilla.

There are some foods, on the other hand, which to most people appear plainly emblazoned with a warning of their inauspicious nature, but which other people, perhaps because of mental quirks or defects—not to say stupidity—utterly fail to see. As an extreme case, we have the grim and grisly example of the Aztecs, who indulged on a massive scale in that unluckiest food of all, human flesh.

Anthropologists had long held that cannibalism has never been practiced as a source of nutrition, but rather, simply as a religious and magical ritual. But in 1975, the anthropologist Michael Harner proposed, in a famous paper read to an anthropological association, that the Aztecs, though they may have covered their cannibalism with a religious veneer, practiced it because they were sorely in need of protein. The population of the Aztec world had ballooned to over four million; agricultural land was limited; they had no domestic animals other than turkeys and dogs; there were no large wild game animals in the valley of Mexico. Other scholars point out, or at least hint, that under these circumstances the consumption of human flesh becomes a very practical alternative to the prospect of a largely vegetarian diet. The cannibal does not have to feed expensive grain to his victim, except for a very short period, after capturing him in war. Humans can fatten themselves for many years at no cost to the ultimate consumer.

We can also surmise that the Aztecs had developed a great liking for the taste of human flesh. One of the virtues of the tapir, a sixteenth-century Aztec manuscript records, is that its flesh had the taste of every other beast, including that of human flesh.

Whatever the truth, it seems evident that the Aztecs—those who could afford it—consumed human flesh in a routine manner, and on an almost daily basis. Many Spanish chroniclers and historians of the Conquest recorded this fact, but the information had long been disregarded and ignored. In *The Conquest Of New Spain*, Bernal Diaz del Castillo speaks repeatedly of cannibalism. He tells, also, of the horrific aspect that the Aztec temples presented: bespattered with blood, caked and drying on the floors and the walls, and smelling "like a slaughterhouse in Spain," the Aztec priests themselves covered with blood which matted and knotted their long hair. A frightening testimonial to the appalling excesses into which a natural cruelty combined with religious fervor can sink a people.

In addition to Diego Duran's horrifying description of the various sacrificial rituals in the temples of the Aztec gods, we have Bernal Diaz's account of how the corpse of the sacrificial victim was kicked down the steps of the towering pyramids, at the bottom of which the butchers waited to carry it away, to be consumed "with a sauce of tomatoes and chili peppers," or in a dish known as *tlacatlaolli*, a stew prepared with human flesh, cooked corn, and garnished with squash flowers. In one battle during the final struggle for Mexico City, Bernal Diaz says, Aztec warriors flung the roasted limbs of sacrificed Spaniards at Cortez's men, shouting tauntingly, "Take back your limbs! The meat is so bitter we cannot eat it!" For the Spaniards had been fighting so long, unrestingly, and bitterly, that the prolonged flow of bile and adrenaline had tainted their flesh.

Fray Bernardino de Sahagun, Clavijero, Acosta, Gomara, Tapia and others, agree with the simple and unscholarly observations of Bernal Diaz: the Aztecs, from the emperor himself down to the lowliest classes, routinely consumed human flesh. Bernal Diaz even expressed the suspicion that human flesh was traded in the market place. In his third letter to King Charles the Fifth, Cortez describes how an Aztec army abandoned their provisions—sacks of corn and *small roasted children* along the trail—as they retreated from one of his forces.

It can be seen that the most disastrous of ill fortunes finally descended upon the Aztecs for their dietary excesses. Crushed by Cortez and massacred by their lifelong enemies, Cortez's Tlaxcaltecan allies, then further devastated by smallpox, their reeking temples and pyramids razed and the stones used to build churches and cathedrals, their culture wiped off the face of the Earth—what could be worse luck, for a people and a race?

Another people who had an excessive love for their fellow man were the Caribs. Columbus and his chroniclers recorded that they would even pen up captives, like pigs or fowl, and fatten them for several days before consuming them. And where are the Caribs now? Only their memory survives in the word "cannibal" itself, which was derived from their name. And whenever we hold a convivial barbecue in our back yard, grilling delicious pork, beef, and sausages, we might reflect that the original barbecue was the *barbricoa* on which the Caribs grilled chunks and gobbets of human flesh.

In our own time, medical investigators in certain uncivilized islands of Melanesia, where cannibalism still occurs occasionally, have recorded the incidence of several cases of Creuzfeldt-Jacobs disease, which they say were the result of eating the brains of diseased victims. This, we might say, is an example of the more direct and immediate results of eating unlucky foods. For, as I have already suggested, despite the callous and impersonal nature of the Fates—and despite the contradiction to be seen in the examples of many ruthless historical figures who died peacefully in bed, heaped with honors and glory—there resides, somewhere within their scheme, the faint indications of a system of justice.

Ancient peoples, we have said, had a better grasp of the importance of food as a factor in their luck than we do. When Moses laid down his laws for the Children of Israel, telling them what they could eat, and what they couldn't eat, it was supposedly because Jehovah had given him this list of clean and unclean foods. But perhaps Moses, in his overzealous wish to protect his people from the consequences of eating unlucky things, erred greatly by including many perfectly safe foods. The list of prohibited foods was further lengthened by his devout followers who included, though Moses did not specifically name it, the lobster, because it is among those creatures ". . . that have not fins and scales in the seas, and in the rivers." Moses was right to include the horse, however, though he did not cite the same reasons I do. Rather, he simply included it by inference, marking it as unclean, i.e., unlucky, because it "cleaveth not the hoof."

Moses was right about many things. He had received many illuminating insights into the workings of fate and destiny, although he attributed all his knowledge to commandments from Jehovah. All of us shy instinctively away from eating anything as disgusting as buzzards and snakes, or as vaguely disquieting as owls, hawks, and bats. We do not need to be aware of the biblical injunctions to feel this way. Some tribes of people, driven by hunger and necessity, will eat some of these things, true, but it can be seen that those peoples are hopelessly stuck in the quagmire of brutishness and poverty. As to whether they are in this state because of their diet, or whether their diet is forced upon them by that same state of wretchedness, it is actually the same thing, as I have already stated, and which I will try to further clarify later.

The rabbit is another animal included in Moses' list of prohibited foods, because it "cheweth the cud, but divideth not the hoof." Here, I think that Moses again erred on the side of caution.

I myself find the jackrabbit and the cottontail to be lucky foods, and I eat them at every opportunity. But Moses could still be right, in a way. Domestic rabbit, such as can be found in supermarkets, is most likely a very unlucky food. This would be for reasons related to that biblical prohibition which says, "Thou shalt not seethe a kid in its mother's milk," or related to the "Negative Confession" found in the *Egyptian Book of the Dead*, which says, "I have not caught fish using bait cut from the same kind of fish." That is to say, these two acts entail a certain heartless cynicism, while eating domestic rabbits seems to be a cruel violation of an innocent little creature's trust. For the same reasons, I will not eat anything labeled as lamb, although I have nothing against eating a grown sheep. In fact, at one time I had a great liking for sheep heads, because of the tenderness of the meat around the jowls. But one day, as I was preparing to boil one in a large pot, a great fat maggot-like worm dropped out of its nostrils. This was a lucky occurrence, because it has cooled my enthusiasm for sheep heads ever since, and I have lately come to the realization that (for me, at least) almost all heads are unlucky food.

To continue with Moses and Leviticus: It seems evident that Moses had a deep mystic knowledge of many things, a knowledge perhaps acquired from the necromancers of Egypt during the years that Moses lived in that land. In his long list of clean and unclean foods, by the way, I find something curious. Although his people could not eat many delicious foods, such as pork, lobster, and jackrabbit ("All these things shall be an abomination unto you," he says), it was okay to eat bugs, grasshoppers, locusts. . . .

"Even these of them ye may eat; the locust after his kind, and the bald locust after his kind, and the beetle after his kind, and the grasshopper after his kind." (Leviticus, 13:22)

If it was all right to eat locusts—both the bald and the hairy kind—and beetles, I draw the conclusion that these must be very lucky foods, to be thus included in the diet of a people otherwise so meticulously scrupulous and picky as to what they eat.

As further evidence that Moses, whether consciously or not, was speaking mainly of lucky and unlucky foods, he said, speaking of these prohibited animals, ". . . whosoever toucheth the carcasse of them shall be unclean until the even," and he went on to stipulate that that person should wash his clothes, and that any earthen vessel contaminated by the flesh of any of those creatures should be broken. These are clearly injunctions designed to conjure away bad luck.

The bad luck attendant upon eating some foods is often only regional in nature, and it will not have the same effect everywhere or on all peoples and races. The ancient Egyptians—and the Greeks, too—were aware of this. Herodotus tells of the inhabitants of Marea and Apis, on the fringes of Egypt with Libya (actually, what is today known as the Sudan; Herodotus referred to all of Africa as Libya), who consulted the Oracle of Ammon to see if it was not safe for them to eat cows, prohibited at that time to Egyptians. They thought they were perhaps not bound by the interdiction, because they considered themselves more Libyan than Egyptian. But the oracle told them this was not so, that all the people who lived below Elephantine and drank the Nile's waters were Egyptian.

Also, the Egyptians would not eat the head of any animal, but would throw it away, or sell it to any Greek who happened to be in the area. And the Greeks would unconcernedly eat those heads, knowing that it was safe for Greeks to do so.

The dietary taboos of many primitive tribes are hard to understand. We cannot understand them because we are in ignorance of the provenance of these taboos, but if we could see into their origins we would perhaps find a certain logic.

Primitive peoples, by the way, do not have the same grasp of "good luck" and "bad luck" that we do. With them, an unlucky action or omen usually carries a specific result, even though they may sometimes be uncertain as to what that specific result may be. In the Peruvian Amazon I discovered that the Achuara Indians will not eat *capybara*, although it is not too different from another large rodent, the *pacarana*, which is eaten all over South and Central America, wherever it is found. Nor will they eat eggs, although they keep chickens. I questioned an Achuara named Cucush, who lived on the Sinchiyacu River, as to why they would not eat *capybara* or eggs. But his reply was vague. He could only tell me that *capybara* and eggs were bad. His wife, however, thought that eating *capybara* would cause a person to break out in spots upon the skin, and that chicken eggs made a person weak and flabby.

It is frequently the same with other peoples and other taboos. When questioned as to the reasons for these taboos, the answer given is often a quizzical smile and a shrug, or else a very specific misfortune is mentioned. Such as the belief of the Huambisas on the Marañon River, who say that using *chuchuhuasha* vines in the construction of a house causes the inhabitants of that house to age prematurely.

I think the Huambisas are mistaken. *Chuchuhuasha* vines are probably simply unlucky material in all regards. And I think that eating *capybara* on the Sinchiyacu River is unlucky in other ways besides causing spots upon the skin. I proved this to my own satisfaction by one day flouting the Achuara belief (not without a faint sensation of unease and fear, I might mention), feasting on a *capybara* gumbo with thick brown gravy and then promptly falling into the rain-swollen river when the little promontory I was camping on collapsed.

Among primitive peoples, the real reasons for prohibitions against various foods are usually lost in the obscure annals of tribal history. And these prohibitions are not fixed and permanent. As the members of a tribe or race intermix socially with other peoples, or as time passes, the taboos are frequently abandoned and forgotten. This is because of the aforementioned effects of time and place. Sometimes the ill effects of the taboo have waned and passed away, diluted among the teeming descendants of the original subjects for whom they were intended. Sometimes they have not. Sometimes they may have survived, now hidden from sight because they do not apply to all those descendants, but only to a select few, just as in the case of genetic characteristics.

Even if no disaster immediately follows the breaking of a superstitious or dietary prohibition, we can often feel the deleterious effects of breaking them. We experience a vague and undefined feeling of fear and unease. We can, if we want to, heighten these feelings by deliberately eliminating the natural resistance of our consciousness to the knowledge of what we have done, and it then becomes easy to see whence these feelings of unease come. This is a good way, incidentally, to begin conjuring away the inevitable results of the transgression. In this way we take our punishment quickly, rather than deferring it for later, or even shunting it on to our children and other descendants.

Let us look some more at the question I brought up earlier, as to whether the poor person is poor because he eats unlucky foods, or whether it is simply the fact that he is forced to eat unlucky foods because he is poor. I said it was actually the same thing. As far as the Fates are concerned, the cause can just as well come after the effect as before, because time does not have the same meaning for them as it does for us. Thus, a people will be condemned by destiny to a lifetime of poverty, and their poverty condemns them to a diet that contributes to a perpetuation of that poverty (such as the jungle dweller, condemned to a diet of cassava and monkey meat).

For example, the Bolivians, like the ancient Egyptians, have a great aversion towards eating any part of an animal's head, whether it be a wild animal or a cow. Eating the head of an animal is apparently very unlucky for Bolivians, just as it was for the ancient Egyptians. I never heard a Bolivian say so, but it is easy to imagine that when they are forced by misfortune to eat an animal's head, more misfortune is sure to follow. In the village of Rurrenabaque, where cattle were flown in by plane from El Beni, to be butchered before being transported to the city, the impoverished natives were glad to pick up the discarded heads, to be taken home and eaten, and their poverty was perhaps living evidence of the fact that misfortune and acts that beget misfortune are mutually self-perpetuating.

For this same reason, then, we can deduce that eating lucky (i.e., rich) foods can wrench a person out of his poverty, because our diet is, to a large degree, a determining factor in the color of our thread of fate. If a poor family could dine for a long period on such lucky stuff as Chateau Briand steaks, Lobster Thermidor, truffles, all washed down with the finest French champagne, they would find, eventually, that they were no longer poor. The problem, of course, is that no one could eat that way for very long unless they were very prosperous to begin with. So my contention becomes hard to prove. But it is true, nevertheless.

As a concrete illustration of the above, and the manner in which it can be applied, let me share with the reader the workings of a very valuable trick: Some chapters ago I told of an effective little procedure for subtracting ourselves from observation by the

Fates by thinking in code in order to carry out certain little chores designed to improve our luck. At this point in time I feel I can safely reveal what, in my case, one of those little chores was.

This was some years ago. I had a one-hundred-fifty-six-dollar wine bottle—not a one-hundred-fifty-six-dollar bottle of wine, but just the empty bottle—which had once held Mouton Rothschild, 1976, with the price sticker still intact and in pristine condition. At the appropriate moment, I would think to myself, "Nun ich bin rayih alashan foolamento meinen botteille von boch," or something nonsensical along those lines.

This is a medley of several foreign languages, and it means, "Now is a good time for me to fill my wine bottle." (Or at least that is what it meant to me.) Then I would scurry off and quickly fill my wine bottle with cheap four-dollar-a-gallon burgundy, such as winos in California drink (it was the best wine I could afford in those times). I would put it away and go back to whatever I had been doing. At supper time I would set that bottle of wine at the table and act for all the world like I was drinking Mouton Rothschild, 1976, uttering expressions such as, "Ahhh! What a superb and heavenly wine. Only in France could such an exquisite delight be brewed!" The change produced in the flavor of that wine by this procedure was uncanny.

But that was not the principal benefit I would reap. I can imagine the frustration the Fates must have felt whenever they would see me enjoying one-hundred-fifty-six-dollar Mouton Rothschild, and wondering how I had managed it. I am convinced that this little trick, which I repeated several times, contributed mightily to the change in my financial situation.

Unfortunately it also caused a certain degree of unpleasantness in my household. I couldn't tell my wife that I wasn't really drinking one-hundred-fifty-six-dollar wine (because the trick must be kept secret in order to be effective). So she was constantly scolding and nagging, pointing out how many dresses and shoes she could have bought with the money I spent on wine. I couldn't offer to share the wine with her, to shut her up, because she might then burst out with something like, "What a fool you are! You paid one-hundred-fifty-six dollars for a pint bottle of wine that tastes just like that cheap wine you say California winos drink!" My wife wasn't very smart.

In the case of that poor family mentioned above, who would actually be consuming the real thing, they would have to follow this rich diet in a very cautious and measured manner. Lucky foods cannot be consumed to the exclusion of everything else. Variety of diet still remains important. In fact, the unmeasured consumption of a lucky food by a poor person causes that food to lose its auspicious value, to the point that it actually becomes unlucky. It is easy to see the reason for this. It causes a flaw in the account books of the Fates. They must eventually come to the realization that a certain amount of food intended only for the fortunate is unaccounted for. Because the poor family had no business consuming all those Chateau Briand steaks and all that champagne.

So that this little treatise shall not degenerate into another fad diet book, I will say no more about food. Let us return, instead, to the color of our thread of fate.

When we talk about changing the color of our thread, it must be remembered that just as it is easier to dye a white sweater black than to dye a black one white, so are some colors of fate harder to change than others. Different colors require different approaches. I have been speaking throughout about the need to deceive the Fates in order to force this change in color. Some readers might still find it hard to believe that the Fates can be deceived as easily as I say they can be—that we can slip one over on them in the way I have related above, thereby changing our color and our destiny. But the Fates are actually quite childlike, and in some respects they can be fooled and tricked quite easily. "As easily as fooling a Chinaman," as the Spanish saying goes (which is not really an aspersion upon the intelligence of the Chinese, but rather a testimonial to their honest and trusting nature).

Many tribes of primitive people know this fact, and use it extensively in religious and magical ritual. It can take the very simple form of pouring water onto the ground to induce rain, for example. Or whistling in imitation of the wind to make the wind blow, as many different tribes of people do (including European sailors, as Frazer has observed in *The Golden Bough*).

Nor have primitive peoples or the people of antiquity ever felt greatly constrained to accept whatever fate has been dished out to them. The ancient Greeks and other peoples of the Mediterranean were always quick to complain to the gods if they felt they had been unfairly dealt with. In Arcadia, Theocritus tells us, hunters would thrash an image of the Great God Pan with squills if they returned from the hunt empty-handed, and in Herodotus we can see how Croesus complained bitterly to Apollo for the ambiguous oracle delivered to him. I do not believe that the Fates deserve any more respect than was accorded to Pan or to Apollo.

However, I do not agree with Machiavelli that fortune should be "jogged and beaten." Just as it does no good whatever to thrash your wife, as many generations of wife beaters should by now have learned (in fact, beating your wife is a very unlucky thing to do), it would do no good to thrash an image of the Fates, if such images existed. There are other more subtle and refined ways to get what you want from fortune.

Now, although I have said that in something such as the lottery such a tremendous amount of luck would be required to win it that luck becomes irrelevant, we do not want to win the lottery unless we have substantially improved our luck. For, what good would it do you to win the lottery if it turned out to be nothing but a curse in disguise? That is exactly what it would be if, through some fluke, as often happens, you should happen to win the lottery while still tainted with the colors of the loser, the unlucky person. For a very short while you would be ecstatic with happiness, but then the Fates would see to it that you broke your neck on a motorcycle; they would involve you in a disastrous law suit; they would have your beautiful new wife poison you. . . .

Why would they do this? Would it be sheer, malicious spite or anger because you had had a tremendous stroke of good fortune? No. It would be simply because you have come into some good fortune without first changing the color of your thread from that of the loser to the winner—from the color of the unfortunate person to that of the lucky and fortunate. If we stop to think about it we can see that this would necessarily cause a smudge—a blemish—in the tapestry of the Fates. Your great stroke of luck has imparted an uncertain shade to your thread of fate. To restore it to its pristine perfection, the Fates find themselves obliged to take certain steps. (Please remember that I am speaking mainly in an allegorical sense.) The easiest and quickest solution for them is to change your color back to what it originally was, to the color of the accursed and unfortunate. This they accomplish by simply cursing you with whatever disaster or misfortune they have at hand.

But wait! the astute reader will interject. If we first change the color of that thread, aren't we causing them the same problem? No, because we are doing it gradually, in such a manner that the change we effect in our present seeps back to the remote past, to the time *before* it was woven into the tapestry. Or, more accurately speaking, we are doing it by moving steadily through realities, to reach one in which our thread has the desired color.

However, let us keep in mind that it is possible for a person to lead a long life of poverty and wretchedness while all the time tinged with the color of the blessed, to then suddenly break out into the life of success, prosperity, and happiness that his true colors merit. This is the case, for example, with those who struggle for long years in an endeavor in which the odds loom always before them like almost insurmountable barriers. Those people are usually recognizable as persons of great determination and willpower. They have always been lucky and fortunate, having dwelt in the shadow of defeat only until their predestined moment. These special persons are not coming into undeserved and unearned good fortune, and therefore are not subject to those drastic adjustments of which we speak above. For years they may have hung by a thread in their miserable condition, and then, upon breaking that thread, they have emerged into the life for which they were destined.

This fact lends more reason to my initial premise: No matter what it is we aspire to, it makes sense that our first step towards its achievement should be an improvement in our luck. Moreover, in affairs ruled by chance we have seen that the Fates, despite their commitment to a complete impartiality in their administration of the laws of chance and probability, nevertheless appear to favor certain categories of humans over others. This means that for a great many of us the odds are not truly impartial.

Therefore, we can greatly improve our chances without violating those laws of probability, simply by restoring our chances to what they should have been in the first place. As to going even further and increasing our chances beyond the probabilities, I have already explained how this can be.

Chapter 20

Wise Decisions by the Flip of a Coin

For the illustration of one approach to this matter of improving our chances beyond the probabilities, let us return to that reliable testing ground and laboratory, the race track. Let us suppose that all of our betting strategy at the track was based strictly on the esoteric theories I have outlined in previous pages. That is to say, pure hunch betting; choosing one out of two or three horses with similar names; or betting on a horse because, for example, its name is similar to a relative's name from whom we have just received news after many years. Or maybe for reasons such as the examples I have mentioned involving horses named Stinger and Leaky Luke, or the incident involving the bony woman in black. What percentage of winners can we expect to have?

It would be very low, of course. If you routinely discarded the favorites which turned up among your choices, perhaps you would wind up with something like five percent of winners. If you retained the favorites, your percentage would be considerably higher, but you would still see no profit.

In the first case your winning horses would always produce rich payoffs, but they would be very few and far between. And when you take into account the expenses involved in attending the race track every day, you can see that you would invariably end each season in the red.

Making money at the track is what it's all about, but when we get right down to it, the nub of the problem consists in the fact that making money at the race track goes against the laws of chance and probability. We come up against what I call the "Tuxedo Effect," named thus after one of my divining cats, which made such consistently disastrous picks that it completely nulli-fied the success I had enjoyed with Precious. The Tuxedo Effect, in other words, is a balancing out of their books by the Fates. We can't indefinitely outmaneuver the Fates (at least, not in an open manner) and not have them bring us up short eventually.

This is the reason we are returning to the track only to test my theories, to see if we have managed to improve our luck to any degree (and also to relax and have a good time, of course), but not with any great expectations of actually coming out ahead. We must remember that we are trying to improve our luck only so that we may apply it in such a manner that the "Tuxedo Effect" will not eventually crush us.

Paradoxically, the Tuxedo Effect is what almost renders my entire theory of coincidence and good fortune completely null and void, and illusory. But there are ways to outmaneuver (remember I said, "not openly") this aforesaid Tuxedo Effect to a certain degree, and in so doing, incidentally, prove its existence. Since the Tuxedo Effect is, I admit, nothing more nor less than a manifestation of the laws of chance and probability, it follows that one of these ways is by carefully taking these laws into con-sideration. Another way, as far as the race track is concerned, is by becoming a good handicapper, and combining your handi-capping skill with the aforesaid consideration.

To be frank, I am not the person to give the reader any meaningful advice on the subject of handicapping. I am only a marginal handicapper at best, despite my many years—never mind exactly how many—of patronizing race tracks from Woodbine to Patagonia.

Those of us who believe in hunches, coincidence, and div-ination know that we can run into long stretches of very lousy luck. Sometimes it may even appear as if the person who sticks to pure handicapping methods has a clear advantage. But we should remember one little fact. Unless that person is a top-line handicapper (good enough to equal or surpass the record of the track or program handicapper), and has the requisite discipline to stay away from the betting windows for at least ninety percent of the races, he can forget about staying ahead of the game. Most track patrons, if they are honest with themselves, will have to admit that they do not fulfill those conditions. It therefore follows that the hunch-bettor who dilutes his practices with handicapping, or the handicapper who sometimes follows his hunches, has an advantage.

True, the pure handicapper will pick a lot more winners than we do. But he won't show any profit. Unless he is one of those shrewd, astute, cold-blooded, (we might almost say, sinister) types who stick rigorously to only one type of bet and make only a half-dozen or so bets in the course of an entire season. Tom Ainslie says in one of his books that Colonel Bradley, the founder of the vast Kentucky breeding farm, Spendthrift, made the money with which he bought that property by betting exclusively on horses in mile, or over, races, that showed in their last race that they had run the last half mile in a faster time than the first half mile.

But, to determine these speed ratings, it is necessary to use the Charts (the results of each particular race, also carried in the *Racing Form*) in conjunction with the Past Performances, and the arithmetical operations involved can be quite tedious for anyone not predisposed to that type of chore. Not that I'm saying that because there is a little more work involved it isn't a problem worth bothering with. However, at small tracks you will never find a horse that has accomplished this feat in the first place, and even at the best tracks, they are very rare. If you did find such a horse at a small track, it would be impractical to place a large bet on it, assuming you were loaded with cash, because your bet would bring the odds down drastically. Many a time, at small tracks, I have placed a fifty, or one-hundred-dollar bet on a horse which was thirty- or forty-to-one on the tote board, and watched the odds immediately drop to fifteen- or twenty-to-one.

There are other methods similar to that reputedly followed by Colonel Bradley, but nearly all of them are equally restrictive. Moreover, they are all unsuited to the bettor at a small track, and with a small bankroll.

At any track, it can be seen that eliminating the non-contenders is often such a perplexing task that one wonders how any handicapper can do it. Many books on handicapping will tell you that you can usually eliminate six or seven of the horses. But this is true only in very few races. More often than not, it can't be done. If you ask a handicapper, who has happened to pick the right horse in one of these races, how he managed to do it, he will perhaps reply, swollen with pride, that he analyzed the pace and his choice had the best pace rating. Some other bettor, in some other race might tell you that he picked the winner because he shrewdly noticed that this horse had shown a good improvement in its last race, or that he had noticed that the horse liked an outside post position, or whatever.

But actually, in races of this type the only thing that can guide the handicapper to the correct choice is luck. And the best handicappers in the world can fall upon evil times, where their luck seems to be cursed, so that no matter how carefully they analyze a race, no matter how cautiously they bet, no matter how scrupulously they follow every handicapper's rules, they will still lose bet after bet after bet.

Hunch bettors can also run into these situations. But we have an edge on the run-of-the-mill handicapper. The dedicated handicapper is always drawn, by the very nature of his methods, to the low-paying favorites. In order to make any money he must be able to pick more than one out of three winners—a very diffi-cult feat. The hunch bettor, on the other hand, frequently betting on horses going off at odds of forty-to-one or over, only needs to hit on one out of nine or ten to put him comfortably ahead. Sometimes, in fact, one such bet can put the hunch bettor ahead for an entire season, or even for two seasons.

If we further enhance this strategy by learning all we can about handicapping, then our advantage is increased dramatically. Nevertheless, I don't necessarily condemn the practice of follow-ing a hunch without even studying the horse's chances in the *Racing Form*. If we receive a strong feeling about a horse, then it is understandable that we may wish to bet on it without even bothering to check out its Past Performances. In fact, sometimes when we carefully handicap a race, we can tout ourselves off a genuine hunch.

Generally speaking, however, it is advisable that we first study the horse very carefully. Sometimes we will then notice something about it which is not readily visible upon a superficial examination of the Past Performances. Maybe the horse is com-ing off a long rest and, like in the example I have mentioned involving Stinger, the horse does well after a long layoff. Or maybe it's a filly, in a filly race, and it beat colts in its last race. Or maybe it came in eighth or ninth in its last two races, but actually only three and a half lengths behind the winner.

In short, do your handicapping just as conscientiously as if you had no hunch at all.

And, you ask, what if you find nothing in the horse's record to justify the hunch? I am speaking of those occasions in which the hunch nags away at us, but the Past Performances tell us that it's a hopeless bet. I won't be so unrealistic as to tell you that you should pass the race and refrain from betting. How can I tell you that, when I'm incapable of following such sage advice myself?

Sometimes, what I do in those cases is place a two-dollar bet, usually to win, but sometimes even to show. If I do find some hidden indication that the horse is really not as bad as it appears at first glance, then I will place a substantial win bet.

Here is a small example of how this can sometimes work out. Recently, at Turf Paradise, there was a horse running in the fifth race named Singing Seagull. My attention was drawn to it because there had been a filly in the third named Gull's Song. There was no connection between the two, either in blood-lines or stable. It was a coincidence, pure and simple. Gull's Song lost her race, so I believed it was very likely that Singing Seagull could prove to be a factor in his. I combined him in several twin trifecta tickets. But there are limits to how much we can invest in such bets. At the last moment, I noticed that a show bet would provide some good insurance, since he was going off at over fifty to one. A ten-dollar show bet paid off sixty dollars when he came in third, thereby covering all my other losing combinations and leaving me with a small profit.

I have mentioned that there are ways in which we can separate a genuine hunch from a false one. But here, as in everything else which has to do with the uncertain art of divination, there is no foolproof way. We can, to a certain degree, minimize the risk of following a false hunch. The most obvious way is by careful handicapping, as I have suggested above. But if we adhere too rigorously to this system, we will wind up canceling out whatever intuitive knowledge we receive.

Since there is really no foolproof way to differentiate between a genuine hunch and a false one, we can resort to a very simple device: flip a coin. However outrageous the suggestion may seem, I have proved to my satisfaction, over many years, that it is the best way. Stop and think about it. You have two choices: to follow your hunch, or to follow the dictates of the Past

Performances. We have but to remember that only a third or less of the horses singled out by the best handicapping methods come in first, and of these, very few pay enough to compensate for the risk taken.

The flip of a coin will tell you either to follow your hunch or to ignore it. Logic tells us that half the time (half the time out of the few times that your hunch is genuine) according to the laws of probability and chance, the answer will be right. Is our handicapping correct this often? We have already begun with a subtle advantage, when we received the hunch in the first place, or noticed the coincidence. The flipped coin gives us an additional advantage, in that when we flip the coin, we do so within the context of the problem, so that it will show a slight tendency to agree with the preordained outcome of the race.

You should resort to the flip of a coin only on very rare occasions: when you find yourself completely unable to make a decision in any other way. You must be careful to pose the question to your coin in the proper manner. You need to keep in mind that there is no secret force out there interested in providing you with the correct answer to your question; only a force which now finds itself obliged to make the coin either hide the answer from you, or else to simply allow it to agree with the course of events it has already decided upon.

Besides conditioning your hunches with handicapping knowledge, you should also confine your bets to those that will produce a worthwhile payoff when they do come through. Making several two-dollar bets on a single race is the wrong strategy, unless they all involve the same horse and the odds on the total of your bets remain at a rich level. While true that the more horses you involve in your bets, the greater the chances that one of those bets will pay off, it's also true that this almost guarantees that the odds against the total of your bets will be small.

Five or six two-dollar bets on each race can add up to quite a bit, after six or seven races, and if in each one of those races you only had the chance of winning a forty- or fifty-dollar payoff, it doesn't take much mathematical knowledge to show that you are playing a losing game.

In short, you must absolutely take into account the relentless laws of chance and probability. You should carefully consider your probability of winning versus the payoff that the winning horse will produce. Keep an eye on the tote board, and don't buck the odds. If you are betting on a race with a field of twelve entries, and a hunch tells you to bet on a horse going off at four-to-one, you would be bucking the odds to place a bet. Of course, if the number of entries in a race is small, say six or seven horses, and you have a strong hunch about one of them, and the Past Performances further tells you that it has a good chance, then the odds of four-to-one would be very good. In most cases, I maintain we should rely on our intuition and the observance of coincidence mainly when the horse thus singled out is going off at good odds, of at least ten-to-one.

In other words, betting on longshot winners by following hunches need not be an entirely esoteric pursuit. There is a solid actuarial basis on which we can base our strategy. At some tracks, for example, the post positions from one to five in a ten-horse field consistently come in first as high as twelve percent more often than the positions from six to ten. This is especially true at short tracks, under a mile long, with sharp turns and a very short stretch run. I have learned to watch for good horses going off at long odds in one of these post positions. But we should place large bets on them only if we are moved to do so by a hunch, or if some coincidence or other, suggests the name of one of these horses to us.

When a horse in a ten-horse field is going off at ten-to-one, by the way, upon superficial examination it would appear that its chances should be exactly that. It has been examined by a crowd of handicappers, and it seems that they agree on the horse's chances. But this is not the case, even if these odds were an exact consensus of pure, experienced handicappers. The reason it is not the case is the percentage which the track automatically deducts from the pool. When a horse in a ten-horse field is going off at ten-to-one, the crowd is actually saying that it considers its chances to be something like twelve-to-one.

Nevertheless, I usually regard a ten-to-one shot in this type of field as a good bet, whenever it is backed up by a curious coincidence or a strong hunch. Here is an example of that type from my experience: Some time ago I accompanied an acquaintance on a trip from Phoenix to the Los Angeles area. His mother had recently died in Phoenix, and she had willed some valuable furniture to a daughter living near Arcadia. My friend asked me to go with him in his truck to help him deliver this furniture to his sister.

She was waiting for us in her home when we arrived, and after we had unloaded the furniture we sat in her kitchen drinking coffee before starting on our trip back. She was a handsome, buxom woman and as she conversed with her brother, I surreptitiously admired her. But I wondered why she was concealing her hair, which everyone knows is a woman's crowning glory, under an ugly bandanna. I soon got an answer to my unspoken question. She didn't have any hair.

"Why are you wearing that silly bandanna?" her brother asked her, and after she cast an embarrassed glance in my direction, she revealed to him that she had recently lost all her hair through a misadventure involving an amateur beautician, who had attempted some sort of hair beautifying process in her

home—I didn't quite catch all the details—with disastrous consequences. It was growing back, she assured him, and she would
only have to conceal her bald head for a few more weeks.

When we started back, I said to my friend, "Why don't we
go to the track?" Santa Anita was nearby, and I don't often get
the chance to go to a high-class track. He accepted my suggestion
and we made the slight detour necessary.

Despite all the disparaging remarks I've made about small
tracks and the difficulty of picking a winner when all of the
entries are of such poor quality, I must admit that at the classy
tracks the chore can often be just as difficult, because all of the
horses are so good. The first four races were disappointing. But
when I turned the *Racing Form* pages to the fifth race, a six-and-
a-half-furlong turf affair, my gaze was immediately riveted to the
name of the filly in the number three position. Hairless Heiress!
And she was going off at about ten-to-one.

Without another moment's thought, I strode purposefully to
the windows and laid down a hefty hunk of cash on Hairless
Heiress to win. I have never, before or since, felt more confident
about a bet. The filly, which had never run on the turf before, or
gone six-and-a-half furlongs, took a one-length lead from the
start and kept it all the way to the stretch, where she widened it
to a comfortable two or three lengths. An easy win.

I hadn't mentioned to my friend that I was betting on that
filly. Partly, I suppose, because I was afraid he would guess at the
reasons for my choice and look upon it as a callous and merce-
nary act.

But I'm only human, and I couldn't conceal the vast satisfaction I felt after I cashed in my ticket. As we rode home, me with
my pockets bulging with cash, he with his empty, he was more tac-
iturn than usual. I have always wondered whether his mood was
occasioned by resentment because I had cashed in on his sister's

misfortune, or because I had failed to point out the coincidence to him. Or if it was simply a reaction of annoyance, akin to the one many of us experience when we are at the track and, as we watch our horse lose the race, someone next to us is whooping and shouting with glee to see his horse coming in first.

Out of respect for the feelings of the people around me, I usually manage to conceal my smug feeling of satisfaction when my horse wins the race. I think it is the decent thing to do. No one with any common sense and the slightest notion of decency would display glee and hilarity at a funeral. We should remember, as we watch our horse taking the race, that there are many people around us who, figuratively speaking, have just lost their shirts.

Aside from this consideration, I admit that I have a sort of superstitious belief about the inadvisability of exhibiting undue exuberance at a race track.

Chapter 21

The Honeycomb of Alternate Realities

In our model of Destiny and Reality we began with a simple concept. We have the three Fates sitting at their loom, spinning and weaving, constructing life as we know it. Their mother, Necessity, perhaps rests nearby on a couch, admiring her daughters' handiwork, mostly letting them do as they please, interfering only when it becomes necessary to point out that they are losing control of the original pattern and design.

This world of the Fates is timeless. Time does not exist for them in the same form that we know it. If sound exists only when there is an atmosphere to transmit its energy, and living creatures to hear it, time, likewise, does not exist unless there are living creatures to measure it and record its passage. For the Fates, therefore, time is only a by-product of the tapestry they weave, a by-product which is then incorporated into the work itself.

When we look closely at this simple concept with which we are cloaking our system we seem to find discrepancies and short-comings. The cloak appears to be insufficient to cover every naked aspect of the paradoxical conundrums that are uncovered in this study. The cloak becomes like the tattered rags that covered the beggar in the old Arab story: When he would pull on one end of his rags to cover one vital area he would uncover an even more important one.

But the difficulty is only apparent. If we go over the principal problems, one by one, we will find that, unlike the beggar, if we pull on the proper ends of our rags we can neatly cover every naked aspect of our system. Let us recapitulate the foregoing.

I have mentioned multiple realities, which exist in prodigious numbers, equal to the number of living creatures in the world. These realities are like an infinite honeycomb, with each of its cells corresponding to a living entity. Every man, every woman, every horse, cow, cat, dog, mosquito, gnat, dust mite, and microbe, has its own personal reality. We exist, not in the cell itself, but in its walls (the physical world), while in the center of each and every one of these trillions of cells, the Fates and their mother (and our *Ka* and our *neter*, if we accept these additional speculative hypotheses as fact) reside.

While we each have our own personal cell, that cell must also be populated by each and every one of the inhabitants of the other cells. Reality differs in each of these immediately adjoining cells only in the minutest of particulars. But the differences grow increasingly greater the farther apart they are situated. All living creatures have the ability to migrate through these cells of reality (by passing from the wall of a cell into the interconnecting wall of another cell), striving to reach one of them where things are better for them.

This arrangement means that only one living creature in each cell is real, of course, and the other teeming billions or trillions are only shadow beings, there only to make real the reality that the one true occupant is living.

Now, although there are difficulties with such a view, we should not try to crudely yank and pull on the rags of the theory to uncover its discrepancies. Rather, we should try to carefully and gently pull on the loose ends to cover its entire surface. This requires certain adjustments in our thinking, and the development of certain new ways to look at the problem.

In order to make the said problem as glaringly evident as possible, let us say that you, a humble clerk, or janitor, or peanut vendor (assuming that peanut vendors were allowed on the Senate floor), or what have you, are an observer at a session of the United States Senate. You see and hear that august body, radiating its nimbus of power throughout the chamber, inhibiting your movements and your very thoughts. You dare not even cough or sneeze in the presence of those one hundred representatives of the power of a mighty nation as they argue and deliberate.

Am I saying that those individuals who are forging the laws by which you will eke out your existence in this nation are not real? That only you, the peanut vendor are real? Yes and no. The elements within our reality forge the rules by which we live. They mark the bounds within which we must stay if we would not destroy ourselves. The fact that each of us is the sole legitimate occupant of a cell of reality does not mean that we are all-powerful within that reality; those senators, the laws, the police, your boss, the cars rushing through the streets, your wife, your mother-in-law, the poisonous snakes in your life, all are elements placed in your reality to make the rules whereby you are to live. In that sense, then, they are real. But they are not real in the same sense that *you* are real.

Here is another problematical objection. Adolf Hitler is a prominent element in my reality. Let us assume that millions of persons are reading these lines. To every one of those millions of persons Adolf Hitler is also real. This would seem to show that every one of us is living in the same reality, that this business of multiple realities is surely poppycock. Which one of us would be the real occupant of this cell of reality? Is it the reader, or is it me? I would naturally be inclined to say that I am real, and that those supposed millions of my readers are only shadow beings, out there only to buy my book, to give substance to my fantasies and my reality.

But the reader will of course take exception to this. He knows he is real. He is fully conscious, and knows for a certainty that he is not merely a shadow being. If anyone is a shadow being it would be me, the writer, this reader will say. And besides, he could say, it can be seen that when we die, the world continues as it has before, with no change whatever; whereas, if what I am saying were true, the world would come to an end when the owner of a cell of reality passes away.

But an easy answer to this objection is, how do you know it will not come to an end when you die, since you obviously have not died yet? The people you have seen die, remember, were only shadow beings composing your reality, and that reality cannot come to an end while you are still alive, holding it together.

As to the Adolf Hitler problem . . . of course all figures with a looming presence—historical or otherwise—in our reality must naturally be present in a vast spectrum of realities. By the same token, material from a reality can only reach those realities in which it remains relevant. No doubt there are realities in which Adolf Hitler never existed; realities in which he died as a child, or on the battlefields of World War I. But these realities are very far removed from the ones that the reader and I know. In the reality occupied by a cat, rat, or microbe, moreover, the historicity of Adolf Hitler is quite irrelevant.

Another objection may be, what about our selves in those other trillions of realities? What is the difference between us, in *this* reality, here and now, and those other "I's" in those other realities? This is the easiest objection of all to answer. The problem is not as real as it appears. The answer could take many thousands of words, but it can also be given in one simple sentence: It is perfectly obvious that we can only be conscious of one reality at a time.

One final objection, to thoroughly belabor the point: What if the author were invited to appear on the Geraldo show, or the Jerry Springer show, or whatever, and that the author was foolish enough to accept the invitation, to there be subjected to scathing scorn and ridicule. Imagine several people from the audience, witheringly scornful of someone who is trying to tell them that they are not real, roasting and basting the author, who would be squirming and stuttering, trying to justify his point of view. A detached observer would perhaps smirk grimly, and say to himself: serves the bugger right. Maybe now he realizes how foolish his beliefs are.

This does not prove anything. At those moments, how does anyone know, how can anyone tell, what is real? The only real person is the observer watching all this. Let us remember that for thousands of years everyone firmly believed what their eyes and all their other senses told them: that the sun and all the universe rotated around the Earth, which was the center of everything. In a similar manner, but in an exactly opposite sense, the individual today believes that what surrounds him is real and that he himself is only a microscopic organism in the universe. I am in my own personal reality as I write these lines, and the future reader at those same moments is only a shadow being. When the reader reads this, he will be in his own reality and I will be only a shadow being in his reality.

What if I told you these things face to face? Which one of us would be real? It would depend, of course. Maybe both of us would be real. Realities can intermesh and protrude into each other, and perhaps even procreate with each other. Also, we constantly leap back and forth between realities, sometimes escaping death in this manner, and at other times leaping from frying pan into fire, and vice versa. When we pass into another reality we lose all memory of the previous one, and continue to live the new reality as if we had always been there, which in a way we have.

Sometimes there are glitches in what should be a smooth transition from one reality to another. Sometimes we make such drastic leaps from one reality to another that in the terror-stricken and hectic hurly-burly of the move we unwittingly drag many elements of the old reality into the new, so that in the new reality a vital link in the succession of memories will be missing. This can be seen in certain unclear memories that we all have. We may remember some episode in our lives in which we were in great danger. Our memory of the episode may not include some important detail, something that contributed greatly to the resulting outcome. The string of memories is only clear at that point in which the details become essential for the resolution of the crisis.

Sometimes, even, the most critical detail will be completely absent from our later memories of the incident. Of such an order would be that famous "leap of Alvarado," from the lore of the Spanish conquest of Mexico, as recorded by Bernal Diaz and others.

The normally courageous Pedro de Alvarado, in his terror-stricken determination to escape the certainty of capture by the Aztecs on that "sad night," when six hundred or so other Spaniards perished, apparently leaped across a canal, weighted down with arms and armor, of such a width that even an equally desperate kangaroo would have found it impossible. After the event he was unable to tell, nor could anyone else, how he had accomplished it. Here, it seems that the leap (both the literal and the figurative one) was so prodigious that it defied explanation. Alvarado simply leaped into a reality in which he was safely on the other side, while hundreds of his companions fell to the Aztec warriors, many of them captured alive, to subsequently meet a horrible death, with their hearts torn out on the heights of the Aztec pyramids.

Today there are a great many veterans of the nation's recent wars who could tell of similar experiences. Here is an example from my personal knowledge, an incident related to me by a veteran of the Korean war, many years after the incident had taken place. He was a Private First Class. at the time, a young man fervidly liberal and idealistic. One day he happened to find himself in a jeep with an officer, a second lieutenant whom he knew from previous contacts as a brutal and arrogant bigot. To the best of his recollection, they were alone in the stationary jeep and no one else was within sight for quite a distance. My friend was resentful of expressions he had heard the lieutenant use on other occasions. Now, he found himself bringing these things up, getting into an argument he had no chance of winning. The argument quickly escalated and the lieutenant, his true nature asserting itself over his supposed condition of officer and gentleman, categorically expressed opinions that sorely wounded my friend's racial, humanitarian, and religious sensibilities.

The continued horrors of war with the ever-hovering presence of death and dismemberment had rendered my friend brash and reckless. The next thing he knew, he was saying to the officer, "Let's you and me step down, you so-and-so, and let me hear you say that again!" The lieutenant, who felt his manhood put into question, accepted the challenge without hesitation. He opened the door of the vehicle, and was stepping out. But at this instant, before my friend could follow him (and I suspect, already greatly ruing his hot-headed words) his sergeant, *whom he does not recall being present until this moment*, grasped him by the arm, loudly reproving and scolding him, and prevented him from leaving the vehicle.

From similar experiences of my own, I can conclude that my friend had leaped from one reality in which the sergeant was absent, into another reality in which his sergeant saved him from what without doubt would have resulted in either a court martial or a bad beating (the lieutenant was bigger than he was), or, more than likely, both.

This, by the way, is not a good way to change your reality. The change is too drastic, too sudden. You are leaving your other self in a very ticklish and compromising situation, and making such a sudden leap from one reality to another almost guarantees that, though you may be saving yourself from an immediately present danger, your new reality will not be much better in the long run. Of course, in an emergency, we must take whatever we can get. But making unwise moves puts you at risk of exchanging your reality for one that is even worse. The friend of whom I speak above should never have gotten himself into such a pickle in the first place. The same can be said of Alvarado. For he was the principle cause of the "sad night," as readers of various books on the conquest of Mexico know.

Although it may seem that since these alternate realities already exist it would be superfluous to retreat into the roots of our origins to transfer our consciousness into them, this is not so. A major change in our reality should be made in a legitimate manner. This is glaringly evident, especially if we ignore the metaphysical aspects of the matter and look at it from a prosaic point of view.

But let us lay the prosaic viewpoint aside, for now, and continue with our metaphysical explorations. Let us say that you are a weak, puny, nondescript, timid, unassertive, nearsighted, and poor high school dropout. How can you migrate into a reality in which you are strong, handsome, forceful, have a college education, and a high-paying job? It isn't easy, but it can be done. Anyone can see, though, that it would have to be done slowly and gradually. You must use each reality as a stepping stone into the next, pausing at each one to carefully consider your next move.

We have all seen examples of seemingly powerful personages who, without pausing, have shouldered and shoved their way to the top, where they ultimately met up with disaster and a miserable end. Napoleon and Hitler are two such examples, but the pages of daily newspapers teem with personages of this sort. What is it that causes their failure? We could simply point to the fact that all people naturally resent pushy persons. But the real reason resides in the fact that these personages made their great migrations through realities without first making the necessary adjustments in their beginnings.

It may appear, at first sight, that I am being contradictory. I have spoken about changing our reality by retreating into the remote past to thereby ascend through legitimate channels into a new reality. And I have also said that we migrate through realities by traveling through the cell of our reality's walls to penetrate the walls of another cell. But if we stop to think about it we can see that it amounts to the same thing. When we penetrate into another cell of reality we are establishing a connection to that cell's origins and we are thereby, to all practical purposes, effecting an incursion into the past.

At any rate, the trick of moving and progressing through realities requires the patience to carry out each move through legitimate avenues, so that in our eagerness to move from one reality to another we do not outpace wisdom. To stay safe from catastrophe, after each migration we must pause for a certain period of time in the new cell, where we will have arrived with subtle changes in our experiences, memories, and psychological baggage. We will have arrived, hopefully, in another reality where things have always been better for us, leaving some of our excess baggage behind, in our other realities.

It therefore becomes true that we have free will and are masters of our fate. But only because we have the ability, restricted though it may be, to move from one fate to another. The part of our being that moves through these cells of reality would perhaps correspond to the ancient Egyptian notion of the *Khu*, or the *Sekhem*, and it would, in fact, be aided in its migrations by information it receives from the *neter*.

The question will occur to many: When we move into another reality, does the shadow-being self that we leave behind still have a *Khu* and a *Sekhem* and all that other baggage, the seven parts of which the ancient Egyptians believed the human being was composed?

A facile answer to this question would be to say, yes, of course a shadow being contains those parts. They are what lend a semblance of substance to the shadow being, and by answering thus we would dispel some of the resistance to the idea that only one person is real in the world. But the true answer has to be, no, the shadow beings in your reality are not whole and complete in that regard. That is the reason they are not real. The part of our being that moves from one reality to another, be it our *Khu* or *Sekhem*, or our *Khaibit* or whatever (or possibly all of them together), are what constitute our consciousness, and only the one living creature that inherits your old reality will have all these attributes.

We can find in these concepts an alternative explanation for dementia of various kinds—schizophrenia, most notably. The cause of schizophrenia derives from a loss of the individual's cell of reality. When the owner of a cell dies—when Atropos snips the thread of his life—the Fates pack up their loom and their shuttles; they gather up the remaining scraps and shreds of yarn and thread, and abandon their factory. It will thereafter be inhabited and managed by the deceased owner (the *Ba*, united with the *Ka*, to become a divine being). But sometimes the Fates will abandon a cell before its heir has died. There are various reasons for this. Perhaps the individual has become too much of a pest. Perhaps, because of certain imbalances in his psyche, he has begun to dwell too indistinctly in the walls of his cell and in its nucleus. He has become, in effect, much like a parasitic microbe that proliferates in a host organism, bringing about either the death of the host, or its own extermination through drastic antibiotic remedies.

For a microbe or virus to cause the death of its host is an indication of a very inefficient evolution on the part of the microbe, because when the host dies, the microbe loses its home. A successful microbe or virus is one that can live indefinitely in the host organism, without causing its death. Therefore, when a human being begins to deteriorate mentally, to the point where he can be termed insane, it is a sign of an inefficient intrusion into the nucleus of his cell; or, as a psychologist would say, an inability to cope with reality. Although it would perhaps be more accurate to say that it is an inability on the part of reality to cope with the schizophrenic. The Fates, unable or unwilling to cope with the schizophrenic, abandon his cell, breaking the connection of the *Ka* to its self in the physical world, thereby leaving the insane person without his reality, unable, because of his insanity, to migrate into any other reality in which he is not insane. That is the reason certain forms of schizophrenia are, at present, impossible to cure.

In our endeavors to peer into the future, and in our restless struggle to divine the outcome of a lottery or a horse race, we should not lose sight of this danger. But I do not wish to frighten the reader. The danger is really very small, unless we are already mentally unstable. Most persons who go insane have not been consciously trying to probe into the occult. All of us penetrate unknowingly, in varying degrees, into those depths. But we have natural defenses which keep us safe. We know how to do it without destroying our cell. Those persons who lose their sanity, however, were born without these natural defenses. They were genetically predisposed to this accident at birth.

From medieval times to the present, many people have believed that an insane person, and those afflicted with the related condition of idiocy, can predict the future. In Rabelais' *Adventures of Gargantua and Pantagruel*, we can see Gargantua's friend Panurge consulting an idiot to find out if his wife would be unfaithful to him. He gave the idiot a wooden sword and an inflated pig's bladder as payment for these services, but all he got for his pains was a slap in the face with the bladder. When he continued to press the idiot, trying to get a coherent answer to his question, the idiot then tried to stab him with the wooden sword.

The problem, then as now, is in getting the insane person or idiot to speak in a coherent manner. The same problem arises when we try to use a cat for this purpose, and here the problem is even more accentuated because the cat, of course, cannot speak at all. I mention this because the thought has no doubt occurred to the reader that if an insane person or idiot can foretell the future, because of their undisciplined incursions into the realms of the arcane, then perhaps an insane cat would be even better. But all cats are naturally insane to a certain degree. A creature that spends one fourth of its waking life licking its rectum and private parts cannot be entirely right in the head. This natural insanity of cats is due to the fact they dwell indistinctly in two different worlds— the interior of their cells of reality and the physical world.

We have seen, then, in this model of destiny and reality, how the struggle for eminence and power is a simple progression through realities in search of that eminence and power.

Many questions remain as to how these other realities can coexist with the one we inhabit. First, why do we linger in a reality full of unpleasantness if there is another reality where we are much better off? It is because every reality that exists can only have one true occupant. There is a tremendous competition to enter and occupy these realities. There will always be a huge number of persons who—the same as you—would be better off in that other reality you would like to move into. If you do manage to enter into another reality where things are better for you, you have done so only by displacing its original occupant (either to his detriment or because he has voluntarily moved on to a better position).

A mathematician could probably present a mathematical formula that would show in exact numbers the probabilities against success in moving from one reality to another. This formula would consist, in part, of the number of competitors for the position, and the probable number of realities in which the desired condition can exist. Reduced to these simple elements, the formula would show that your chances of migrating into a reality in which you have won a lottery are exactly the same as the probability of winning that same lottery in your present reality. But the formula could be made to function beyond the stiff rules of the mathematics of probability by introducing some other factors. These mathematically imponderable factors could include, for example, the prejudice that destiny holds against you and the strength of your willpower, both expressed in some sort of quantitative measurement. The result would then vary, from the 25,000 to one that applies to some people, to the many millions to one that applies to others.

Another question: Is it possible to know when we have slipped from one reality to another? Sometimes it is. Those strange sensations of *dejá vu*, *presque vu*, and *jamais vu*, are such instances. They signal tiny leaps forward or backward through realities. When we experience those sensations we have managed to slip into another time and another reality, or we have fleetingly made contact with another reality, only to slip back into the one we have been occupying. Other instances are those in which an object which we have left in a specific place seems to momentarily disappear. We search for it thoroughly on the table, or in the cupboard, where we know we left it, and are unable to find it. Then we look again, and presto! there it is. The object had momentarily disappeared because of what we might call a fibrillation of realities. We have slipped for a short period into another reality in which the object is absent.

Sometimes, also, the object will never reappear again. These are instances in which we have successfully completed the migration, but have carried residues of one reality into another; we have migrated into another reality, unwittingly dragging with us the memory of the knife, or can opener, or scissors that we had in the other reality.

A disbeliever will say, "This is hogwash. If we look long enough the first time, we will find the object we're looking for. Very rarely will the disappearance of an object remain unsolved. And in such rare cases, it will be simply because someone has stolen it."

Yes, this is true. Sometimes some small object or other will mysteriously vanish. Then the object will reappear, sometimes months later, and then we will remember that we absent-mindedly put it there ourselves. But there is one thing we must keep in mind: the existence of those other realities can never be something that is obvious to us. There will always be a simple, ordinary explanation for every manifestation of those said alternate realities. That is to say, if we try hard enough to prove that the disappearance of an object is due to some unexplained phenomenon, we will inevitably find a simple explanation. This is necessary in order to preserve the integrity of each reality.

By the way, in this migration through realities we also have an explanation for many a case of conflicting versions of events, historical or otherwise. For example, you and your wife or husband may have witnessed an event together, and yet you will have greatly different memories of it. You are positive that you are right and you may try to convince your mate that he or she is mistaken. But though you argue until you are blue in the face, you are unable to convince your mate that you are right. These are instances in which contiguous and adjoining realities—inhabited respectively by husband and wife (and their children, friends, and other relations)—contain visible differences, not recognizable as anything other than evidence of faulty memory in one or the other party.

This is possible because realities can intermesh, as I have pointed out before. Elements from contiguous cells of reality always protrude into each other. In your migration through realities you have taken a pathway in which a past event has occurred in a manner somewhat different from the way it has transpired in your mate's adjoining reality.

These differences become increasingly greater with time, thereby all the more easily attributable to faulty memory. I remember running into an old acquaintance from my grammar school days. Reminiscing on those long-gone times, I reminded him of how once, when he had talked me into performing a certain illicit action (the exact nature of which is irrelevant here), promising that he would stand guard for me while I carried it out, he thereupon treacherously betrayed me so that I was caught in the act.

But my friend denied that this had ever happened. I was mistaken, he said. He would never have done such a thing. My first impulse was to insist that I was not mistaken. I could remember it clearly. But then I reflected that quite possibly, as far as my so-called friend was concerned, it had *not* happened. Our realities had been bumping together at that moment in my recollection, but there was no telling what wide expanse of realities we had both traversed in those intervening years.

The reader may be wondering, "How much can we change our reality? How hard would it be to migrate into a reality in which I would have a better wife, or a better husband?"

The answer to that is that great changes in reality are hard to achieve. The problem consists in the fact that we would have to travel very far through the honeycomb of realities to find one in which those things that most annoy us are absent. And if that thing that most annoys you is a powerful person, or one whose life interacts intimately with your own, then it becomes much more difficult.

Equally as difficult as leaving a wife or husband behind when you move into another reality is leaving behind your excess psychological baggage. This baggage will continue with you across a wide spectrum of realities. An important requirement for successful migration is learning to leave anything that is excess baggage behind. When we move we must learn to leave our self-destructive habits in the garbage can of our old reality, while carefully packing up everything we wish to keep, such as our capacity to acquire wisdom, and our knowledge. And especially our luck, or at least that part of it against which we have no complaints. Knowing how to do this will guarantee that we will move into a *better* reality, and not simply into a *different* reality.

If we are incapable of learning how to do this, then we can often supplant this knowledge by a careful observation of superstitious taboos.

Chapter 22

Spinning the Thirty-Million-Dollar Dream

The reader is perhaps wondering at this point how I have acquired all this valuable knowledge I am passing on in such a selfless manner. As I have mentioned before, I have not always known all these things. Gradually, little by little, with one small step after another, I have reached my present more or less sheltered position. Because up until relatively recent times my life was a long series of minor disasters and calamities, one after another.

I have been broke and without a job more times than I care to remember. When traveling I always went to the cheapest hotels and patronized low-life chili joints; I drank generic beer; my female companionship before I married were the humblest of hotel maids in Latin America; I have wandered through the desolation of Mosquitia, jobless and broke, and with a wife and two small children to feed. I have been—I hesitate to mention it—imprisoned on the Mosquito Coast, falsely accused of violating the forestry laws. It was only for two days, but it was prison, nevertheless. I have been stranded in Panama after missing a flight, penniless and with only the clothes on my back; I have been almost hounded into a premature grave by a nagging wife; I have been . . . but I think I have communicated the general idea. I mention these things only to illustrate the change I have wrought upon my condition, and which I attribute to the application of the metaphysical truths I have discovered.

The reader may be saying, this guy is irresponsible and evidently not very smart to have gotten himself in those fixes. That is precisely the point. I have never claimed to be very smart. That is what comprises the principle misfortune in my life, which I have managed to vanquish, and that is what gives me the authority to advise other equally unfortunate people on how to triumph in life with that handicap.

The unfortunate aspects of my life are rooted in my childhood years in the San Joaquin Valley. As I have mentioned, we were very poor, and it seems I was always hungry. I was the next youngest in a large family, and I had to be on my toes to stay fed. I don't know if things were actually as bad as my memory tells me, but I do know that food was always the foremost thought, overriding all else, in my mind. Even when I was replete with beans, and tortillas and jackrabbit, I would be thinking about the next meal, and wondering if I would get my fair share. For a long time I misheard the words of the popular religious hymn, ". . . When the roll is called up yonder," as "When the roast is scalloped yonder," associating the refrain with roast beef and scalloped potatoes, which I knew of only by hearsay. Mother Goose rhymes would make my mouth water, with the references to four-and-twenty blackbirds, baked in a pie, and Miss Muffet eating curds and whey. I didn't know what curds and whey were, but I knew it must be something exquisitely delicious.

One particular memory I preserve highlights this matter of my preoccupation with food. I was about seven years old. We had discovered a clever way of toasting a tortilla by placing a flatiron over the tortilla on the warm, wood-burning stove until it was toasted to a rich, golden brown. One of my sisters was engaged in this pleasant task one day, with a tortilla that had been left over from dinner. I watched enviously. When she momentarily turned her back, I swiftly approached the stove, removed the iron, and appropriated the aforesaid tortilla.

I headed quickly for the door, to exit from the scene of my crime. But I was scarcely outside when my sister noticed the theft and let out a shriek of rage. Clutching the stolen tortilla I fled as if for my life. I headed for a grassy field nearby, intending to hide in the tall growth, I suppose, like a fox with a stolen hen. But I ran straight into a taut strand of barbed wire, invisible in the tall grass, which put an effective end to my flight. I bear scars on my shins to this day, to remind me that crime does not pay, and I have shunned toasted tortillas ever since.

I have often reflected that my intellectual development was stunted as a consequence of this preoccupation with food. Who knows what transcendental discoveries, other than the ones consigned in this work, I might have contributed to the world if an abundance of food had allowed me to apply my mind to other problems in life. My preoccupation with food, strong residues of which remain with me to this day, was not something normal, such as can be seen in the obese person, because I have never been obese. It was born of an awareness, nurtured by the wretched barrenness of those times, that getting a square meal was not something that could always be counted on.

The above anecdote is intended only to illustrate the great change from my origins to my present position. Whereas in those days my condition was such that I could callously steal a toasted tortilla from my own flesh and blood; and whereas I was so bereft of shame, because of my impoverished state, that the decent course of returning what was left of the five dollars to poor Lam was never so much as a glimmer in my mind, today I can unhesitatingly return a multimillion-dollar-lottery ticket to its rightful owner, as evidenced in that dream I mentioned earlier. This should indicate, to anyone willing to give the matter some thought, that my methods for attaining this improved condition must surely have some merit.

But let me return to my thesis.

We agreed, some chapters ago, that we have never relinquished the right to probe and pry into the hidden mysteries of the future, to thereby bring about a change in the past and a consequent revision of the present. Whether the powers that guard that information like it or not should be of no great concern to us, except for the natural care we should take to do our probing and prying in an efficient manner, avoiding any approach that might stiffen the resistance against us, or otherwise cause us harm.

Sometimes we make our intrusions into the arcane in a conscious manner, as when we consult a fortune-teller, or when we peer into a crystal ball. And sometimes we do it involuntarily, such as when we have prophetic dreams. Even long before Joseph and the pharaoh of Egypt, dreams have always been the most obvious way of divining the future. But besides their prophetic content, dreams can also carry a wealth of information of a more prosaic nature. In *The Act Of Creation*, Arthur Koestler told of how the solution to a vexing problem in chemistry came to a famed scientist in a dream, after he had all but given up trying to solve it. Possibly, a visionary dreamer among our remote cave-dwelling ancestors was first guided into making fire by a dream.

We can therefore expect to extract both types of information from our dreams: prophetic visions of things to come, and practical solutions to problems in the present. A common error in the interpretation of dreams is trying to interpret them by attaching set formulas to situations and objects in them, as the ancients did. The applicable meanings will differ vastly from one individual to another. More often than not, the meaning is impossible to decipher until after the event announced by the dream has occurred.

However, warnings of impending unfavorable events can often be intuitively divined, even if the specific event remains a murky puzzle. Such as the dream of Polycrates' daughter, as told by Herodotus. In a dream, she saw her father suspended in the air, washed by Zeus and anointed by the sun. Deeply disturbed by this dream, she tried to dissuade her father from heeding the summons of the Persian Oroetes, who had requested his presence in Sardis. Polycrates ignored his daughter's warning and went anyway, only to be crucified by the treacherous Oroetes, who left him out in the rain and sun to die—to be "washed" by Zeus and "anointed" by the Sun.

I have found little of any value in those books on dream interpretation I have read, but perhaps the reader may wish to look into them anyway. *The Complete Book Of Dreams*, by Edwin Raphael, is a voluminous treatise on the hidden meaning behind a long list of things the human mind can dream of. The list goes from Abacus ("An indication of financial improvement through careful work") to Zulu (To be surrounded by Zulus, in a dream, means release from danger that has been threatening you). The book is a compilation of dream-meanings culled from the ancient literature on the subject, and further broadened with many modern additions.

Then there is *Dreams and Omens*, by James Ward. Both authors apparently went to the same sources for much of their material, which seems to originate in Artemidorus and his *Interpretation of Dreams* and in other ancient Greek and Roman writings. But, except for the interesting introductions to these books, the long list of dreams and their meanings do not, in my opinion, contain any profound insight as to how dreams should be interpreted. In these books nearly every dream, with a monotonous regularity, seems to herald either trouble or an end to trouble. Raphael's book, for example, records the fact that to dream of eating fleas "signifies problems." Most of us would agree that if you dream you are eating fleas, then you indeed have problems. And anyway, life is nothing but one long problem. Therefore, a dream announcing problems seems redundant.

Moreover, I feel that most of these dream meanings, originating as they did thousands of years ago, have long since ceased to hold the same meaning as they did then. Not only for the obvious reasons that both Ward and Raphael acknowledge, but for the more subtle reason that the guardians of the arcane will have long ago taken steps to cloak their mysteries with other garb.

In a slender volume, *Los Sueños y Los Numeros*, a very popular treatise in Central America (where a small weekly lottery consisting of numbers from one to one-hundred is played) we find another theory on dream meanings. The author leaves aside all preoccupation with any other meanings of dreams and reduces them all to numbers. His conclusions, though simplistic, have a certain appeal. To dream of a bicycle can be a reference to the number eight; a chair would refer to the number four (because of its four legs); a table, being larger than a chair, can mean the number forty; anything long, such as a banana or a cigar, can signify the number one.

As to this last example, however, anyone with even a superficial knowledge of Freud knows that a banana or a cigar can also be a symbolic representation of the male procreative organ.

Freud had a liking for cigars by the way, and someone once observed to him that perhaps, in accordance with his theories, his addiction to cigars revealed a subconscious, unmentionable proclivity. Freud is said to have replied in an irritated manner, "Sometimes a cigar is just a cigar."

And of course Freud was right in this.

Things are never just one thing in a dream, either. A chair can mean a great many things, depending on the prominence that it had in the dream, whether we were sitting on it or it was simply there, seemingly present only because the nature of the dream dictated that a chair had to be present. It is wrong, then, to ascribe a single meaning, symbolic or otherwise, to any thing, object, or animal in a dream.

More important than the thing or object in the dream, is the way we *felt* about it as we dreamed. Sometimes we may feel expectant, or depressed, or irrelevantly happy. We may dream of gold, or money, and yet we may feel inexplicably disturbed. A dream which could be described simply as, "I dreamed I was fishing, and I caught a big fish," could possibly take as many as twenty pages, or even an entire volume, to describe its every last nuance, and its twists and convolutions. Every last detail, from the kind of line and bait you were using, to the vaguely perceived notion of the place, and the time, and the people around you, whether actually present or only lurking faintly in the back of your consciousness, would be of importance for the correct interpretation. And more often than not, this correct interpretation would still elude us.

Sometimes a dream that defies interpretation, whether with a superficial or a detailed dissection, can still reveal to us the most astonishing information. Some years ago in Brazil, there was the much publicized story of a poor gold seeker who found a very large nugget of gold, weighing over fifty pounds. He had gone to the gold fields in a desperate effort to remedy his impoverished situation, although he had never in his life wielded a pick and shovel or used a gold pan. One night, after several days of fruitless digging and worrying about the family he had left behind in the city in straitened circumstances, he had a dream. In this dream he saw his daughter covered with fecal matter from head to toe. Strange to say, the sight of his daughter in that distressing state did not disturb him greatly in the dream. Rather, somehow or other, it led him the next morning to don his best suit of clothes, and then walk directly to a certain spot on the mountain, where he proceeded to dig out the fantastic chunk of gold, which rested just beneath a thin layer of overburden.

This was undoubtedly a strange occurrence, and it provides us with a clue as to how dreams should be considered. We should not give too much importance to the things in our dreams, but instead, let the underlying current of the entire dream serve to propel us, in a subconscious manner, towards certain courses in life that we should take.

Sometimes, however, we may receive specific, prophetic information in a dream, such as the upcoming numbers in a lottery. I once lived for some time in La Ceiba, a small city on the north coast of Honduras, where the small lottery I have spoken of is played weekly. Since it involves only the picking of one number out of one hundred, the amount of money to be won is small and divining the number to play is not such an extraordinary occurrence. But the people of La Ceiba are greatly engrossed in the pastime of their lottery. It is held on Sunday morning, and for the entire week one can hear discussions on the prospects for one number or another. "What did you dream last night," is a question one hears frequently; usually among women, since I must admit that these preoccupations slant towards the feminine in nature. Several times in this lottery I spotted the number to be played, which was revealed to me in various cryptic dreams.

I was living alone by this time, and I had a maid, a very poor young girl named Rosa, who did my housework and laundry. She was a quite plain and unattractive girl, who spent a good deal of her free time counting her meager savings, and talking to me of how she was saving her money in order to get married some day, sometimes asking for my advice on the matter.

Despite her poverty, Rosa was always a cheerful soul, seemingly unaware of the pathos-evoking quality of her situation. She would notice me sitting at my desk, staring blankly at the wall, and mistake these reveries for depression. She would lay aside her broom and mop and sit beside me on a stack of books, endeavoring to cheer me up by telling me stories of her family and neighbors in her impoverished village of San Juan Pueblo. But her stories would sometimes depress me. Then I would go to bed at night wishing I could do something of real consequence for Rosa.

One night I had a peculiar dream. I was giving Rosa some money and telling her, "Go into town and get me some umbrellas; I want fifteen of them." And as Rosa hurried away, carrying a ragged umbrella that an uncle had given her on her twelfth birthday, to shelter herself from the rain that was threatening, I felt an inexplicable warmth and satisfaction, as if by sending her on this curious errand I had done something good for her.

The next morning was Sunday, normally Rosa's day off, but she intended to hang around the house, she told me, because she didn't have any money to go anywhere. I gave her some money and told her, "Take the day off and go into town. Buy yourself some lottery tickets. Get number fifteen." But Rosa had no great faith in my psychic powers and she only bought two tickets, using the rest of the money to buy some underwear that she was badly in need of, and some ribbons for her hair. She won, I think, about forty dollars, which was a considerable sum for her.

A few weeks later, I had the following dream. I was sitting on a bench in the city park. Two young women whom I had frequently admired from a distance strolled by and sat on the bench beside me. We began to talk, and in the course of the conversation they asked me, "How old are you, anyway?" "I'm thirty-five," I answered. "I only look this way because I've worked so hard all my life."

They acted astonished and said, "Why, no. You look very young!"

Then, in that state between dreaming and waking, and as the young women walked away, I said to myself, "They will never believe I'm thirty-five, but it's a good number." For the truth is, I was considerably older.

The next morning I again gave Rosa some money and told her, "Go into town and have yourself a good time. Buy some lottery tickets—number thirty-five."

This time Rosa had a little more faith in my prediction. But, as she told me later, she had had doubts, finding it hard to believe that I would divine correctly twice in a row. So, again, she had not spent the entire sum on the lottery. Nevertheless, she won over eighty dollars that day.

But the guardians of the arcane tend to set traps for us when we too consistently uncover their secrets. One Sunday morning I gave Rosa another number that had been revealed to me in a dream. This time she invested, not only the money I gave her, but a large part of her own as well, and lost everything.

More recently, driven now, not by an altruistic desire to help a poor girl, but rather by a consuming wish to win a large sum of cash for myself, to indulge my yearning for travel, to see other parts of the world, and to enjoy fine wines, champagne and caviar, I have pondered deeply over ways to refine and perfect a dreaming technique that might possibly reveal to me, not one number, for a measly, small-potatoes prize of thirty or forty dollars, but six numbers, which might pay off to the tune of twenty or thirty million dollars. Here, I must immediately state, the task becomes infinitely more complicated. And yet, several times I have seen evidence that it could some day happen.

Revelatory dreams, then, can be of two different types. They can be visions of things as yet nonexistent, visions of the future, and the information can come in a completely disguised shape, more often than not defying interpretation. Or they can be transmitters of physically existing information which would normally be hidden from the dreamer, and indeed, hidden from all human knowledge, as in the case of the Brazilian gold seeker and many other such cases. In dreams of this type, the information may manifest itself only in an obscure impulse.

This is the best way in which we should try to receive both types of information. That is to say, we should not try to interpret our dreams into explicit language, or scrutinize them too closely for hidden meanings. We should only let our dreams serve as a subconscious impulse that will incline us towards one course of action or another in our everyday affairs. We should let those hidden meanings come to us in sudden, epiphanous moments, without thinking about them too intently. We should expect only to receive subconscious impulses and information from our dreams. While those instances in which a dream plainly and unequivocally reveals a set of lottery numbers to us are quite spectacular, they are also very rare, and consciously exerting ourselves to have dreams of this sort only makes them that much scarcer. Additionally, when we struggle too openly to decipher the meaning of a dream, the guardians of the arcane find the means to further confound us by providing us with an erroneous interpretation.

Do dreams always contain a prophetic content? Probably not. No doubt there are many occasions in which the dream arises purely from a physical disturbance in the body—the result of a disturbed digestive process, for example, when the dreamer has indulged too liberally in his favorite dish of pig feet, or pasta, or whatever, just before going to bed. Of course for the condemned prisoner scheduled to die at dawn, added to the profound psychic disturbance caused by the fear of his approaching death, is the fact that there are no future events in his life to dream about.

Notwithstanding this last, however, we can dream of other realities, other realities that touch upon our own and that transmit their impressions upon our consciousness as we sleep; other realities with which we fleetingly make contact but are unable to penetrate and move into because of the isolated state of the human body in sleep. But the aforementioned condemned prisoner will not make contact with any reality in which he has escaped from his sentence of death, because any such reality is far removed from the one in which he finds himself. All his dreams on that final night's sleep, therefore, will necessarily be filled with the ominous portents and shadows of his approaching death.

On the other hand, it could be that I am mistaken in my view of the condemned murderer and his dreams. After all, when we see the execution of the murderer, or read about it, we are only seeing the execution of his husk, since it is happening in our reality, and not in his. It could be that the murderer, in whichever reality he may be, does escape into another reality, a reality in which he never committed his crime or was never caught.

This would seem to suggest, then, that we never die, but live on and on into eternity, escaping always into another reality at the moment of death. But a reality cannot go on and on forever. It has to have its fixed bounds, a beginning and an end. Nevertheless, those particles of time through which we live our days are always there, eternally, and it can therefore be rightfully said that we never die. Perhaps this is something that the ancient Egyptians knew very well, and maybe that is what was meant in those very ancient tomb writings that say, "You will live for millions of years, for millions and millions of years."

We know that animals dream too, dogs especially, as can be seen when they whimper and whine as they sleep, with quivering movements of their limbs as they apparently chase a dream-world rabbit, or flee from a larger dog. The dreams of the dog or the cat probably contain a much greater portion of prophetic content, because the power hiding the future from the consciousness of living creatures does not need to worry too much about a dog or cat. The intelligent dog, as compared to the stupid dog, is better equipped to extract guidance from its dreams, which provide it with a better connection to its *neter* (making it a "lucky dog"), and this better connection to its *neter* is what constitutes the principal difference between a smart dog and a dumb dog.

Chapter 23

"Of Divination, What Good Has Ever Come to Men?"

In ninety-nine billion realities—to use a specific figure—is there a reality in which your non-insane cat or non-stupid dog can read and write, has a bank account, is the president of the United States, or has won a lottery? No, there isn't. It would have to be an entirely different creature for any of these conditions to exist. Likewise, in that vast spectrum of realities in which you have a presence, there cannot be one in which your own situation is entirely removed from the life pattern dictated by your basic nature.

That is to say, what we are in each of those countless billions of cells of reality is determined, to a large degree, by our genes, which are the visible manifestation of the fate laid out for you by the Fates, by destiny, by fortune, whatever you wish to call it.

A radical change in any particular person therefore means a change in the composition of that person's genes, and it would carry with it a consequent change across a large spectrum of realities. It is a change in the tapestry of creation itself, quite unlike a simple transference of a life into an already existing reality. All this should illustrate why it is so hard to change ourselves.

The methods for self-improvement advocated by psychologists and other experts sometimes work, just as some primitive medical remedies sometimes work, and just as the Ptolemaic system worked. But if the theories being proposed here were developed and applied, those methods would work much better. Self-improvement experts never take into account this truth: the present is unchangeable. How could it be different? Any alternative behavior in the past would necessarily have entailed equivalent changes in the lives of those people we are in contact with, and in the entire reality surrounding us—an entirely different reality. If we could have brought about this different reality by behaving differently in the past, then this separate reality would absolutely have to have had a *prior existence* to accommodate this different behavior.

This means that a simpler and more direct way to effect a change (a minor change, not a radical change) of our character would be to concentrate on a way to pass into that reality, rather than the much more cumbersome procedure of bringing that reality into our present life. Could this perhaps be the lesson that Mohammed was trying to teach his followers when he opted for going to the mountain rather than having the mountain come to him?

One of the most important tools that we can use for passing into those other realities is, of course, by foreseeing events in the future. Thomas Hobbes said, "The present only, has a being in Nature; things past have a being in the memory only, but things to come have no being at all, the Future being but a fiction of the mind . . ." Marcus Aurelius and Saint Augustine also assert that only the present exists. I, however, find more sense in P. D. Ouspensky, who points out that it is ridiculous to suppose that life and the vast universe only exist in that split fraction of time in which we are living it. Once we have recognized that the world undoubtedly exists through all time, whether past, present or future, then we have to accept that the things in that world must necessarily also exist in the past and in the future.

Therefore, somewhere in the future, every dip and rise in the stock market has already occurred; every lottery has been played; every horse race has been run, and the results are known. We need but to devise a way to journey to that future, to collect that information, and then bring it back to the present—to the same reality in which that information will remain valid—without impairment.

Some kinds of information are easier to access than others. In some areas we can deceive fortune by pretending to acquire that information by logical deduction, such as when we handicap a horse race, or analyze the stock market. The effects of chance upon these events in the future are partially rooted in the present. But the outcome of anything that rests *entirely* upon the shifty and unstable bases of chance and probability gives the appearance of having nothing whatsoever in the present that can be used as a tool, nothing that would give us a clue as to which event has a greater probability of occurring. But this is a mistaken view. There *are* clues and indicators. It is just the fact that they are more securely hidden away, and that they are not mathematically or physically demonstrable. A para-mathematical science (as yet undeveloped) is necessary to uncover the methods required to develop the art of predicting the outcome of events of chance. The powers that guard the arcane will withhold the secrets of this new science from man for as long as they can.

But man will eventually triumph over fate, and have his way. A time will come when the ability to divine the future will be a routine accomplishment. But it is a time many aeons away in the future of man's evolution. It is that day announced by the prophet Joel, when he says,

> And it shall come to pass afterwards, that I will pour out my spirit upon all flesh; and your sons and your daughters shall prophesy, your old men shall dream dreams, your young men shall see visions. (Joel, 2:28)

When we know where to look, proofs can be seen that there is a power which strives to hide the future from us. These proofs become faintly visible when we pause to ask ourselves why it is that the more important the future event, the more securely is it hidden away. As an illustration, I have no doubt that a great many people who read these lines have experienced at least one very minor flash of intuition, the sudden illuminating answer to a hidden secret of no great importance. But how many of you have won the lottery in a similar way? And yet, the two events are very much alike, the principal difference being the extreme importance of one of them as compared to the other. Against this reasoning, it could be argued that the mathematical reality of the odds is what makes the principal difference. But these odds are only the visible pretext furnished by the guardians of the arcane to justify the greater difficulty in correctly divining these more important matters. For all these reasons, then, it can be seen why magic would be quite ineffectual for something such as winning the lottery.

Even in the days when divination of the future was devoutly believed in by kings, statesmen, and great leaders of nations, there were scoffers, too, and people who, while pretending to believe, only used the faith of others towards their own ends. Plutarch tells us, for example, that Lysander, the Spartan statesman and general, tried to bribe the priests at the oracle of Zeus Ammon in Libya to emit an oracular pronouncement favorable to his own purposes. The priests, however, not only refused the bribe, but traveled from the Libyan desert to Sparta to denounce him. Other priests, seers, and prophets, were not always so honest. The Athenian Onomacritus, Herodotus tells us, was expelled from Athens for forging and falsifying the oracles of Musaeus, which he collected. From Athens he went to Persia, and contributed to Xerxes' decision to invade Greece by reading to him, from his edited and falsified oracles, those parts which seemed to augur great success for Xerxes.

Even in those days before this constant harassing of the oracles finally led to a closing of those fountainheads of arcane knowledge, the information that was thus garnered of events to come was always couched in obscure and sometimes incomprehensible terms. Sometimes even in a language unknown to the person consulting the oracle: "And Pythian oracles are Greek, yet hard to read," says the chorus to Cassandra in Aeschylus' *Agamemnon*.

Elsewhere in that same work the chorus intones, "Of divination, what good has ever come to men?" Aeschylus no doubt had in mind those countless cases of oracular pronouncements that have been recorded from ancient times in which it is hard to single out one that prevented the recipient from embarking on a rash course, or that saved him from disaster. The most spectacular case which seems to illustrate the futility of trying to avoid one's fate is the long and involved story of King Laius, his wife Iocasta, and their son Oedipus. It was foretold to the first two that their son would kill his father, so they exposed him to die on a mountain side. To Oedipus, saved from certain death by a shepherd and adopted by Polybus and Merope, it was foretold that he would kill his father and fornicate with his mother.

So he fled from his home in horror, determined to go so far away from his mother and father that the oracle would never come true, so no one could ever call him a mother-fornicator. But he didn't know he was adopted, and he fled directly to Thebes, where his real parents lived. Along the way he ran into his father Laius along a narrow mountain pass, and killed him in a dispute over who had the right of way. He then continued on to Thebes, and there after some time married his mother, who did not know it was he who had killed Laius.

There are, no doubt, innumerable cases in which a person who consulted an oracle and correctly understood what was announced to him, saved himself from many an unpleasant occurrence. Since the disaster did not occur, the case is mostly forgotten. For there is no way of knowing if the thing would have happened if that person had not heeded the oracle.

Cassandra herself, the most famous prophetess of ancient times, contributed greatly to this view of the futility of divination of the future. Even in our time, I have more than once seen people improperly use her name as an example of doomsayers who are constantly seeing trouble and disaster ahead, when there is really nothing to fear. Cassandra, however, was a very accurate prophetess. In fact, she was never wrong. But no one ever believed her.

When her brother Paris was born, she recommended to her parents that they pick him up by the heels and bash him against a wall, for example, and horrid as the act would have been, it would have avoided many far worse horrors: ". . . the broken wall, the burning roof and tower and Agamemnon dead," her aged father Priam killed, her sister Polyxena sacrificed, her mother, driven insane with grief, barking like a dog on a Thracian plain, and eventually, her own death, murdered by Clytemnestra, wife of her captor, Agamemnon.

The reason no one ever believed Cassandra, by the way, was because she had welshed on her promise to the god Apollo, who had bestowed upon her the gift of prophecy in exchange for some sex. But once Cassandra found herself gifted in this way, she then refused to come across for Apollo, who, unable to take back his gift, had then laid that curse on her.

There were a great many oracles in the ancient world, but only a few of them have preserved their fame down to our day— the Delphic Oracle, the Oracle of Zeus Ammon, the Oracle of Zeus at Dodona, the Oracle of Apollo at the Lycaeum, the Oracle of Demeter at Patrae, the oracles of Amphiaraus, Mopsus, Amphilocus, Trophonius. Great intrepidity was sometimes required to consult these oracles. To consult the Oracle of Trophonius, for example, the suppliant had to crawl into a dark, narrow cave, feet first, holding a honey-cake in each hand. Halfway down, two pairs of hands would suddenly grab his feet, drag him into the darkness, club him over the head, and take the honey-cakes. In a dazed state, the suppliant would then hear an invisible voice revealing the future in a sepulchral tone.

Hey, one might have said to Trophonius, if you wanted honey-cakes that bad, you could have just asked. I, for one, would have thought more than twice about consulting that oracle, even with a twenty-million-dollar lottery as the prize, for it sounds like a dangerous undertaking.

I once visited the site of an ancient oracle on the island of Malta. No one could tell me what its name had been. It is a large, hollow cavern, with an opening skyward. Within, carved out of the rocky wall, is a small, smoothly hollowed-out basin, which, if one speaks into it, makes the voice reverberate imposingly throughout the chamber. I frightened my children as they cowered at the entrance by speaking into it, announcing dire events in store for them if they disobeyed their parents.

The ancient oracles are silent now. One by one they fell into disrepute and disuse, victims of the force of destiny, which conspires to keep man in ignorance of the future. But human enterprise and ingenuity has replaced them with a myriad of tricks and devices—Tarot cards, dream interpretation, tea leaves, crystal balls, palmistry—all of which devices and methods have survived from those same times.

Where dreams are concerned, I have already said that we should not strive too openly to interpret them. They can be a valuable tool for divining the future, but just as you can ruin a tool by trying to make it perform beyond its designed purpose, so could you render your dreams useless by looking for too much in them.

The more you consciously try to look for occult knowledge in your dreams, the more care will the guardians of the arcane take to make sure they are properly encrypted and shrouded. We should only concentrate our attention on learning how to remember them when we awake, and learning how to open our consciousness to the subtle messages they sometimes imprint on us.

Even when we have learned to receive messages from our dreams in this manner, we must still exercise the maximum caution before we act on that information. You might be thinking, "If in a dream I receive a suggestion of four numbers to play in the lottery, I could wheel them with every other number, and I would have a sure thing." On the surface of it, this would appear to be a clever thing to do. It would only cost you, unless my arithmetic deceives me, one thousand and eighty dollars in a fifty-number lottery to collect a prize of several millions. But actually, it could be a foolhardy thing to do, unless the dream were of a portentous nature, far beyond a simple suggestion. We would not allow a simple dream to prompt us to quit our job, or to sell our house. Nor should we put so much faith in a dream that we would plunge, in this manner, into something such as the lottery. Because dreams often lie, for reasons which I think I have made clear in the above.

Since I am dwelling at some length on the lottery as a dramatic example of a change of fortune, I must acknowledge that some chapters back I hinted that I could show the reader how to increase his chances of winning it by a thousandfold. And the reader might be thinking that I have still not delivered on this promise. But I have already detailed many insightful approaches and ways in which the matter of chance and probability should be viewed. Taken all together, they constitute an approach to the problem whereby we reduce the odds against us many times over.

Here is an additional ploy towards that end: subtract eight or ten numbers in your lottery from all consideration. Choose those numbers that you dislike, and play the lottery as if they did not exist. Often, these numbers you are thus arbitrarily subtracting from the lottery will still show up in the drawing. But the intuitive knowledge that has prompted you to eliminate those numbers gives you a powerful advantage, represented by the eighteen or twenty to one probability that the numbers you have eliminated will not figure in the drawing, which means that five percent of the times that you play the lottery in this fashion you have reduced the odds against you by several millions.

I will not vouch for the mathematical sense in the above, but when you proceed in this manner you also give yourself a subtle advantage of another sort. When you eliminate those numbers you make it a little tougher for the Fates to frustrate you. You give them the additional task of seeing to it that the numbers you have eliminated do figure in the drawing. Eventually, the day will come when they will not want to be bothered with this extra chore.

Speaking of subtle advantages, recently I became acquainted with a most curious problem in probabilities. In a famous television game show, a contestant is given the chance to win a car by guessing which of three doors conceals it. The other two doors hide a goat. After the contestant chooses one of the doors, the game-show host opens one of the two remaining doors, to reveal one of the goats. Then, he gives the contestant the opportunity to switch his original choice of doors to the other.

Now, common sense seems to show that in the two remaining doors, chances that the car is in either one are even. But the columnist Marilyn Vos Savant, in *Parade* magazine, has correctly pointed out that it would be greatly to the contestant's advantage to always switch. Les Krantz, in his book, *What the Odds Are*, tries to explain why she is right, but he only succeeds in muddying the waters of what should be a simple problem for practitioners of the esoteric.

In order to understand the matter more clearly, look at it in this manner: imagine that you are the contestant. Instead of trying to choose the door which hides the car, try to choose one that hides a goat. The chances that you will be right are sixty-six percent. Now, the host will reveal the door that hides the other goat. (He must know, obviously, where the two goats are.) Then he gives you the opportunity to change your first choice. It can immediately be seen that you will of course change, since you chose the first door on the assumption that it hid a goat, and you now know (or think you know) where both goats are. By proceeding in this manner you thereby increase your chances of choosing the door that hides the car from thirty-three percent to sixty-six percent.

It is easy to see the logic in this. The strange part is that even if your first choice of doors was prompted by the belief that it hid the car, it would still make sense to switch, and you would still increase your chances from thirty-three percent to sixty-six percent. But it becomes extremely difficult to recognize the truth of this when we have proceeded in that manner.

Similarly, it's hard to see how eliminating numbers from the lottery could produce any mathematical advantage. Well, let us consider: We have compared the odds against winning the lottery to a living room full of beans, with the winning set of numbers represented by one bean, painted white. But in this living room full of beans, the white one remains in one spot as we try to draw it out of the pile. In the actual lottery, on the other hand, this white bean is constantly shifting around, moving, now to the top of the pile, now to the bottom, first to one corner, then to the other. When we eliminate numbers from the lottery, we are thereby reducing that pile of beans, and we are doing it without permanently tossing out the marked one. Because it must eventually be returned to the pile, to the reduced area in which we have concentrated our search.

Chapter 24

Incursions Into the Future to Beat the Lottery

If we can catch occasional glimpses of the future, such as in a dream or crystal ball, then of course it should also be theoretically possible to consistently look into the future, and even into the outcome of all events ruled by chance and probability.

In the previous chapter I suggested that in coming millennia it is something that will be sure to happen. When that time comes, of which the prophet Joel speaks, the nature of time and chance will have changed. This change will actually be in man himself. A great evolutionary leap will some day allow us to gain legitimate entry into that world of which we now catch only foggy and obstructed views now and then in dreams. When the first man (or woman) learns how to do this, the knowledge will spread from the highest of tribes to the lowliest (or vice versa), just as the art of making and using fire has been universal amongst humanity from the remotest of times. If all this seems too preposterous to swallow, let us remember that I am speaking of something that will come to be in a time hundreds of thousands, or even millions, of years in the future.

Speculations of this sort, however, immediately meet the familiar objections. Probing into the future and the past is equivalent to time travel, and the paradoxes this sort of activity would give rise to prove that it can never be done. Not to mention the fact that if it were possible, we would surely have seen evidence of it already, in the form of time travelers journeying from the distant future to visit us.

As to this last item, however, it is very possible that repeated instances of this are continually occurring. If flying saucers really exist, this is what they would have to be. They must surely come from a greatly distant future, since it is almost certain that they cannot come from any of the planets or from the stars. They are in fact time travelers, who have been journeying backwards through the ages from an incredibly distant future, where man has long since solved the problem of time travel and all of the paradoxes which it supposedly should give rise to. This is such an obvious conclusion that it is amazing the belief is not more widely held. To my knowledge, only Marc Davenport, in his book, *Visitors from Time*, has proposed the idea.

But then again, perhaps it is not so amazing. Our present concept of time presents many irresoluble objections against the idea of time travel, which contribute to keep the notion confined to the fantasies of science fiction writers. The first of these irresolvable objections is that principal one, often cited: If we could travel into the future, we would be able to modify our present in such a way as to change the future, in which case it would no longer be the future.

But in these cases we would not be changing the future. We would only be transposing one reality for another.

Another objection, raised by some scientists who recognize that time travel is theoretically possible, is the mind-boggling technology that would be necessary to accomplish it, such as in the manipulation of cosmic strings, (I don't know what cosmic strings are), or gravitational balloons (nor these). But here we can point to the enormous technological advances achieved by man in a mere one hundred years. What can he not be capable of doing in one *million* years?

At present, we are severely restricted in our ability to tamper with the past or the future, even if we were to suddenly discover the secret of time travel, because we would find that man in a distant future has reserved for himself that right, and will not countenance any further interference from any other time.

Furthermore, let us suppose that those time travelers come from a time several million years in the future. They would be so evolved as to be no longer human, and they would have no desire to resort to the sophomoric shenanigans that we imagine ourselves engaging in if we could travel through time, to say nothing of passing on tips for the lottery or horse races. In other words, man in the future is the master over past, present and future. He is, in fact, in confabulation with destiny itself, and any interference from this source in our present-day affairs would be of an invisible nature. Finally, in the very distant future we/they will find that there is no longer any reason to change anything in the remote past.

Many witnesses who seemingly have had personal encounters with these time travelers will swear that this last is not so. The occupants of those flying saucers appear to have some sort of obsession with pregnancy tests, as if each of those witnesses was important in some grave way to those visitors. These witnesses, any psychologist can testify, are quite normal, level-headed people, who appear to genuinely believe that they saw what they say they have seen. But what those persons have seen and experienced is distorted, for several reasons.

Those time travelers are not in confabulation with any present world government, nor are they abducting people, or implanting monitoring devices in anyone; and they are certainly not doing pregnancy tests. But these are the only impressions that persons who are somehow touched, probably accidentally, by these time travelers are able to perceive. They receive those distorted impressions because the human mind in its present state is incapable of apprehending what it has really experienced when it is thus affected by time travel. The human mind naturally translates the impressions it receives into the equivalent of familiar stimuli and experiences.

There is one more detail I would like to touch upon, while we are on this subject of flying saucers and time travel: How do those time travelers accomplish their trips through time? The shape, itself, of the saucer provides us with a clue. They are round for a good reason. When those travelers initiate their voyage, the first step they take is to rise into space above the Earth. Here, the outer ring of the saucer, which is independent of the nucleus, or core, of the craft, begins to spin, propelled by magnetism or some other force we are presently ignorant of. It spins faster and faster, until it reaches a speed very nearly the speed of light. At this speed, as the theory of relativity has taught us, time does strange things. When the outer ring of the saucer has been thus transposed into the time of the occupants' choice, they stop the spinning. They can then leave the nucleus of the saucer, and by means of a chute enter into the ring and into that other time. When they have finished their visit, they simply retreat back into the nucleus. By a reversal of the spin, they can then bring the ring back into synchronicity with the nucleus, and presto, they are back, all in one piece, in their own time.

These are perhaps the very first time machines. Over the centuries, however, other models will have been developed in which the saucer shape is no longer necessary. And this would be the reason that these unidentified flying objects are reported in many different shapes.

What are those time travelers doing when they appear in our time? What are they looking for? They must surely be simply watching over what is their property, just as the owner of a vast ranch must occasionally ride the boundaries of his land, to check his stock and his fences. Flying saucers are range riders, keeping an eye on the millennia which surround their own time.

In short, the changes inherent in that world of the future render all seeming inconsistencies and paradoxes nonexistent. In millennia to come, our preoccupation with those paradoxes will appear no less absurd than was the childish contention in olden times that the world could not be round, because then the people standing on the bottom of the Earth would fall off, trees would grow down instead of up, and rain would fall up instead of down, according to the arguments against the roundness of the Earth used by the oft-quoted Firmianus Lactantius, who was tutor to the son of the Emperor Constantine, no less, as late as the fourth century of our era.

In that world of the very distant future, time and chance will not exist in the same manner as they do for us now. The only reason that events of chance are presently so chancy is because we have no foreknowledge of them, of course. Once we gain the ability to foresee these things, then chance and happenstance will cease to exist.

Such a state of affairs seems extremely strange and impossible to us now, but we have only to remember the experiences we undergo in dreams to see how this could be. We do strange, and sometimes impossible, things in dreams. We take long flying leaps over wide rivers, propelling ourselves across by sheer willpower; we swim tirelessly across oceans; we commune with persons long dead; we wander around a teeming mall completely naked, unnoticed by the shoppers bustling about around us. Another strange aspect of dreams is their dichotomous nature. Things are often simultaneously more than one thing. In the world of dreams, a dog can suddenly and inexplicably become a mouse; a crocodile becomes an iguana; a trip to a familiar town turns subtly into a safari in Africa.

But the most intriguing part of dreams is the vaguely perceived notion of the unrealness of time. In dreams, time is suspended, with the cause of an event sometimes taking place *after* the event.

This is because, in dreams, we are on the borderline territory of that other world where the real nature of time and chance rules. Just beyond this borderland and within that other world, which is within the center of the cell in that honeycomb of realities I spoke of earlier, the result of every event of chance and probability is known.

When we find ourselves in this borderland territory, we can sometimes hear or see deep secrets. Since each one of us is the sole owner and legatee of his cell of reality, the secrets we learn in this way are usually of a subjective nature, tinged with the aura of our personal affairs. At the present stage of man's evolution the greater part of this secret information must necessarily elude us. Fate's grip on our destiny is still too strong.

How is it, then, that we can sometimes discover these secrets? In *Moby Dick* Herman Melville gives us an idea:

"The weaver-god, he weaves; and by that weaving is he deafened. . . . For even so it is in all material factories. The spoken words that are inaudible among the flying spindles; those same words are plainly heard without the walls, bursting from the opened casements . . . "

Imagine the Fates sitting at their loom in their factory in the nucleus of your cell of reality. They sit there weaving, chatting away, perhaps, to relieve their boredom. Sometimes they have to shout, to hear each other above the sounds of their whirring shuttles. And you, standing out of sight, with one ear glued to the wall of your cell, will sometimes catch a stray word or two of their conversation. Just as when you are standing on the banks of a bayou, perhaps, and two acquaintances pass by in a motorboat. They wave to you as they go by, and then begin to make derogatory comments about you, in loud voices, to hear each other above the high-pitched whine of their motor. They do not realize that to you the sound of the motor is only a minor background noise, and that you can hear every word they say.

The fates often commit this same error. As I have indicated before, they are not necessarily very smart. In this manner we can sometimes catch fragments of their conversation—the name of a horse they have scheduled to win a race, perhaps; or, even more tantalizing and exciting, a number or two they have scheduled to be drawn in a coming lottery.

In that borderland there are possibly waste dumps from where, just as detectives will sometimes sift through a person's garbage to learn his secrets, we can pick up information. But no doubt there is a security system of some sort on the fringes of that forbidden area, security guards who patrol the inner surface of the wall to keep unauthorized personnel—specifically, *you*—away. If they catch you looking through a peephole, or sifting through the Fates' garbage can, they will treat you just as any trespasser or peeping-tom is treated in our world. They will pick you up by the scruff of the neck and the seat of your pants to fling you ignominiously out of their precincts.

You can probably recall instances in which you were having a peculiar dream, perhaps a pleasurable dream, and then, at the most interesting, pleasurable, or intriguing part of it, you suddenly awoke. You are always denied the fulfillment of the pleasure. These are instances in which you were coming perilously close to hearing or seeing a forbidden secret, and were caught out just in time by the Fates and their security guards.

If we can learn valuable information this way, by listening at the wall, or peeping through a hole, what a wealth of information could we not gather by actually penetrating into the center of the cell itself, to wander unseen through its store rooms; to venture into those areas where the Fates have stretched out their finished product to dry, to then return to our world with maybe a list of twenty or thirty horses scheduled to win a race, and the numbers to a lottery or two.

But keep in mind the fate of the cockroach that dwells in the hidden crevices of your kitchen. You enter the kitchen at night for a glass of water; you suddenly turn on your light, and there the disgusting little creature will be, brazenly feasting on the crumbs you left on your kitchen sideboard. You will certainly crush it if you can, and probably you will spray the crevices and seal them up tight. The same thing will happen to you if the Fates suddenly turn on their light to find you poking around where you should not be. But the danger is really not very great because most of us have natural defenses which prevent us from entering that region. So, unless there is a history of schizophrenia in your family, you are most likely safe.

Even when we do manage an occasional incursion into those forbidden regions, we can rarely return with any of the knowledge that is found there. Because the shape of that knowledge is adapted only for that *other* world, and when we bring it into our own it becomes unrecognizable. Once we have returned to a point in which we can place a bet on a horse or buy a lottery ticket, we have left that knowledge behind in that other world. For these reasons we should not try to penetrate into that world itself. We must reach into that other world while maintaining a firm foothold in our own, peeping and eavesdropping from the other side of the wall, so to speak, reprehensible as this may sound. In this manner, any information we manage to snag will retain a recognizable shape when we bring it back to reality.

Everywhere at hand, in this world of dreams, we see and hear information, mundane and arcane, cloaked in symbolic shapes and forms. In part, this is because, as Freudians say, the truth is painful for us, and we disguise it in that manner. But it is also because the powers that guard those secrets labor to disguise and twist them into those strange shapes, never mind what Carl G. Jung said, ". . . dreams are a part of nature, which harbors no intention to deceive, but expresses things as best it can. . . ." They have garbled our dreams in order to preserve their mysteries. It is only incidental that they have also garbled the other, more mundane and personal, knowledge that we find in dreams. The woman who dreams of eating a banana could be overhearing a private conversation from beyond the wall, where the number one is being discussed. Or she could, as Freudians suggest, be expressing a repressed desire.

The Fates, just to be on the safe side, thus disguise the true meaning of all dreams, whether it impinges on their domain or not. In fact, they also disguise almost all occult information that we are able to capture in our waking life, so that indisputable evidence of the existence of that vast river of esoteric information that flows through all human affairs will forever be placed in doubt. Frequently, whenever we divine an event in the future, they will provide the non-occult means by which the information was obtained after the fact itself. This applies, especially, to those paranormal events that are subjected to intense scrutiny.

We should realize, therefore, that every bit of knowledge we acquire has elements of the esoteric. Some of it is almost purely esoteric, without ever being recognized as such. The successful horse race handicapper, though he may honestly believe that his success is based purely on his knowledge of horses and horse races, actually derives most of his success from luck—from extracting hidden knowledge from the future. The powers that guard this knowledge preserve the integrity of their tapestry, the fabric of reality, by providing the visible means through which this success is accomplished after the fact itself. The same can be said, to a large extent, of successful investors in the stock market, and to many other endeavors in which luck plays an important part.

To attenuate the element of absurdity in all of the foregoing, it should be noted that the secrets of the future, including the outcome of horse races, remain secret because there is a part of us (perhaps that part of us that the ancient Egyptians called the *Ka*) that is actually in confabulation with the powers that strive to keep those secrets from us. And in the very fact of this confabulation we can find the essence that gives being to those same powers. Thus, it could be said, the powers that disguise our dreams are our own creation, and it is with our help that they guard their secrets.

I have said that the inhabitants of the distant future are also in confabulation with destiny. But these creatures have gained, through many millennia of strife and struggle, a privileged position within the hierarchy of fate. They are vastly superior in intelligence, and their confabulation is not, like our own, under duress, and designed to keep them in an inferior position, but rather a confabulation which confers upon them all those rights and powers which to us are only unrealizable dreams.

Going even further, it is quite possible that these creatures, evolved from man, are now so powerful and all-knowing that it is they, even more than the Fates, who manipulate our destiny and our position in life.

Chapter 25

The Last One to Remain Clinging to the Wall

Now let us return for a last look at the race track, with these further considerations and observations on time travel and dreams added to our view of fate, coincidence, luck, and sound handicapping practices. I only wish to make a short comment about the application of time travel in the picking of winning horses at the track.

Even if humanity has not yet mastered time travel, the rudiments of the ability are probably present in the psyche of every living man and woman. Therefore, I think it is a good idea, if we are using the race track as a work shop and laboratory for the investigation of these things, if we take every opportunity to peruse old racing charts and racing results. *Why?* you ask. Because it's possible that when you receive a hunch about a horse it's because you have captured that knowledge somewhere in the future. When you look at the results of a horse race in the *Racing Form* charts today, it's possible that you sometimes transmit that information to yourself in the past, and that this is what produces the hunch.

Speaking of the *Racing Form*, most handicappers agree that the *Racing Form* should be studied at home, and not the track. This gives you the time and tranquillity essential to study each horse to the minutest detail. Many very good handicappers do not need more than half an hour to study all the races in a day's card, but most of us need more time than that. The racetrack, with all its noise and distractions, is not the best place to do a thorough job. To give ourselves every advantage, then, we need to choose the best possible time and place in which to do our handicapping and forecasting. If you are not already doing it, you should make a practice of buying the *Racing Form*, or at least the program, the day before the races, instead of buying it at the track.

If you are using divining methods—peering somehow into the future—then this rule becomes even more important. There are ideal moments, varying from person to person, in which a divining method works best. For daytime racing, I have had better success by studying the *Racing Form* or program at night, from eight-to-ten, and I have found that most of the divining methods work very well in the early morning hours. The golf ball method is excellent at one o'clock in the morning. But using it at that hour can be a problem. If there are other members of your household trying to sleep, the clatter of golf balls across a hardwood floor can be very disturbing, or even the sound they make rolling over a carpet and thudding into the cardboard. With the cat-in-the-cage method, I found that Precious did best between nine and ten in the morning.

For nighttime racing, more or less the same rules apply, but we run into the complication that if we go to the track at night, then this interferes with our quiet hours of study and prognostication that we should do in those nocturnal hours. Each individual must resolve that problem as best he or she can.

Dabblers in the occult already know all these things, of course. People who have used Tarot cards, for example, know that they should be treated in certain ways to obtain maximum performance. They know that they shouldn't be used in a brightly-lit room, that they produce the best results on a dark velvet surface, and that there are many other rules for the proper care and handling of the cards. Likewise, any horse-picking method you use will work best if you achieve the proper atmosphere, preferably a quiet, softly-lit room, far away from the television set, radio, or any other distraction.

Before you begin, be sure you won't be interrupted, whether by your wife screaming at you because she stepped on one of your golf balls and almost broke her neck, or by your children, who think you are mistreating the cat. Also, very important, you should not be watched by anyone who thinks the whole idea absurd, or even worse, hilarious. An attitude of tolerant amusement in a spectator is not too harmful, but if someone is jeering or laughing at you, you will lose your train of concentration and be unable to follow through to the point in reality where your horses are running true to your predictions.

If you have faith in the beliefs outlined on the preceding pages, and if you religiously observe all superstitious taboos, and if you further temper your practices generously with sound handicapping knowledge, how can you go wrong?

To be realistic, we must acknowledge that you could still, conceivably, continue in a rut, if that is where you have been. Sometimes it becomes necessary to make drastic changes in your lifestyle to wrench yourself out of your present reality and improve your luck. At the same time, you must take care that you don't allow superstition to take control of your life in such a way that you become fearful of life itself.

In the treacherous sea of the horse racing world, once we understand that we are trying to make a profit by consistently sailing against the prevailing wind and tide, represented by the large percentage—in some states nearly twenty percent—that goes to the track, we can then take the tack necessary to offset this disadvantage. We also need to understand that everybody can't win. Why should you be one of the very few who frequent the track to consistently come out ahead? What is your special virtue? Perhaps you consider yourself an excellent handicapper; perhaps you consider yourself smarter than the average specimen of *Homo sapiens race-trackensis*, which swarms around you at the track.

But you would have to be considerably smarter, because everybody at the track is trying to take everybody else's money. And returning again to that matter of the twenty percent, that little fact is the reef upon which so many bettors eventually leave the shattered skeleton of the vessel of their hopes, their forlorn hopes, of making money at the track. Many of those bettors are well served, because they have been too greedy, not knowing, or caring, whose money it was that they were so intent on taking.

Many of those people whose money you are trying to take, are little old ladies, widows, and pensioners, who can ill afford to lose it. I have found that my luck improves if I occasionally try to help some of these people, by steering them onto a hot thing if I happen to know of one. Another superstition? Yes, but one with noble roots, and also one for which I have found a possible logical foundation.

The Fates, in their ceaseless endeavors to plug up the rents through which we can see into the future, become confused if we use the knowledge to benefit a third party. The only way in which they can plug up these leaks is within our conscious mind, and when we use our mind only as a way station for information to pass on to a third party, they somehow are unable to catch it. This forbidden information apparently becomes, to a large degree, invisible to the Fates when it flows only through the altruistic portion of our psyche. This also explains why fortune-tellers and mediums who ply their vocation gratuitously are more reliable than those who do it for a fee.

There is something else we can say, to show that man, in his apparently hopeless task of trying to outwit the Fates, has a subtle advantage. The Fates already know all they are ever going to know. They can learn nothing new. Mankind, on the other hand, continues to expand his knowledge and his wisdom, generation after generation. Even the coyote, will eventually manage to frustrate Mother Nature, by learning to see through the nesting bird's deception. When the first coyote learns, this new awareness will begin to spread through the species, because of what Rupert Sheldrake calls the "Theory of Formative Causation," which says that learning is contagious. This theory, by the way, is only something which millions of children all over the world have always known, just as they have always known that the continents were once a solid land mass and are now drifting apart.

In our endeavors to learn how to pick winners at the track, then, we racing fans, who are often looked upon as sleazy, shiftless, grubbing characters, are contributing mightily to the progress of the human race. Because when we finally hit upon a dramatically new way to pick winning horses, the entire population of the Earth will benefit, since the divinatory science will slowly spread by way of contagious learning. It will be more than horse racing outcomes we will be able to accurately predict.

So, have I told you anything new here, which has not been said before and in a better way? I think that the one thing of importance which I am saying is that learning to divine the future, though it is not something which is fated to be, in the sense that the Fates themselves have written it into their design, is nevertheless something which will eventually come to be a common accomplishment for the mass of humanity. A second thing of importance is that the arcane has the ability to actively evade scrutiny. Also, I hope that the reader is convinced of the very real consequences which are sometimes incurred when we contravene a superstitious belief.

However, so that no one can accuse me of fostering unfounded fears in the race-goer's heart, I'll concede this much: if the reader is coming home from the racetrack every day with more money in his pocket than when he left, then don't worry about superstition. Forget I even mentioned it. But if you are losing money, what harm can there be in knocking on wood, or tossing some spilled salt over your left shoulder, or in taking care not to walk under a ladder? Observing these little precautions will not take up much of your time, and it might do you a world of good.

We'll leave the matter of superstition aside now, and mention some other little precautions that I'm sure no one will disagree with. When you're at the racetrack, you should allow nothing to distract you from the business at hand. Don't put yourself in the position of having to say, after a race has been run, something like, "Why didn't I notice that Silver Street Gal was going off at sixty to one!" or, "Why didn't I notice that there was a Jack B. Nimble and a Quick Jack running in the same race!"

You didn't notice because your mind wasn't entirely where it should have been. You should stay wide awake at the track, and absorb every detail of what is found in the *Racing Form*, and watch every detail of what goes on in the paddock, in the post parade, and on the tote board. At the same time, you must stay relaxed, and avoid the sort of tenseness and frustration which leads to blunders and errors.

To end this chapter, here is another little trick of prognostication which I have saved, like a delicious little tidbit. On little strips of bond paper, write the names of the horses in a given race. Put them in a glass of soapy water. Fling them against a wall. They should all stick to the wall and remain there for several minutes. This will take a bit of patience, because you must now stand there and watch until all but one has fallen off the wall. The last one to remain clinging to the wall, will be the one corresponding to the winner of that race. You must do this, by the way, using an outside wall, as you would quickly ruin your living room walls otherwise, and cause additional discord in your home.

It will take a bit of experimentation to discover the correct amount of soap to use, so that the strips of paper will not stay on the wall too long. The first time I tried this method, for a race which was to be run the following day, I waited patiently by the wall for two hours, and finally had to give up when every one of the strips continued to stubbornly cling to the surface. The next morning, however, I stepped out on the porch and checked the wall. All of the shiny, white strips of paper had fallen to the floor except one, which remained shining high on the flaking paint of the wall. And the name of the horse written on it was Shining High.

This gelding had been running at—if I recall correctly—Montana and Idaho, where it had won three out of its lifetime total of five races. But now, in its first appearance at New Orleans Fairgrounds, it was up against some comparatively classy horses. It looked like a very chancy proposition. But it validated the merit of my new-found method of divining by coming in first at fifteen-to-one.

Chapter 26

Struggling Against Ourselves for Our Future

I must repeat again, at the risk of sounding repetitious, that all of the foregoing ideas upon the origins of fortune and misfortune and the true nature of fate and destiny have been of a metaphorical bent, intended only to serve as an empirical base from which we can study ways to improve our luck, change our destiny, and build a better life for ourselves.

The critical reader may interpose many objections. He will say: The only way we can make changes in our life is by using our common sense; by developing our willpower; by forcing ourselves to steer clear of evil influences; by dedicating ourselves more assiduously to our work; by tempering our greed and the love of sensual and ephemeral pleasures; by ending this habit of looking for someone or something upon which we can place the blame for our condition—by ceasing to blame our condition on our bad luck.

In a way, I would agree with this critical reader. But the fact remains that it was our lousy luck that caused us to be cast forth into the world with the defects of character with which we are cursed. And the very fact of having been cursed with these defects is what prevents us from correcting them. If we live in a house whose walls and roof are cracking and shifting because its foundations are rotting away, we should not waste our time and our resources repairing the walls and the roof. The first step we take should be to repair the foundations.

Where our life is concerned, those foundations rest in the very beginnings of it, before we were born. So it becomes necessary to tackle the powers responsible for the way we are. I have talked of ways in which we can do this, and I should now mention that a great deal of courage and resolution is also needed. We must not be intimidated or discouraged by any initial resistance to our efforts. In this endeavor of bettering our luck we should have more persistence than a dumb animal. Animals, much more so than humans, may often have an intuitive notion of what course they should take, but will still fail to act upon it, because the immediate discomfort they would undergo discourages them. Under the pressure of minor pain or discomfort, the menace of death itself will not convince them to bear it and act in their own best interests.

An example: Some years ago I was keeping a young stray tomcat, feeding it whenever it came around my apartment (which was every day, in fact, since it was a cat evidently used to the good life). I would let it hang around inside my apartment during the day and would put it out at night. At first, this was an arrangement it seemed to object to. When I would put it out in the evening it would return to my door and scratch insistently upon it, trying to gain reentry. But I soon put an end to that non-sense. I would take a glass with a small amount of cold water to the door, open it suddenly, and fling the water in its face. After two or three evenings of this treatment it learned not to scratch on my door. This is one of the respects in which it can be seen that cats are quite intelligent.

But one evening, long after it had learned to respect these rules, it suddenly cast its learning aside, and returned after I had put it out for the night, to scratch with a sort of desperate urgency upon my door. I grimly filled a glass with water, marched to the door, and opened it suddenly. But I only caught a fleeting glimpse of the cat as it fled, tail high, down the walk-way. Something had prompted it to scratch on the door, but it had lacked the resolution to continue through with its insistence. It knew about the cold water.

Why had the cat scratched on my door when it knew full well that it would not be admitted inside? The next day I waited for it to return early in the morning to be fed, as was its custom. But I waited in vain. Later in the day a neighbor told me that my cat would never return. It had been reduced to the semblance of a sad little door mat by a vehicle, as it tried to cross the street.

It seems to me that this cat somehow knew that its death lurked in the vicinity, and it had tried to escape it. It had made a desperate effort to communicate to me that it was in great danger, but I had failed to listen.

Now, some people might say that it was simply a coincidence that the cat chose that evening to forget what it had learned about scratching on my door and the cold water in its face. Yes, of course it was a coincidence. But every coincidence has its hidden reasons and causes. Moreover, the cat had not forgotten about the cold water. It seemed to know that there was grave danger for it if it remained outside that night, but in the final showdown the immediate threat of cold water in its face overrode all other considerations. It refused to endure this discomfort, even though it's possible that if it had stoically endured this punishment and then continued to plead for entry, I would have relented, ashamed of my cruelty, and allowed it back inside.

The Fates have stratagems somewhat akin to flinging cold water in our face when we scratch too insistently at the gates of the arcane. And many of us have no more intelligence or determination than a cat, quickly losing our resolution and fleeing from their door to avoid a minor discomfort, failing to understand that with a little persistence we could avoid a much more serious calamity.

However, we should persist in a quiet, unobtrusive way. If the cat had accepted the water in its face, and then continued to persist, meowing piteously, instead of using the grating, annoying method of scratching at the door, it might possibly have succeeded and escaped its fate. I do not mean that we should seek pity from the Fates. I have already said that they are pitiless. But we should not annoy them, and prompt them to actively resist us, by using grating and obtrusive methods. Because, as I must repeat, the Fates are not interested in revealing the future to you, or in changing anything in it just to please you. They do not love you, or me. If anything, I am sometimes inclined to think that they hate our guts.

But, the reader may say, what about lucky and fortunate people, people blessed with rare talents, with superior intelligence and abilities, born into wealthy and happy families. Don't the Fates love them? Doesn't their great good fortune show that they are held in special esteem? No. All it shows is that their thread of fate happened to have been dyed with a certain color—a color that was needed at the moment for a certain place on the tapestry of the Fates, and it is in the interest of the Fates to preserve that color, to save themselves the labor and trouble of redoing their work. The rest of us, if we manage to change our color by receiving revelations of the future, accomplish this because we have peeked and eavesdropped at the wall, and caught bits and fragments of forbidden information. Those visions come to us purely as a result of an intrepidity, courage, and resolution that we have found in the depths of our psyche, where it never occurred to the Fates that we would ever probe.

A revelatory dream, therefore, does not belong in the same category as an omen or a coincidence. A dream of this sort is information of an impending event that we capture at its very source. A coincidence, on the other hand, comes about for the same reason that causes the clustering effect that can be seen in lotteries, keno, and other numbers games. It is because the powers that have charted the results of these things are often impelled by expediency and propinquity when they schedule their events. Having once picked one thing, or number, they will sometimes then pick the one immediately adjoining, because they cannot be bothered to go to the trouble of choosing something entirely unlike it, or opposite.

They do make desultory efforts to avoid coincidences, however, and across the centuries the Fates have managed to eliminate a good many of them. At one time coincidences were much more common than they are today, as witness the widespread and quite successful use of omens in antiquity to forecast impending events. The people of those times regarded omens as divine messages, but they are really nothing more nor less than coincidence.

Although the occurrence of coincidences is becoming less frequent as time progresses, yet it can be guessed that the powers that are bringing about this elimination of coincidence will finally be overwhelmed by the task. The fates will eventually throw up their hands in disgust, and surrender the last of their secrets, frustrated by man's relentless and ceaseless probing into the arcane. That will be when that era arrives that the prophet Joel speaks of, in which our sons and daughters will routinely prophesy, and the outcome of all events of chance will no longer be hidden. This will naturally entail the final demise of the Fates, insofar as their ability to dictate the terms of life to us is concerned. Unfortunately, it will also mean an end to horse races, lotteries and all other games of chance.

I have spoken of revelations of the future that we sometimes capture in dreams, and of how these revelations are disguised in symbolic shapes and forms. But of course when we surprise these revelations at their source we see them in their true shape and meaning. It is only when we try to bring them with us, out of the world of dreams and into our waking consciousness, that they assume those weird shapes. When we do succeed in bringing out legitimate information as to the future, it is because we have rushed quickly to the well, like the Danaids with their leaking pitchers, to pour out the essence of the information before it has leaked out again.

It was the same with the ancient oracles. In the writings of Herodotus, and in Plutarch, Pausanias, Livy, and others, we can still read the exact words of many an oracular pronouncement, and we can see that almost always those revelations were presented in the form of a riddle. Sometimes it took great skill and astuteness to correctly interpret them. In fact, after consulting an oracle it was almost always necessary to then consult a seer or diviner to interpret the oracular message received, and very often this interpretation could be erroneous.

It can also be argued, of course, that the most famed oracles of those days preserved their fame and their reputation by that quite common device of the diviner: their pronouncements were always couched in ambiguous and ambivalent language, so that the oracle could always claim that the petitioner had misinterpreted the words. The most well-known of such cases is that of Croesus and that criminally ambiguous oracle about the destruction of a great kingdom.

According to Herodotus, Croesus had first tested the accuracy of the Oracle by sending envoys to inquire of the priestess what he, Croesus, was doing at that precise instant. (The priestess no doubt had tolerance for such a frivolous question because of the rich gifts that Croesus sent.) The priestess immediately answered with a five-line hexameter verse which ended,

". . . a hard-shelled tortoise with lamb,
Bubbling and boiling in a pot,
The cauldron of bronze, and of bronze the lid."

And that was exactly what Croesus, in faraway Sardis, was doing—boiling a tortoise with lamb in a bronze pot—on the very day he had arranged for his envoys to ask the question.

As to that most unfortunate prophecy about the destruction of a mighty kingdom, when Croesus later complained bitterly to the oracle for having been deceived, the oracular priestess pointed out to him that the pronouncement had been entirely truthful, that he should have consulted the oracle again, to ask whose kingdom was meant.

Another such ambiguous message was the one delivered to the Lacedaemonians, who were told by the Delphic priestess:

I will give thee Tegea to dance in with stamping feet
And her fair plain to measure out with the line.

So the Lacedaemonians tried to conquer Tegea, but wound up as enslaved prisoners, threshing grain with their stamping feet and measuring out the fields of Tegea for their masters.

The most important thing about these oracles, then, was the way in which they were interpreted. There was a class of professional interpreters for this purpose, but they were as fallible as everything else that has to do with divination of the future. A famous oracle delivered to the Athenians during the Persian invasion announced a great disaster for Athens, and further stated that only the "wooden wall" would not fall.

The professional interpreters thought that "wooden wall" meant the Acropolis, because it had once been fenced in with a thorn hedge, which could be interpreted as a wooden wall. Fortunately for the Athenians, Themistocles was there to point out that the wooden wall could only refer to the ships, that Athens itself should be evacuated and that the Persians should be met at sea.

The professional interpreters, however, were disturbed by the final two lines of the prophecy, which said, "Divine Salamis, you will bring death to women's sons/When the grain is scattered, or the harvest gathered in."

But Themistocles provided the correct interpretation for these lines, too. Since the oracle had used the word "divine" instead of "hateful," he said, this surely meant that the women's sons who would die at Salamis were Persians and not Athenians. The great victory of the Athenian fleet at Salamis proved the wisdom of his interpretation.

Occasionally, a message might be quite clear and unambiguous, such as the oracular message left by the famous seer Bacis, who made this prophecy:

By Thermodon and Asopus, where the grass grows soft,
Shall be a gathering of Greeks and of foreign tongues;
And there, beyond lot and portion shall many Medes fall,
Armed with the bow, when the day of doom comes.
(*Herodotus, ix 56, Aubrey de Selicourt translation*)

Before this prophecy could come true, Tisamenus, who became the diviner for the Spartans during the Persian invasion, consulted the Delphic oracle, seeking a solution to certain personal problems. The oracle failed to answer his questions, but did tell him that he would be the winner of "the five greatest contests." Tisamenus thought this must refer to the Olympics, and therefore began to train for the pentathlon. But the Spartans knew that the oracle was referring to war, and they made a determined effort to recruit him into their army as their diviner, although Tisamenus was not a Spartan. Tisamenus, who realized how badly the Spartans wanted him, told them he would accept the offer, but only on condition that he be granted Spartan citizenship.

But this was something which apparently was not lightly granted, and the Spartans refused, "with great indignation," Herodotus says. Then came the Persian invasion, and the Spartans approached Tisamenus again. But now Tisamenus upped his price. He no longer wanted citizenship just for himself, but for his brother as well. And the Spartans, greatly alarmed at the approach of the vast Persian hosts, had to agree.

Tisamenus was therefore the diviner for the Spartan forces at the great battle of Plataea, "By Thermodon and Asopus, where the grass grows soft," and remained with the Spartans as their diviner in four other very important battles, all of which were won by the Spartans, thus fulfilling the prophecy.

Divining the future, in our time, has become mainly an occupation followed by women, whereas in ancient times it appears to have been an equal opportunity endeavor. Why is this? It would seem to be simply because women, with their opportunities curtailed in many other fields, have across the centuries been able to gradually make ever greater inroads into this occupation, greatly neglected by men since those days when Plutarch wrote his essay, *Why Oracles Are Silent*, early in the second century of the Christian era. So that now men have become reluctant to engage in something which plainly appears to be a female avocation, just as they are reluctant to become secretaries and telephone operators. Divining the future has thus acquired an effeminate and unmanly veneer.

But in olden times, no one would have considered a seer and diviner unmanly simply because of his divining ability. In fact, many of the famous seers of those times often have retained their renown as much for their fame as doughty warriors as for their skill in divining the future. The list of these is long and illustrious. There was Mopsus the Argonaut, who died on the Libyan desert, just as he had foretold for himself. Amphiaraus, another prophet,

died trying to capture Thebes, as he had himself divined. Hegesistratus, the diviner for the Persians at Plataea, cut off his own foot in
order to escape from the stocks of a Spartan prison, ". . . the
bravest thing I have ever heard of," Herodotus says of this deed.

At Thermopylae this inscription was raised in honor of the
seer Megistias, who, though he had foretold what was to come,
and had been given the opportunity to leave the pass by
Leonidas, yet refused to leave, and died there with the others.

> "Here lies Megistias, who died
> When the Mede passed Spercheius' tide.
> A prophet, yet he scorned to save
> Himself, and shared the Spartans' grave."
> (Herodotus, Aubrey de Selincourt translation)

Sometimes, when the ancient seers made a prophecy, it was
necessary to change the facts on the ground, so to speak, in order
to thereby fulfill its conditions. Such as when the Plataeans, at the
battle of Plataea against the Persians, moved the boundary stones
of their land, as Plutarch relates, making a present of that land to
the Athenians, so that the Athenians could fight in the vicinity of
certain shrines but still remain on Athenian soil, both of which
conditions had been stipulated in an oracle delivered by the seer
Bacis. Many years later Alexander the Great honored the
Plataeans for this sacrifice. And in the New Testament, of course,
there is the familiar example of Jesus Christ, who went to some
trouble to secure an ass, so that he could fulfill the ancient
prophecy by riding into Jerusalem on its back.

There are many other such examples from ancient times.
This is a significant clue to keep in mind when we ponder upon
ways in which we can make an event come true, whether we have
divined it ourselves or whether it has been announced to us.

As to how this changing of the facts on the ground could possibly have an effect on reality, I have no doubt it is because the change is sometimes so tenuous that the Fates are deceived, and we are, by virtue of these facts, allowed into the reality in which they have complete legitimacy. This "changing the facts on the ground," is also an essential ingredient of magic. We create spurious facts in our reality and thereby either force the Fates to revise their tapestry or else we create a wedge with which we prize ourselves into a reality in which they have a legitimate existence. The ancients knew the effects of this kind of deception, though they probably did not know the reasons. In some respects the Fates, being the personification of Nature itself, can be as easily tricked as Nature's lowliest creations. Just as a chicken can be fooled into hatching a duck's eggs, and as a cat can be tricked into suckling a rabbit.

In fact, the Fates that reside in your particular cell of reality are scarcely any smarter than you are. In a way, their intelligence is limited by the owner of the cell of reality in which they reside, since their actions and procedures within that cell are only a replica of the actions of the creature which owns that cell. Thus, to a certain degree, the same things that have tricked and deceived you in your life will also serve to deceive the Fates. You cannot be smarter than they are. But you can no doubt recall many instances when you yourself were tricked and deceived by someone much dumber than you.

The successful diviner knows that the more important the information he or she seeks, the more securely will it be hidden away. Therefore, in a search for higher information, the diviner should confine his inquiries only to data peripheral to this higher information. The final answer to a question of this sort should then be deduced from the more minor indications that are revealed.

Just as the Fates labor to keep the future hidden from us, we should no less doggedly labor to thwart and baffle them. We should not fear to grapple with the Fates, because, as I have already suggested, when we struggle to divine the future we are actually struggling against ourselves. It is for this reason that we should not fear meddling with destiny, any more than we should fear struggling with ourselves to overcome our bad habits, vices, and thoughts. We can agree that sometimes it is all for the best that the future should remain hidden from us. However, we can learn to selectively divine the future, confining our inquiries to lotteries, horse races, the stock market, and steering clear of such unpleasant and frightening aspects of it as our own death, and other irrelevancies.

All of the foregoing may appear absurd and extravagant to many. And yet, this anthropomorphic view of fate and destiny—the three Fates weaving eternally at their loom, with piles of yarn and thread at their feet, their mother, Necessity, dozing fitfully on a couch nearby, occasionally stirring awake to intercede in matters where her daughters have been too careless and slipshod—adheres strictly to that scientific maxim, "parsimony in hypotheses."

Chapter 27

Storming the Mysteries Sideways

In this book, it has not been my intention to promote a love for gambling, as my frequent references to the lottery and to horse races might suggest. Gambling is an idle, unproductive vice that leads, more often than not, to penury.

However, many mildly addicted gambling fans are not aware of the reasons behind their addiction. Gambling holds an attraction far beyond that of making money in a more or less effortless manner. Many people do not realize that their fascination with games of chance stems from an unconscious urge to vanquish the laws of probability, to discover an unerring way to *divine* the outcome of a horse race, the numbers in a lottery, the rise in a speculative stock, or the numbers in a game of keno. In so doing we would reap benefits far beyond the obvious ones of putting money immediately in our pockets. It will be a gambling man (or woman) who will some day discover the secret that will usher mankind into his next evolutionary step, from where we shall inevitably progress into that stage in which we can grab the Fates by the short hair, as noted at the beginning of this work.

I am speaking, however, of the *mildly* addicted gambler. The severely addicted are sick people. These people have tried too intently to force out the secrets of the arcane, and the arcane, in a defensively reflexive reaction has grabbed *them* by the short hair, inexorably hauling them down the path of financial ruin, to that region of penury from where they must necessarily cease to be such pernicious pests.

But if this is our underlying purpose for hanging out in a casino or at a race track—that is, to discover the evolutionary secret alluded to—then, in order to keep ourselves safe from the insidious damage to our psyche, our moral worth, to say nothing of our bank roll, we should learn to acknowledge that this is indeed our primary goal, and adjust our involvement with the problem accordingly, to minimize our losses. Otherwise, to persist in an endeavor in which the odds are stacked forbiddingly against us is the height of foolishness.

I pride myself on having recognized this truth. My former wife tended to look down on me for what she called my addiction to sleazy race tracks and casinos. (This "addiction," as she called it, was a mere three-or-four times a year thing, and entailed no great financial loss, except for the traveling expenses involved.) For all her high-flown airs and pretensions, my wife was somewhat short in intellect, as I have hinted earlier, and I could never make her understand that my apparent fascination with games of chance was only an absorption with the much more profound problems of fate, destiny, chance, and probability. Throughout my life every venture in which these elements entered into the picture has represented an opportunity to delve into these mysteries.

Several times, when passing through Las Vegas, I devoted a considerable amount of my free time to experiments designed to prove or disprove some of the points I have brought up here. There was the matter of the advisability of eating certain foods, for example, and their effect on correctly picking keno numbers, or slot machines ready to make a big payoff, or winning horses in the simulcast horse races.

One thing I proved to my complete satisfaction is that jackrabbit is a very lucky food for me. One winter, while living in Arizona, I took some cooked jackrabbit with me on a trip to Las Vegas, in order to thoroughly test that aspect of my theories. (Jackrabbit, by the way, should only be eaten during the winter months. In the summer they tend to have boils.) As I played the slot machines and the video keno machines, I nibbled surreptitiously on a leg of jackrabbit that I carried in my coat pocket, wrapped in cling wrap and napkins, to avoid smearing grease on the machines. I had eaten some on the plane, also, during the flight, and in my hotel room after I arrived.

The slight awkwardness this entailed was richly compensated. Everything I touched on that most fortunate of sallies, with the exception of my jackrabbit lunch, seemed to instantly turn into money. King Midas, with his foolish golden touch, would have turned green with envy. The slot machines behaved as if under a charm, producing a constant din and clatter of beeps and bongs and cascading dollars; the video poker machines produced a profusion of flushes, straights, full houses and straight flushes; I hit six out of six twice on the video keno machines.

When the last of my jackrabbit was consumed I went home with my pockets bulging with cash. Every dime of which I scrupulously reported to the IRS, of course, since the IRS always so fairly shares in our gambling losses. I kept the last leg bone of that rabbit for several years afterwards, and it continued to give me good luck. I would have liked to wear it on a golden chain, like a priceless watch. But eventually it lost its power, of course, and I regretfully had to throw it away.

The only thing that didn't produce money for me on that memorable trip was the simulcast horse races, but this was only because I didn't have any time to waste on them, sitting there waiting for the horses to run. Not when the slot machines were belching out cash when I would so much as look at them.

On other trips to Las Vegas, horse races have been a relatively safe entertainment. While I have never made a fortune betting on horses, neither have I ever suffered serious financial harm. But the other inducements of the Las Vegas casinos are another matter. In these, no amount of handicapping knowledge or sound judgment can have an effect. There, nothing but luck, pure and simple, has any value. But ordinary good luck in a casino, in the normal course of events, can only serve to prolong the length of time that our money will last before it inevitably goes down the drain. With this fact in mind I have dedicated those hours when the casino's horse room was closed to long sessions with the video keno machines, but playing only a quarter at a time, progressing to three and four quarters only occasionally, whenever I felt that my good luck was at its optimum peak.

Keno, for those readers who may not be familiar with it, is a game of numbers, not too dissimilar from the lottery. On the video screen are eighty little numbered squares. With an electronic marker one picks six numbers (or four, or five, or seven, or whatever the player wishes), marking the corresponding little squares. A button is pressed and, accompanied by a little bonging, beeping sound, twenty of the eighty squares, one by one, are lit up. If the six you have marked are among the twenty, you are a big winner. Three numbers, and four, and five, also pay off with a lesser return. I spent many hours, and many quarters and dollars, documenting the fact that if you choose your numbers quickly, irreflexively, without thinking, you stand a better chance of choosing correctly. The harder we try to visualize the numbers we should choose, the harder we try to guess as to which numbers will be chosen by the randomly acting device, the worse becomes our luck. The tiniest pause, the tiniest hesitation is fatal to our chances.

When we pause to reflect upon the reasons why this should be so, we can see that it is because hesitancy gives the powers that preserve the integrity of the laws of probability more opportunity to oppose us and regain their control. How do these powers manage to do it? They do it in two ways.

All people who play numbers games have a tantalizing vision in the back of their minds. They feel that it should be easy to pick the correct lottery numbers, or the correct keno numbers. They feel that there is a part of them that *knows* which numbers should be played, that the knowledge resides somewhere within them. Why should it be so hard, really; just six or so lousy little numbers. And yet they unerringly pick the wrong numbers, time after time. Are these people laboring under a delusion, a false notion which makes the task appear so easy, when it is actually so difficult? No. They are not entirely mistaken. We do have that knowledge. But we must remember that we are unwitting confabulators with the Fates and with their laws of probability.

That is the first of the two ways in which the Fates manage to frustrate our goals.

The other way is by changing the reality. In those cases in which we manage to fleetingly free ourselves from the dictates of our traitorous impulses (represented by our submissive *Ka*) that act against our own best interest just to please those three ugly old bags, the Fates, they regain the upper hand by shifting our reality to one in which the numbers we have chosen are rendered invalid.

There is an optimal frame of mind, however, in which we can sometimes evade our *Ka*, the Fates, and their laws of probability. That optimal frame of mind in which we shake off the shackles that bind us to those laws, allowing us to proceed without hesitation, unerringly choosing the correct numbers, is very hard to achieve. Contrary to the secret of success in every other endeavor in life, concentration is not the key. We should not focus our conscious mind too intently on the problem. This can be seen in the example of the ancient oracles.

The officiating seers at those places were chosen from amongst the common rural population. They were generally uneducated, unsophisticated young girls, not inclined to reflective thought, with a tendency to let their feelings—their prophetic utterances—surge involuntarily to the surface. The historian Tacitus speaks of them as, "those girls with frenzied mouths." In other ancient writings the words, "prophetic frenzy," are frequently seen. It is apparently a state in which the two hemispheres of the brain function independently of each other. It is a regression to the primitive bicameral mind, of which Professor Julian Janes speaks.

Unfortunately, we cannot very well patronize a race track or a casino in a frenzied state. People would stare at us, and we would probably soon be escorted to the gate. But the idea within this kernel of truth is that we should not try consciously. We should let hidden knowledge come to us unbidden, striving only to keep our mind free and open, cleansed of static-producing conscious effort. We should try to recuperate certain primitive functions of the brain without lapsing into complete bicamerality, recuperate these primitive functions while still retaining every bit of our modern mental capacities, to sagely guide these primitive functions down the proper pathways.

This tendency of hidden resolutions to come to us when we have ceased trying to force them, can be seen in the example of the scientist's dream from Arthur Koestler's *Act of Creation*, mentioned earlier. Revelations come in the same manner in matters involving arcane mysteries, such as in prediction of the future. We must first probe determinedly and make long and exhaustive investigations upon the defenses protecting the arcane. Then we must make a strong assault upon those defenses. This increases the resistance against us, I have said, but it will do so only at those points we are assaulting. The defenses at other strategic points are consequently neglected. Then we pretend to give up. We withdraw and pretend to sail away. But we return suddenly and unexpectedly, to make a quick assault upon one of those weakened points. Sometimes we can even leave a Trojan horse outside those walls and battlements, and then return to pour into the citadel of the arcane through an opened gate.

In other words, although we should strive to resolve occult mysteries, we cannot succeed if we concentrate too openly and intently on it. It must be done in a sideways manner, maintaining a casual and carefree attitude as we approach specific, minor goals within the greater corpus of the problem. Because the arcane is like an extremely cautious and wary wild creature. It knows if you are even so much as thinking about it. Some wild animals can be approached quite closely if you refrain from looking at them. Turn your eyes to stare at a feral cat as you walk by it and you will see it immediately go tense with caution. Turn to walk towards it and it will of course immediately vanish.

Do not directly strive, therefore, to win a lottery, or other similar great stroke of fortune. Don't try anything as futile as trying to make keno or lottery numbers come up through an exercise of willpower. In these matters willpower is utterly useless. Of course we should try to develop our willpower, but we will be wasting this valuable resource if we direct it towards games of chance, or if we try to use magic, which is a disreputable cousin of willpower.

But we are perhaps losing sight of the original theme of this book, which was how to improve our luck. Let us wind up all the foregoing by repeating, again: The way to change our luck for the better is by tackling the chore through small increments, with each little victory over our destiny strengthening us for the next assault . . . improving our luck in such small ways that often the benefits won may even be completely invisible to us.

There are any number of decisions that we make almost every day in life in which this invisible luck is of the greatest importance. Perhaps you are studying an offer of employment that would necessitate a move to a distant city. Or maybe you are pondering upon whether you should make a long trip to visit a family member. Maybe you are trying to decide if the time is propitious to refinance your mortgage, or trade in your old car, or whether you should invest your scarce spare cash in the stock market. Or maybe even such a minor thing as whether you should take the garbage out now or leave it for later.

Whatever you decide, the decision can be either felicitous or it can lead to grief and regret. To a large measure, the considerations that lean you towards your decision will depend on your luck. If you are naturally lucky you will be impelled towards the correct choice. But if you were born unlucky, you can partly neutralize your natural inclination towards misfortune; first, by recognizing the fact that you are unlucky, and then, by learning to receive warnings from your subconscious—by learning to reestablish a link with your *neter* and allowing it to guide you and keep you safe from harm.

Arcane knowledge has a natural tendency to become useless when everyone has access to it and accepts it as truth. So, the reader should not feel disappointed if all I have said appears to be of little use to him. Perhaps by passing the ideas and speculations in this little work through a fine strainer you might find there a lump or a morsel that can be boiled into a digestible truth. Perhaps there you will find a clue or two that will help you to uncover some truths of your own, of even greater value than any I have tried to express on these pages.

About the Author

When he's not figuring out new ways to outmaneuver the Fates, Armando Benitez works in Houston, Texas, as a professional translator. Born in Fresno, California, Benitez has traveled widely, and worked as an oil exploration land surveyor, gold prospector, red snapper fisherman, shrimper, merchant, and since 1980, as a writer. Besides studying the vagaries of fortune, luck, and destiny, Benitez has written about the mythic centaurs and alligator hunting in Guatemala, and completed a mock-epic poem about the fall of Berlin. In 1992, Hampton Roads published his Fate, Coincidence, and the Outcome of Horse Races.

Index

A

abilities, psychic. *See* psychic abilities
Achilles, 100, 192
Achuara Indians, 219
Acosta, 214
Act of Creation, The (Koestler), 258, 314
Adventures of Gargantua and Pantagruel (Rabelais), 250
Aeschylus, 273
Affy David (race horse), 37
Agamemnon (Aeschylus), 273
age, 142–43
    and fortune, 134–35
Ainslie, Tom, 229
A Lotta Moolah (race horse), 72
altruism, 292
Amazon tribesmen, 209–11
Amphiaraus, 305
    Oracle of, 274
Amphilocus, Oracle of, 274
Anabasis (Xenophon), 145
ancestors
    of Amazon tribesmen, 209–11
    wisdom of, 50, 57, 61
animals
    dreams of, 266–67
    and earthquakes, 61
    entrails (for divination), 84, 118
    intuition of, 298–99
    and lottery numbers, 127–28
    luck of, 17–19
    outwitting the Fates, 89
    superstitious behavior in, 7–8, 141
    See also specific animals
Apollo, 224
    Oracle of, 274
Apt To Do (race horse), 169
arcane knowledge. *See* knowledge, arcane

Arcolano of Siena, the Spendthrift, 150
Argus Panoptes, 146–47
Artaxerxes, 145
Artemidorus, 259
Athenians, oracle to, 303–4
athletes, and thirteen, 160–61
Atropos, 24, 97, 107, 143, 248
    as weak nuclear force, 138
    See also Fates, the
attitude
    and beginners luck, 112–13
    and intuition, 92
    for outwitting the Fates, 312–16
    towards change, 151
Augustine, Saint., 270
aura
    and age, 142
    of daydreams, 131, 136
    horses', 109, 110
    at racetrack, 56, 58
Aurelius, Marcus, 270
Aztecs
    and beans, 191–92
    cannibalism of, 213–15
    and thirteen, 162–63

B

Ba, 202, 248
Bacis, 304, 306
ball and pendulum, 84
baloney and luck, 187
barbricoa (barbecue), 215
Bargain Fun (race horse), 72
bastos (cards), 4
beans
    and Aztecs, 191-192
    eating, 190–91
    magic, 158–59
bears, polar, 7, 141
Bed of Cash (race horse), 46

"beginners luck," 112, 118
behavior, superstitious, 7–9
    See also beliefs, superstitious
beliefs, superstitious
    distribution of effects, 161
    effects over time, 57
    extremes of, 167
    inclinations toward, 64
    and industry, 165
    respecting others, 39–40
    as survival mechanism, 7–9
    taboos, 63–64, 80, 165–66
    worldwide, 40–41
    See also specific beliefs
betting, 55
    and courage, 117
    on "duplicated horses," 171–76
    strategies for, 233–34
    See also horse racing
birds, flights of (for divination),
        118, 128, 144, 145–46
Blowing Sand (race horse), 172
Bolivians, 221
bottles, cracked (for divination), 85,
        118
Boutiquos (race horse), 72
Bradley, Colonel, 229
Budge, Wallis, 76, 202

C

camels, eating, 189–90
cannibalism, 213–15
Cantonese, 193
Capricorn Sun (race horse), 71
capybara (food), 219–20
Carbony (race horse), 35
cards
    playing, 84, 118
    Spanish playing, 4
    Tarot, 50, 84, 118, 290
Caribs, 215
Cassandra, 273–74

cassava, 187, 210
caterpillars, 7, 141
Catlore (Morris), 193
cats
    for divination, 28–29, 118,
        127–28, 290
    eating, 188–90, 192–93
    relation to man and spirit,
        194–96, 250
chance
    law of, 97, 174–75
    and luck, 135
    and magic, 160
    "Tuxedo Effect," 228
Change of Motion (race horse), 172
character
    changing our, 14, 21–22, 135,
        152, 270, 297–98
    and daydreams, 137
charity, reason for, 75
charms, good-luck, 153–56
Cheiron, 192
chess, as metaphor, 181
chuchuhuasha (vines), 219
Clavijero, 214
Clean As a Whistle (race horse), 72,
        73
Clorox, metaphorical use of, 151
Clotho, 24, 97, 107, 143
    as strong nuclear force, 138
    See also Fates, the
clover, four-leaf, 153, 156
coin, flip of a, 232–33
coincidence, 25–31, 42, 45, 80
    cause of, 300–301
    and divination, 118, 128
    and "duplicated horses," 172–74
    and horse races, 33–43
    and the nature of reality, 38
    and primitive man, 62
    and "Tuxedo Effect," 227–28
    and twins, 170–71
color, of life threads, 120

changing, 121, 133, 151–52, 223–26
Columbus, 215
commerce and superstition, 165
common sense, 80, 297
Complete Book of Dreams, The (Raphael), 259
concentration, effect of, 65, 151, 312–15
Conquest of New Spain, The (Diaz del Castillo), 214
contract, with life/destiny, 25, 141–42
   See also Fates, the
Cortez, 215
cosmology, early, 95–96
courage, 117, 298, 300
Crazy Lea (race horse), 109–10
creation, code of, 93, 94
Creuzfeldt-Jacobs disease, 215
Critique of Pure Reason (Kant), 27
crocodile hunter, Malay, 62
Croesus, 48, 224, 302–3
crossing the fingers, 58–61
crow, talking (for divination), 84, 110–11, 118
crystal ball, 84, 118
Cup of Wind (race horse), 172
customs, as superstitions, 67
Cyrus, 145

D

Danaids, 302
Dance A Bunch (race horse), 169
danger
   of changing realities, 246
   of daydreaming, 131–37
   of resisting the Fates, 105, 151–52, 293
   of seeing the future, 93, 249
Dante, 93, 120–21, 150
Davenport, Marc, 280

daydreaming, 131–37
   and age, 142
de Alvarado, Pedro, 244
death
   cheating, 142–44
   illusion of, 266
dejá vu, 251
Delphic Oracle, 49, 145, 274
dementia, 248
Demeter, 191
   Oracle of, 274
de Sahagun, Fray Bernardino, 214
destiny
   changing, 77–82
   and coincidences, 27
   contract with, 25, 141–42
   control over, 11, 180–81
   flexibility of, 102
   and food, 199, 211
   immutability of, 99, 101, 148–50
   imperfection in, 177
   and *Ka,* 182–83
   model of, 95, 201, 239
   personification of, 24–25
   will of, 77–78
   See also fate; Fates, the
determination, 180, 226, 298, 300
determinism, 101, 141
Diaz del Castillo, Bernal, 214, 244
diet, 186–96
   affect on mental state, 198
   and poverty, 199, 220–23
   See also food
disease
   conquering, 138
   Creuzfeldt-Jacobs, 215
divination, 269–79
   arcane resistance to, 37, 48–50
   atmosphere/time for, 290–91
   and dreams, 128, 258, 262–65, 275–76
   learning art of, 25
   list of methods, 118

methods for horse racing, 28–29, 84–85, 88, 110–11, 294–95
methods for lottery, 127–28
relationship of words and events, 27
and women, 305
See also specific methods of divination
divinity, fear of, 119
Djeta, story of, 205
Dobbs, Adrian, 45
dogs
  eating, 188–90
  luck of, 17–19
double. *See Ka*
Double Deficit (race horse), 72
Dream Feather (race horse), 174
dreams, 258–67, 300
  disguises of, 286–88
  interpreting, problem of, 275–76
  time and chance in, 283–85
Dreams and Omens (Ward), 259
Duncan, Mrs., 3–6
Duran, Fray Diego, 191

E

earthquakes, 60–61
Egyptian Book of the Dead, 76, 203–4
Egyptians, ancient, 41, 50, 76, 182
  and cats, 196
  and food taboos, 191, 218
  religion of, 202–5
electromagnetic force, 139
employment and superstition, 164–65
enchantments, 153, 159–60
End Gun (race horse), 72
entrails, animal (for divination), 84, 118
etzalli (food), 191
events

foreseeing, 79–82, 270–72
occurring in sets, 40–41, 62–63
and relationship to words, 27
evolution, 98
  human, 177, 279
  and unlucky actions, 58
Exciting V. (race horse), 72

F

faculties, paranormal. *See* paranormal faculties
Fast Buck Phil (race horse), 34
fate
  anthropomorphic view of, 24–26
  changing the nature of, 137
  contract with, 141–42
  fear of, 56–57
  and free will, 97
  and inaction, 178, 180
  and moving through realities, 246–48
  mutability of, 46
  personification of, 24–25
  randomness of, 67
  using coincidences, 27
  See also Fates, the
Fates, the, 24–26, 97–98
  and aging, 142–43
  and altruism, 292
  challenging, 93, 152, 206–7, 293
  and changing realities, 102–07, 313
  and daydreams, 131–32, 136
  and dreams, 287
  and fortunate people, 300
  human frailties of, 27, 177, 224
  and *Ka,* 182–83
  markers for, 185, 199, 211
  outwitting, 66–67, 83–89, 112, 177–81, 222, 284–86, 307–8
  and race horses, 46–47, 71–73

and time, 98, 239
and "Tuxedo Effect," 227–28
and unlucky actions, 58
fear, 211–12
of divinity, 119
of fate, 57–58
fingers, crossing the, 58–61
flatworms, experiment with, 197
Fleet Reflection (race horse), 71
flights of birds. *See* birds, flights of
Flying Admiral (race horse), 72
Flying Rosario (race horse), 71
flying saucers, 279–82
food
cannibalism, 213–15
childhood memories of, 256–57
and *Ka,* 204
lucky and unlucky, 186–96,
198–99, 210–11, 216–21
and poverty, 199, 220–23
and psychic abilities, 200–201
See also specific foods
forces, four, 138–39
foresight, 45, 79–80
fortunate people. *See* people, fortunate
fortune
and age, 134–35
and connection to *neter,* 77
distribution of, 74–75, 292
and luck, difference between,
23–24
substituting superstition for, 163
See also luck
fortune-tellers, 118
Gypsy, 84, 91–92
Selena, 158–59
four forces, 138–39
Frazer, Sir James George, 1, 29, 62,
224
free will, 97, 101, 247–48
frenzy, 314
Freud, 260

Frothy (race horse), 172
Fucci, Vanni, 150
future
and changing reality, 78
foreseeing the, 45, 47, 93–94,
270–72, 301–2
inhabitants of, 288
seeing in dreams, 262–65,
275–76
time travel, 279–82

G

Galawac (race horse), 72
gambling, higher purpose of, 293,
309–10
generosity, reason for, 75, 292
genes, 269
Golden Bough, The (Frazer), 1, 30,
62, 224
golf balls (for divination), 28, 84,
88, 118, 290
Gomaro, 214
Grand Unified Theory, 138
Grant, Ulysses S., 68
Graves, Robert, 90, 162
gravity, 96, 138
Greek Myths, The (Graves), 90, 162
Greeks, ancient
and food taboos, 218
resistance to Gods, 224
See also oracles, ancient
Gregorio, 169–70
guardian angel, 76, 77
guilt, 211–12
Gull's Song (racehorse), 232

H

habits, as superstitions, 67, 141
Hairless Heiress (racehorse), 236
hallway, whistling in, 163
handicapping, 33, 43, 228–31
and hunches, 37–38, 115–17

studying the *Racing Form,*
  289–90
See also horse racing
Hannibal, 145
Harner, Michael, 213
Harris, Marvin, 189
Harrison, E. R., 96
Harvie, Paul Robert, 71
heads, eating, 217, 218, 221
Hegesistratus, 306
Hera, 146–47
herbs, 155–56
Hercules, birth of, 58–59
Hermes, 147
Herodotus, 191, 196, 203
  on dreams, 258
  on food, 218
  Histories, 41
  on oracles, 272, 302, 304–6
  on resisting the gods, 224
Herutataf, 205
Histories (Herodotus), 41
Hitler, Adolf, and reality, 241–42,
  247
Hobbes, Thomas, 13, 206, 270
Homo sapiens race-trackensis, 83, 291
honeycomb, as symbol, 240
horse racing, 55–56, 113–14
  arcane resistance to, 65–66
  and coincidence, 28, 33–43,
    71–73
  and crossing the fingers, 60
  and divination, 84–89, 118,
    290–91, 294–95
  duplication of names in, 169–70,
    171–76
  hunches and handicapping,
    37–38, 115–17
  improving chances at betting on,
    37–38, 227–37
  and neophytes, 112–13
  significance of winning at, 293
  and time travel, 289

horses
  eating, 188–90
  See also horse racing; race horses
Huambisas, 219
hunches
  and betting, 229–33
  and handicapping, 37–38,
    115–17

I

illness
  conquering, 138
  mental, and seeing the future,
    250
  as metaphor for bad-luck, 165–66
inaction, 178, 180
Inferno (Dante), 93, 120–21
insects
  eating, 211, 217–18
  as metaphor, 83
Interpretation of Dreams
    (Artemidorus), 259
intuition
  about foods, 212
  and dreams, 261
  and seeing the future, 272
  and unlucky objects, 154
Io, 146–47
Iocasta, 273

J

jackrabbit, 157–58, 310–11
  See also rabbit
Jackson, Michael, 104
jamais vu, 251
Jaynes, Julian, 202–3, 314
Jesus Christ, 306
Joel (prophet), 271
Jung, Carl, 71, 287
jungle, as habitat, 209–10

K

Ka, 182–83, 202–5, 240, 248, 288
Kammerer, Paul, 71
Kant, 27
keno, 312
Khaibit, 202, 248
Khat, 202
Khayyam, Omar, 133
Khu, 202, 205, 248
Khufu, Pharaoh, 205
Kleoitas, 47
Knock on Wood, 68
knowledge, arcane
    expansion of, 292–93, 316
    protection of, 65, 111, 272, 287
Koestler, Arthur, 61, 71
    Art of Creation, The, 258, 314
    Roots of Coincidence, The, 26, 45
Krantz, Les, 277

L

Lacedaemonians, 303
Lachesis, 24, 97, 107, 143
    as electromagnetic force, 139
    See also Fates, the
Lactantius, Firmianus, 283
ladder, walking under, 163
Lady Don (race horse), 72
Laius, King, 273
Lam, 123–24
lamb, eating, 217
languages, foreign, 179
lapsus linguae, 47
laziness, 180
Leaky Luke (race horse), 36, 227
Levi, Peter, 191
Leviathan (Hobbes), 206
Levi-Strauss, Claude, 64
Leviticus, 217
life
    changing your, 20, 120–22,
        151–52, 223–26, 297

contract with, 25, 141–42
tapestry of, 98, 104
    See also reality
Life of Lysander, 47–48
light, speed of, 282
lightning, being struck by, 126
Lights of London (race horse), 41
Livy, 302
London Bells (race horse), 41
longevity, 143
Loomis, Louise Ropes, 90
Lord Catcher (race horse), 172
Los Sueños y Los Numeros, 260
lottery
    and dreams, 263–64
    and magic, 160
    method of winning, 276–78
    odds of winning, 124–29
    winners and age, 142
    winners and daydreaming, 134,
        135
    winning and misfortune, 186
luck
    beginners, 112
    changing your, 12–14, 20–22,
        135, 222, 225–26,
        315–16
    charms for, 153–56
    and concentration, 65, 151–52,
        312–13
    distribution of, 74–75
    for a dog, 17–19
    and food, 186–96, 198–99,
        210–11, 218–21
    and foresight, 79
    and fortune, difference between,
        23–24
    and *neter,* 77
    to primitive peoples, 219
Lysander, 272

M

Machiavelli, 134–35, 224
Mademoiselle Fu (race horse), 47
magic, 106, 159–60, 307
  "sympathetic magic," 29
Mahl, Huey, 113
Making the Cash (race horse), 46
Malta, oracle on, 275
mandrake, 156
Man O' War (race horse), 47, 52
Mar Della (race horse), 71, 72, 73
Marie Helene (race horse), 47
McComb, Black Cat, 55
medicine and fate, 138
Medieval Mary (race horse), 47
Meet General Grant, 68
Megistias, 306
Melanesia, cannibalism in, 215
Melville, Herman, 97, 191, 284
memories and reality, 252–54
messages, subconscious, 79–81
Metamorphoses (Ovid), 25
Metcalf, Olga, 128
Midas, King, story of, 15, 16–17
Millie's Snowflake (race horse), 36
miracles, 104, 106
Moby Dick (Melville), 97, 284
Mohammed, 270
monkeys, eating, 210
Mopsus, 305
  Oracle of, 274
moralists, and luck, 135
Morris, Desmond, 193
Mosaic law, and food, 216–18
Moses. *See* Mosaic law
Mozart, 22
multiple realities, 99, 101–7, 239–54
Musaeus, Oracle of, 272
My Nadia (race horse), 47
Myrtilus, 114–15

N

Napoleon, 247
nationalities and food, 188–96
Native Joe (race horse), 172
Necessity, 97–98, 239
  as gravity, 138
necessity, 97
neophytes, racing, 112–13, 118
neter
  connection to, 77–79, 81, 183,
    267, 316
  and free will, 248
  and good-luck charms, 153
  meaning of, 76, 202, 205
  and reality, 240
Noble Napper (race horse), 55
Norman's Promise (race horse), 169
Northern Dancer (race horse), 173
nuclear force, 138
numerology, 118

O

objects
  disappearance of, 252
  unlucky, 154
Ocyrhoe, 48
Oedipus, story of, 273
Oenomaus, King, 114–15
Of Cannibals and Kings (Harris), 189
Oh How Right (race horse), 71
omens, 41, 71, 80, 301
One Jose (race horse), 172
oneness, of all, 85
Onomacritus, 272
On Superstition (Plutarch), 57
oracles, ancient, 47–50, 272–75,
    302–6, 313–14
  See also specific oracles
Ore D'Argent (race horse), 174
*Origin of Consciousness in the
    Breakdown of the Bicameral
    Mind, The* (Jaynes), 202–3

Ortona (race horse), 174
Oughtado (race horse), 169
Ouspensky, P. D., 270
Ovid, 25
owl, porcelain, 154

P

pacarana (food), 219
palmistry, 275
Pan, 224
paranormal faculties
    and courage, 117
    and food, 192, 201
    waning of, 91–92, 111
paranormal phenomenon, 50–52,
        61, 71
Paris, birth of, 274
"parsimony in hypotheses," maxim
        of, 308
past
    changing, 11, 14
    experience of, 122, 124, 270
patience, 30–31
    and changing realities, 247
Pausanias, 47, 191, 302
peacock, 146–48
peanuts, and horse racing, 58
Pelops, 114–15
people, fortunate
    contact with *neter*, 76, 79
    and daydreaming, 133–34
    and the Fates, 300
    power protecting, 30
    qualities of, 15–16
    and superstition, 67–69, 163–65
people, primitive
    Achuara Indians, 219
    Amazon tribesmen, 209–11
    and coincidence, 62
    and food taboos, 210–11,
        218–20
    rituals of, 224

Warao Indians, 64
phenomenon
    observation of, 41, 62– 63
    paranormal, 50–52, 61, 71
Phineus, 48
physics
    Grand Unified Theory, 138
    and time, 99, 100
Pie Woman, story of, 3–6
Planetiades, 49–50
Plataeans, 306
Plumovent (race horse), 174
Plutarch
    on ancient oracles, 302
    Life of Lysander, 47–48, 272
    on Plataeans, 306
    On Superstition, 57
    "Why Oracles Are Silent," 49–50,
        90, 305
Poe, Edgar Allan, 22
Polycrates, 258–59
pork, 189
Potter, Carole, 68
poverty and diet, 199, 220–23
power, protective, 75–76
Precious (cat), 29, 85, 127, 290
present, unchangeability of, 269
presque vu, 251
Prevailing Winds (race horse), 172
primitive people. *See* people, primi-
        tive
probability
    law of, 29, 97, 174–75
    and magic, 160–61
    and moving through reality, 251
    problem in, 277–78
    "Tuxedo Effect," 228
problem solving, in dreams, 258
prophecy
    in dreams, 262–65
    See also oracles, ancient
protozoa, 59
prudence, 6–7, 11

"psitrons," 45
psychic abilities
    and courage, 117
    and food, 192, 201
    waning of, 91–92, 111
pyramids and the lottery, 128
Pyramid Texts, 204
Pythagoreans, 190–91

Q

quantum theory, 85

R

rabbit
    eating, 216–17, 310–11
    foot, as charm, 153–57
    See also jackrabbit
Rabelais, 250
race horses
    blood lines of, 172–73
    condition of, 109–10
    names and coincidence, 34–37,
        46–47, 169–70
    See also horse racing
Race is Pace, The (Mahl), 113
race tracks
    difference in sizes, 42
    See also horse racing
Rachel, story of, 156
racial groups and food, 188–96
randomness, 67, 169
Raphael, Edwin, 259, 260
rats, eating, 193
Raw and the Cooked, The, 64
reality
    effect of daydreams on, 131–32,
        136
    changing, 75, 78–79, 95,
        120–22, 151–52, 306–7
    and dreams, 266
    model of, 201, 239–40

multiple, 99, 101–7, 239–54
nature of, 38–39, 73
relativity, theory of, 282
Ren, 202
revelations
    disguised nature of, 301–4
    in dreams, 261–65
rituals, 224
Ritzie Pirate (race horse), 71
Roots of Coincidence, The (Koestler),
    26, 45

S

salt, spilling, 56–57, 163
Salud y Pesetas (race horse), 174
santeria (magic), 106
Sara Toga (race horse), 33
schizophrenia, 203, 248–49
Seabreeze Whisper (race horse), 71,
    73
Sekhem, 202, 205, 248
Selena, Queen of the Gypsies,
    158–59
self-improvement
    conventional methods of, 13–14,
        297
    effectiveness of, 269
Sextus Empiricus, 191
Shakespeare, 133
shanja (bird), 211
Sheldrake, Rupert, 293
Shining High (race horse), 295
Silanos, 145
Silver Sally (race horse), 26
Silver Supreme (race horse), 174
Singing Seagull (race horse), 232
slugs, and lottery numbers, 128
smallpox, 138
Socrates, 145
Solid Silver (race horse), 26
sota de copas (card), 4

Special to Us (race horse), 71
sports and superstition, 165
Stepping Emily (race horse), 36
Stinger (race horse), 36, 227, 231
subconscious
    and foods, 200
    link with, 316
    messages, 79–81
success
    and daydreaming, 133–34
    and superstition, 163
Summer's Callin' (race horse), 172
Summer's Glory (race horse), 173
Summer Time Guy (race horse), 173
superstition
    derivation of word, 57
    "fear of divinity," 119
    and the fortunate, 163—64
    as observed phenomena, 62
    overall effect of, 161
    premise of, 7, 11
    See also beliefs, superstitious
sweeping, 163

T

taboos
    food, 210–11, 218–21
    knowledge of, 63–64, 80
    and symptoms of bad luck,
        165–66
Tacitus, 314
Take it Home (race horse), 72
talking crow (for divination), 84,
        110–11
Tantalus, 200
Tapia, 214
tapir, eating, 213
Tarot cards, 50, 84, 118, 275, 290
tea leaves, 84, 118, 275
technology
    changing fate, 137
    for time travel, 280

tectonic plates, 60–61
termite, simile of, 201, 205–6
Thamus, 90
Themistocles, 303–4
Theocritus, 224
"Theory of Formative Causation,"
        293
Thermopylae, 306
thirteen, 160–63
thoughts
    affect on reality, 131–32
    in foreign languages, 179, 222
threads, of life, 120, 151, 300
    changing color of, 121, 133,
        223–26
three
    sets of, 40–41, 63
    significance of, 25
time, 270
    ancient, 49
    in dreams, 283–84
    and the Fates, 98, 239
    reality of, 99–101
    travel, 279–82, 289
Tisamenus, 304–5
tlacatlaolli (food), 214
To B. Noble (race horse), 55
tortillas, toasted, 212–13, 256–57
tree, as metaphor, 20
Trophonius, Oracle of, 274, 275
Tubro (charm), 153
"Tuxedo Effect," 227–28
twins, identical, 170–71
two, sets of, 40–41

U

umbrella, opening, 163
universe
    model of, 95
    order of, 71
Upset (race horse), 47, 52

V

Van Gogh, Vincent, 22
virtues
    for changing life, 297–98
    courage, 117, 300
    determination, 180, 226, 300
    and good fortune, 15–16
    patience, 30–31
    prudence, 6–7, 11
    willpower, 132, 226, 315
    wisdom, 6–7, 12, 14
Visitors from Time (Davenport), 280
Vos Savant, Marilyn, 277

W

wall, clinging to (for divination),
    294–95
Warao Indians, 64
Ward, James, 259, 260
Westcar Papyrus, 205
What the Odds Are (Krantz), 277
"Why Oracles Are Silent" (Plutarch),
    49, 90, 305
will, free. *See* free will
willpower, 132, 226, 297, 315
Winds a Callin' (race horse), 173
Winds of Life (race horse), 172
Windy Valley (race horse), 172
wine, fooling the Fates with, 222
wisdom, 6–7, 12, 14
    interrelationship with luck,
        18–20, 22
    source of, 77
witchcraft, 106
women, modern diviners, 305
words, relationship to events, 27
Works Like Cash (race horse), 46

X

Xenophon, 145
Xerxes, 272

Z

Zeno, 100
Zeus, 146–47
Zeus Ammon, Oracle of, 49, 272,
    274
Zeus at Dodona, Oracle of, 274
Zog, 145